Lawyers, Guns, and Money

Lawyers, Guns, and Money

ONE MAN'S BATTLE WITH THE GUN INDUSTRY

CAROL X. VINZANT

First published 2005 by
PALGRAVE MACMILLAN™
175 Fifth Avenue, New York, N.Y. 10010 and
Houndmills, Basingstoke, Hampshire, England RG21 6XS.
Companies and representatives throughout the world.

PALGRAVE MACMILLAN IS THE GLOBAL ACADEMIC IMPRINT OF THE PALGRAVE
MACMILLAN division of St. Martin's Press, LLC and of Palgrave Macmillan Ltd.
Macmillan® is a registered trademark in the United States, United Kingdom
and other countries. Palgrave is a registered trademark in the European Union
and other countries.

ISBN 1-4039-6627-3 hardback

Library of Congress Cataloging-in-Publication Data
Vinzant, Carol X.
Lawyers, guns, and money: one man's battle with the gun industry/Carol X.
Vinzant.
    p.   cm.
  Includes index.
  ISBN 1-4039-6627-3
  1. Firearms—Law and Legislation—United States.   2. Gun control—Law
and legislation—United States.   3. Products liability—United States.   4.
McDermott, Tom—Trials, litigation, etc.   I. Title

KF 3941.V56   2005
344.7305'33—dc22
            2005045943

A catalogue record for this book is available from the British Library.

Design by Letra Libre, Inc.

First edition: November 2005
10 9 8 7 6 5 4 3 2 1
Printed in the United States of America

CONTENTS

ACKNOWLEDGMENTS

Tom and Rosemary McDermott let me enter their lives and write an account of their journey that was more personal than we'd originally set out to make it.

This book was possible only because hundreds of people generously gave me their time, some sharing painful experiences, others offering esoteric financial expertise.

My fiancé David Lidsky has campaigned seemingly relentlessly to be recognized favorably here. Staying up grueling nights, taking time off from *Fast Company* to work on this, abiding detours of vacations to gun sites, being relentlessly supportive and sweet—oh, there is nothing that man wouldn't do to be cited here. Fine, fine, enough already, David, you win, I couldn't have done it without you, okay? It wouldn't have been half as clear or interesting without you.

My editor David Pervin always believed in the importance of this book and gave good advice that I often didn't want to listen to. I'd also like to thank Amanda Fernández, Yasmin Mathew, and Heather VanDusen. Heather Florence and Enid Stubin gave this project not only their expertise, but also their enthusiasm and editorial flair.

My sage agent Joe Vallely gave me advice and lots of help.

Susan Woodward did the tough economic number crunching. I handed her a pile of data, and she magically made sense of it.

Andy Kupfer, my editor back at *Fortune,* gave me the chance to check out this story.

I stood on the shoulders of many journalists and researchers. I especially relied on the diligent work of Matt Bai, Alix Freedman, Paul M. Barrett, Maureen Fan, Robert Sherrill, Sharon Walsh, Robert J. Spitzer, Jason Kaufman, and Tom Diaz.

Lots of people helped me with my research: Patricia Neering, Fortune's amazing researcher, helped me tremendously. Cindy Vinzant helped me compile enormous quantities of tedious price data.

My parents, Mary Lou and Guy Vinzant, worked many hard jobs, raised six kids, and sent me to college when they hadn't been able to go themselves. My mom especially made lots of sacrifices. My sisters Mary Ann Fuller and Karen Vinzant Asa helped me get through this project like they've helped me through everything.

Cora Daniels is a true friend and inspiration; she keeps me going and laughing. Amey Stone supports me no matter what. Gary Vinzant, Chanoine Webb, and Tess Chi were my Excel elves. Gunnar Hellekson, Rob Kolb, and Elizabeth Finch gave me good advice.

S. Ollenberg dug up historical documents for me in Germany.

Editors like Rob Norton; Larry Yu; Bob Arnold, and the folks at *BusinessWeek Online;* Steve Hendrix; Craig Stoltz; David Plotz; Patrick Boyle; Hildie Anderson and the Bobs, Bob Andreas and Robert Sullivan, at *Life* gave me fun and interesting work that supported me through this project. Turns out there's more money in writing about the stock market than there is in writing about guns and insurance.

David Groff did his special textual jujitsu and guided me to tell a better story.

Joe Queenan; Jeanne, Barb, and Kathryn Lightfoot; Bette Ruttman; Patricia, Alan and Tadex Avidan; Alice Couch; Mary Ann Stark; Dr. Dave Ores; Andy Johnson; Helena Adams; Tim Prairie; Patrick Rogers; and Robert Weinberg each helped in their own way to make this a better book. Norma and Sylvain Lidsky raised a son who is almost as smart and considerate as they are, then welcomed me into their family.

Ken Labich made sure I didn't get thirsty. James Hampbell and Victor Sanchez gave me the full hospitality and friendship of the Scratcher. TV's Frank Tantillo taught me about Long Island.

I'll always be grateful to my best teachers: Peter Stallybrass, Lynn Dieter, Phil Loveall, and Steve Granzyk.

Thanks to the institutions that let me use their materials: the Queens County Farm Museum, the New-York Historical Society, the Springfield Armory, the New York Public Library, the University of Massachusetts library at Amherst.

Jolly Vinzant, through his eternal vigilance, kept my office free of squirrels throughout the writing of this book.

PREFACE

This book, like a few others, started out as a story for *Fortune Magazine*, when I worked there in 2000. I hoped to tell a story about how the emotional gun issue might just be determined by something as obscure, mundane and apolitical as liability insurance. Smashing idea, you may be thinking, take an issue that involves political passion and murder and turn it into the tedium of actuaries. Isn't it supposed to work the other way around?

The deeper I got into the story—which never actually ran in *Fortune*—I found that people on either side of the issue knew little about the actual business of making guns. The companies are mainly privately owned and secretive. Also, the industry is uniquely shielded from public scrutiny by its lobbying forces. While I was writing this book, for example, an ATF spokesman told me a new rule prevented the agency from giving out most gun data and said the law even applied retroactively to data that had previously been released.

Any story about gun companies and insurance will inevitably end up in the epic bankruptcy of Lorcin Engineering, a maker of cheap handguns known as Saturday Night Specials. Lorcin was once the country's biggest gun maker and its low quality guns inordinately found their way into trouble. Gun experts told people to steer clear of the guns, because of their tendency to jam or even blow up in gun owners hands. Despite a slew of gun owners suing Lorcin for those kind of accidents, what got all the attention were the more political lawsuits over negligent distribution of handguns.

After years of battling over this case, even the lawyers were weary of discussing the insurance issue. *There's only one guy who even wants to think about this anymore. A lawyer in New York. He worked on Hamilton. He was a shooting victim himself,* one told me. *You should call Tom McDermott.*

And that's how I met Tom, the main character of this book, who takes us on a tour of the gun issue, starting when he's shot and knows nothing, through his battles with the National Rifle Association, lobbying Congress, jousting on talk shows, investigating and arguing in court. As a former white collar crime prosecutor, Tom also wanted to look at guns like any other business. And he shared my high tolerance for financial minutia.

So, this book follows Tom's story and his extraordinary investigation. When Tom got shot, he decided to do something about gun crimes. The NRA was a giant roadblock to any meaningful public dialogue or new laws. Some tried to do an end-run around new laws by going to court, but because the laws were weak, that hasn't worked. Tom's quest was, in effect, an end-run around and an end-run. Tom had the good sense not to try to get tangled with in the NRA. He went on to work where he could do the most good: dissecting a complex, international financial scheme that others ignored. This book relies heavily on his account.

I looped back and did my own research to back up the tale. My job is telling his story in context. Way too many books have been written about the gun issue already, so I've concentrated on what's not out there: the dependence of both the gun industry and the NRA on government funding; how American gun culture is largely borrowed from Germany; the way gun crimes have gone up when gun prices went down.

Everyone's attitude towards guns is shaped in their upbringing, so I think I should reveal mine. I'm from Des Plaines, Illinois. My dad grew up in Arkansas during the Depression. His father would get him up before dark to go hunting for food and sometimes all they'd get was squirrels. As someone who had to go hunting, he didn't understand why some men thought it was fun. He didn't have any qualms about guns (or even shooting animals he thought were menacing his garden), but he seemed to wonder why, of all the wonderful parts of farm life, that was the one suburbanites grasped onto. My biggest experience with guns was going shooting with my country cousins in Arkansas—unfortunately with inadequate hearing protection. It was fun—something most Yankees don't grasp about shooting. But it was very memorable, as I have chronicled in the *Washington Post,* because it left me with a permanent ringing in one ear, known as tinnitus.

To learn as much as I could about guns, I took a class to get a hunting license. I learned as much about the ethics of hunting as I did about gun handling. I learned from my friends who hunt and my gun class that hunters and hikers are basically out for the same thing: a good time in the woods with their friends. In a peculiarly New Agey interlude of the hunting class, we learned that a hunter only evolves through several stages into a true sportsman. First they try to maximize their shots, then their kills. Next they get selective: trophy animals and then difficult techniques: bows, historical weapons or handguns. They only become a true sportsmen in the fifth stage, when they care about conserving wildlife and teaching the next generation. Indeed, hunters have been crucial to conservation.

But as much as the class tried to imbue a sense of responsibility, the instructor also tried to impart the NRA viewpoint. The state class actually showed an NRA video. They don't do that in every class, but the class is run by the International Hunter Education Association which acknowledges some states are better than others in keeping "gung-ho" gun rights advocates in check. Still, it means that gun tax dollars earmarked for wildlife conservation go not only to hunter education and recruitment, but also to NRA recruitment. The effect is to convince hunters that mothers who worried about handguns harming kids are secretly conspiring to confiscate hunting rifles. Hunters are essential to fighting gun control because they are far more socially palatable than the other main gun constituencies, militias and the crowd that wants 9mm's in their waistband, nightstand, car, and high school teacher's desk to fend off would-be attackers.

The gun class reminded me mainly that the gun issue has many alluring side avenues to explore, but it takes someone wise like Tom McDermott to forget all that and focus on getting things done.

I've tried to differentiate in the book between responsible gun companies and gun owners and others that are more reckless.

I tried to pick up the gun culture so I wouldn't lapse into the easy habit of calling those who believe in gun rights "gun nuts." I think a more apt term is "gun geek," someone who is so enthralled with the minutia, grandeur and idealism of the gun hobby, they start to value it more than human life.

What I've tried to do here is to tell Tom McDermott's story, but put it in the proper historical and sociological perspective.

One

THE SHOOTING

MURDER ON THE LONG ISLAND RAILROAD
5:33: DECEMBER 7, 1993

KRIK-KRIK KRIK-KRIK

The sound pulled Tom McDermott up from reading his newspaper. The Long Island Railroad train chugged away from the New Hyde Park station, the first stop outside New York City.

It was December 7, 1993, so even at 6 P.M. it was already dark. It was cold, but people on this crowded 5:33 P.M. train bound for Port Jefferson still clung to fall and their overcoats instead of trading them in for winter's down jackets.[1]

Tom, 50, looked the part of an Irish-Catholic family man. He had the general look of John McCain, if the Arizona senator were a typical suburban commuter: suit, briefcase, trench coat, blue eyes, receding white hair. Tom wanted to return to the *New York Times* without investigating the sound. On the train this morning he had somehow missed a story about one of his cases. He was the lawyer fighting a tiny Long Island company that was trying to hang onto its contract to build a phone system across Georgia, in the former Soviet Union.[2] He was now excited to be able to show his wife Rosemary the story when he got home to Garden City, just a couple of stops away.

Tom used to see his cases in the paper all the time, back when he was a white-collar crime prosecutor. He had gone after the mob on New York City's waterfront and crooked politicians on Long Island. But his days of socially momentous cases were long gone. For the past decade he'd had a small private practice and was counsel to the New York State Thoroughbred Racing Capital Investment Fund, an unheard-of agency that financed and supervised improvements at New York's three thoroughbred racetracks. It was just a steady job to support his family.

KRIK-KRIK-KRIK

Those damn boys, throwing rocks at the train from the platform again, Tom thought to himself. *And at this time of year.*

McDermott had arrived at Penn Station just in time to take the 5:33 train. By the time he got to the platform, the crowd was three deep in front of him. This was a standard Long Island Railroad commuter train: two sets of doors that opened on both sides, forming two vestibules that divided the train into small front and back sections and one large middle seating area.

McDermott had gotten on at the rear door of the third car. He had turned right, toward the back section of the car. That back area was too crowded, though, so he turned around and got a window seat in the third row of the middle section. He was now dimly aware of some commotion in the rear, where he had tried to sit. . . . As the train chugged forward he was on the right (or south) side of the car. The cars all have two-seaters on one side and three-seaters on the other. Tom was in a three-seater that faced toward the rear of the train. Two Asian men had taken the seats next to him.

Suddenly a hulking man in a suit planted his foot on the armrest of Tom's vinyl seat as he scrambled forward in the car. The man sounded no warning; he just lurched onward, clutching his briefcase and nearly whacking the head of the Asian man sitting on the aisle end of Tom's seat. There was more commotion from the back of the train.

A crush of business-suited passengers followed the lurching briefcase man. They crammed into the aisle. No one was shouting or screaming. They were just frantically, instinctively pushing away from some danger in the back of the car that the rest of the passengers couldn't see. This went beyond typical New York rush-hour rudeness. These scrambling people were the same normally methodical Garden City commuters McDermott saw everyday; to be the first off the train at Merillon Avenue, they got in the third car (the first two overhung the small station and didn't open there) and anticipated their stop by lurking in the doorways. They were the only ones who understood someone was shooting a gun at passengers. Everyone else's view was blocked by the ads covering the vestibule's plexiglass partitions.

McDermott normally would have been among these people standing up. He wasn't today only because he had driven his car to Mineola station, the next express stop, to catch an earlier train. McDermott usually felt lazy if he bothered to take the car to the Merillon Avenue stop because it was just a 5-minute walk from his house.

KRIK-KRIK-KRIK

Finally McDermott recognized the sound as gunshots. As an army specialist, fourth-class, in Vietnam, he had realized why people said "the crack of gunfire." That's what the sound was, like a firecracker. Not just a pop.

Not a boom, either. More electric. An overpoweringly loud but short crack that stings your ears.

KRIK-KRIK-KRIK

The mind works in funny ways. When it is confronted with an impossibly horrible event, it tries to soothe itself by coming up with mild and acceptable explanations. McDermott explained the gunfire to himself as a shoot-out. His mind instantly jumped to what he figured was the most likely scenario for gunshots on a train: police confronting a suspect who pulled a gun.

KRIK-KRIK-KRIK

Despite the continued gunshots, McDermott tried to calm people down: "Don't panic, don't panic," he said.

He slowly prepared to get ready to join the throng pushing forward. He worried about a ricochet or stray bullet, but that was all the danger he thought he faced. The man who nearly got decapitated by the briefcase went into the aisle, then the man next to McDermott. Now it was McDermott's turn. No one could move, though, because the aisle was jammed. McDermott was the last one in the line.

He looked backward and saw a neatly dressed, pudgy black man holding a gun in the vestibule. The man was serenely calm. His jeans had been ironed so fastidiously they had a crease in them. His black shoes were shiny, and he wore a clean tan jacket.

McDermott could not see past the man who turned out to be Colin Ferguson, or he would have seen blood splashed on the windows and walls. The partitions hid McDermott's view of commuters who were minutes from home, who were now slumped over in their seats, covered in gore. The gunman's bulky frame blocked the sight of Kevin McCarthy, shot in the head and leaning on his now-dead father, Dennis. McDermott could not see this hideous back section of the train car, where Ferguson had done the most damage and where McDermott had tried to sit when he first boarded the train.

All McDermott could see was a man calmly reloading his Ruger 9 mm pistol. *Undercover cop,* McDermott's mind told him. McDermott was about to ask what was going on when Ferguson met his gaze with a blank stare.

Then Ferguson lifted up the gun and pointed it at McDermott. Only then did Ferguson stop being a cop in McDermott's mind and become a threat. The two stared at each other for seconds.

Oh my God, he's going to shoot me, McDermott finally realized.

The army had taught McDermott one sure thing about getting shot at: Don't give the shooter a clean, full, head-on target. At the last second he flipped himself sideways and forward. He curled his shoulder under.

KRIK

The bullet burst into McDermott's left shoulder from behind with such force it pushed him to the floor and threw him two rows forward from where he had been sitting. He tried to crawl under the seat. He tried to hide but his feet still lay out in the aisle. All he could see was Ferguson's polished shoes and meticulous jeans approach. If McDermott moved his feet he might call attention to himself. He thought Ferguson was stalking him, standing over him, preparing to shoot him through the train seat. So he decided he had better stay still and play dead. He expected to die anyway. He said a short prayer: "God, make it quick."

McDermott thought about how he would not get to say goodbye to his two teenage children, Katie and Ryan. He had gotten angry with Ryan because Ryan left a cousin's wedding early and the two hadn't spoken in days. What a stupid way to spend his last days.

Then Tom closed his eyes. The world became dark, as black as a pool of oil, yet calm. He was certain he was going to die, but he was overcome with the unexpected sense that everything would be all right even if he did.

KRIK-KRIK

McDermott heard the gunfire and realized he hadn't been shot again. Instead Ferguson had shot two people hiding under the next seat forward. Then McDermott heard Ferguson's steps moving on again. As soon as McDermott realized the shooter had gone by, he started crawling away under the seats. He wanted to get to the back of the car to pull the emergency brake, the only thing he could think of to stop the shooting. The train car itself was helping Ferguson hold these hostages; if it stopped, at least people could jump off. Pulling the brake would certainly let the conductor know something was wrong.

KRIK-KRIK-KRIK-KRIK

Now that Ferguson was in the car's middle section, everyone could see him calmly walking up the aisle, shooting anyone he found.[3] Terrified, people hid under seats or tried to. Some seats jammed with people piled on each other, searching for the safety of the floor. They knew they would not make it through the throng of commuters trying to wedge themselves through the door to the second car, where passengers were oblivious to the shooting.

"This is real life, people," someone said.[4] The shooting was not like anything anyone had seen in the movies. No one screamed or cried out loud. The passengers were stuck in slow motion, just pushing to get to the front of the car as Ferguson closed in behind them, grinning and systematically shooting people. He did not just shoot into the crowd, which would have both killed and terrorized. Instead he picked his victims one by one, seemingly relishing their anguish.[5]

KRIK-KRIK-KRIK

McDermott continued to crawl under the seats. *Get away, get away,* was his only thought. When he got to the last seat in the middle section, he stood up and scrambled to the back of the car. Only then did he see the people who were shot, slouched in their seats. One bloody man lay on the lap of the man sitting next to him, who had also been shot. Miraculously, one old woman was unharmed in that section. She rocked in her seat, head in her hands, mumbling over and over, "God help us, God help us, God help us."

KRIK-KRIK

Ferguson continued shooting. Now he was nearing the front set of doors.

KRIK

McDermott searched for the emergency brake, but he couldn't find it. Up front, Frank Barker, thirty-six, pleaded with Ferguson for his life. He said that he had seven children. He held up his hand between his head and Ferguson's gun.

KRIK

There was no mercy. The bullet pierced the man's hand and grazed his ear. He was the last one shot before Ferguson ran out of bullets again.

Ferguson had shot his way up to the front vestibule. As soon as he paused, a man held up a briefcase as a shield and charged him. Two other guys helped tackle Ferguson, take away the gun, and hold him in a seat.[6] Ferguson suddenly turned calm and docile. He put up no resistance. "I've done a bad thing," he said.[7]

McDermott finally found the emergency brake, but by then the train had stopped at Merillon Avenue, and the doors opened to suburban Garden City.

The shooting was over less than three minutes after it had started. In that short time Ferguson managed to get off thirty rounds. He shot at close range and seldom missed. He had shot twenty-five people, and six lay dying or dead.

A FAMILY REACTS TO THE SHOOTING: DECEMBER 7, 1993

At first one policeman, then dozens converged on the Merillon Avenue train station.

The station looks like any other you'd find in a suburban bedroom community. Each train track has its own concrete platform a few steps off the ground, and each platform has a few ads and a small glass and steel shelter. The station isn't in a downtown area; there's just a parking lot, a couple of businesses, and then the suburban houses of Garden City, a village of about twenty thousand middle-class or upper-middle-class commuters, mostly married white couples with kids. One-third are Irish-American.[8]

This train splattered in blood was not expected. Kathleen Giblin, an EMT who happened to be riding in another car on the train, ran up to treat the wounded. The smell of blood overwhelmed her. "It just looked to me like someone took a hose and painted the car with red paint," she said.[9]

The cops weren't sure what had happened. Looking at the incredible carnage, they first thought there must be another gunman.

Barker, a Garden City technology manager and the last man Ferguson shot, ran off the train and onto Nassau Boulevard, a usually calm street with just a few one-story businesses. The sight of the bleeding, frenzied man, who had been shot through the thumb, arm, leg, and mouth, was so inexplicable that the first few cars avoided him. Finally he flagged someone down who took him to the hospital. "I wasn't waiting for an ambulance," Barker later said to Tom.

The rescue workers walked through the car, finding some passengers already dead and some just sitting motionless among them, physically unhurt but in shock.

Tom stumbled out of the back of the third car and walked onto the concrete platform. Dazed, he went back in the train car through the front set of doors. This was only a couple minutes after the shooting stopped and Tom saw two young women, one white, one Filipino, on the floor with head wounds. The white woman was clutching her keys in her hand.

A man came in from the second car and said "Oh, God, Oh, God. I've gotta get help." Before he left, he guided Tom to a seat. Tom gave the second man who came by his home phone number and asked him to tell his wife Rosemary that he was shot but okay. A third dazed man came by, took off his tie, and made it into a tourniquet for Tom's left arm. Next, a man came on the train, announced he was a police officer, though he wore no uniform, and then started to leave.

"Where are you going?" Tom, still dazed, called after him. LIRR Police Det. Andrew Roderick, who had been waiting at the station for his wife, was getting his handcuffs from his car.[10] Roderick came back, handcuffed Ferguson, and walked him out of the car. As he passed a few feet away, Tom yelled out, "It's him, he's the one who did it." Tom sat in shock on the train, bleeding from the shoulder, watching as police officers moved up and down the aisle with medical equipment. The man who had put the tourniquet on Tom's arm returned and led Tom off the train to the platform railing, where a line of shooting victims was forming. A woman wearing a badge nearly tipping off its chain approached. She said that she was a cop and also a nurse, and she wanted Tom to take off his jacket to check out his wound.

"Are you really a nurse?" he argued, suspicious of her precarious badge.

When she said she was, he took off his trench coat. She inspected the wound with her penlight and declared that he would be okay. It seemed like hours, given all that was going on, but really it was only about five minutes since the shooting.

A uniformed police officer stood at the end of the train platform directing the traffic of injured bodies to seven Long Island hospitals so that no hospital would be overwhelmed. Many victims wound up nearby at Winthrop University Hospital in Mineola or at Nassau County Medical Center in East Meadow.

McDermott thought of his wife Rosemary, whom he called Roe. Rosemary had grown up in Garden City. She attended Marymount University, a Catholic college in Virginia, then went to work as a secretary on Wall Street. She met Tom when they were both out with friends drinking in New York in the spring of 1970. Back then Tom had a full head of brown hair and an athletic build. He was just home from Vietnam. They married within a year. She was now an administrative assistant to the principal of a local grammar school and the mother of their two children, Ryan, seventeen, and Katie, who had just turned twenty.

Rosemary hated driving outside Garden City. When the policeman told McDermott he was going to South Nassau Communities Hospital in Oceanside, way down in a residential neighborhood near the south shore of Long Island, Tom rebelled. It wasn't even that far—fewer than ten miles—but Tom focused on the mundane part of the situation, not yet fully grasping the enormity of the tragedy.

"I can't go to that hospital. My wife will never find it," he told the cop.

The cop ignored him.

"If you don't send me at least to Mercy Hospital I'll get up off this gurney."

"Okay, fine," the cop said. "You're going to Mercy."

Jennifer Logan, a CBS television reporter who lived up the block from the McDermotts, had run to the train station with her camera. She captured McDermott's bizarre, animated exchange with the cop. In the subsequent TV coverage, the tape was played so often it became a family joke: Tom, moments after getting shot, arguing with a police officer about the logistics of his emergency medical care.

Within ten minutes of the shooting, Tom was in an ambulance. The ambulance back doors opened as it sped up the hill, but the paramedics caught the gurney so that Tom didn't roll out.

Back home, Rosemary did not hear the sirens of ambulances converging on the Merillon station a half mile away. She first heard of the shooting when a neighbor called to ask if her son was there visiting Ryan—if so, Rosemary was to send him home because of what had happened at the train station.[11]

"What's going on at the train station?" Rosemary asked.

"Just turn on the TV," the neighbor said.

Rosemary did and saw the LIRR station only blocks from her home. The McDermotts live on a side street off Merillon Avenue. Their little neighborhood train station was surrounded by police cars and ambulances. Even though her husband almost never took a train as early as the 5:33, she had the sense that he was on that train.

Within ten minutes, her instinct was confirmed. The phone rang again at around 6:30—fifteen minutes after the train had pulled into the station.

"Rosemary McDermott?" a voice she didn't recognize asked.

"You're calling to tell me my husband's been shot, right?"

"Yes."

"But if you're calling me, it's because he gave you my name and phone number and he's okay, right?"

"Yes."

Tom's bit of hospital gamesmanship on behalf of Rosemary turned out to be moot because Ryan had driven the family's second car to the library. She called her niece to drive her to the library, then started packing snack foods and toiletries.

"What are you doing?" her niece asked her when she arrived.

"We're going to be there a long time," Rosemary explained.

The McDermotts find it amusing that one of their son Ryan's rare trips to the library is forever memorialized in family lore because he happened to choose to study there the day his father was shot. Ryan was working on a group project with friends and they had vaguely heard that a crazy man had shot up a nearby train, killing lots of people.

As soon as Ryan saw his mother coming to fetch him at the library, he knew.

"Don't be upset," she explained, "but Dad's been shot."

Meanwhile, Tom lay on a metal slab at the hospital. Off to the side he could see the emergency room doctors examine his x-ray. He saw the doctor shake his head, left to right.

Oh my God, they're going to have to operate, Tom thought.

The doctor approached. "I've never seen anything like this and I've treated hundreds of gunshot wounds. The bullet passed through your shoulder—an area dense with joints, tendons, nerves, major blood vessels— and didn't touch any of it."

"Are you disappointed, doc?" Tom asked, instantly relieved.

"No," the doctor said, "but it is something of a miracle."

By the time Rosemary and Ryan arrived at the hospital, they found Tom on a gurney in the emergency room. Ryan had tried not to cry, but his lips were quivering by the time he saw his father. Rosemary walked up and put herself between Tom and the two cops interrogating him, making clear that their interview was over. Then she pulled Ryan closer and he finally let out his sobs.

"It wouldn't have been fair for you to be taken, Dad, while we were fighting . . ." Ryan trailed off.

Tom and Rosemary, each more worried about the other, told each other it was going to be okay.

All night Rosemary tried to reach their daughter, Katie, who was away at Salve Regina University in Newport, Rhode Island. Inadvertently, she was dialing Katie's freshman-year number, and Katie was a sophomore now.

Katie had been out with her friends and when they came back to the dorm they went down to the TV lounge to watch the 11 o'clock news. Katie found out her father had been shot by seeing him wheeled away on a stretcher from the train station, arguing with the cop.

Her friends ran to get the school nurse. For an hour they dialed everyone in the family, but this was the pre-cell-phone age and everyone was at the hospital. Finally, her mother got university officials to track Katie down just as Katie had figured out which hospital had her dad.

Tom's insistence on Mercy Hospital had saved his family from the pandemonium at the two main hospitals, where practically everyone from Garden City, along with a horde of media, showed up to look for victims. Tom was one of the few patients at Mercy and the mood there was calm and removed from the larger tragedy.

Around four A.M., once Rosemary was sure Tom was safe and just needed to sleep, she finally drove home with Ryan. On the way, even though she had given up smoking years earlier, she decided she wanted cigarettes. She thought nothing of driving to the local 7–11, which happened to be across the street from the train station. Then she saw the scene at the train station, the first of many awakenings of just what had happened that night. The train was still in the station, where it would remain for another day. There were spotlights, and the train doors were open so that forensic investigators could search for clues. Ten hours after the shooting, police still swarmed over the scene and helicopters circled above.

The scene shook Rosemary. She never got her cigarettes.

MEET THE MCDERMOTTS, DECEMBER 7, 1941

December 7 had always been a strange day for the McDermotts. On December 7, 1941, Kathleen Walsh, who had come from County Sligo, Ireland, to work in New York as a housekeeper, married Thomas R. McDermott, whose father had come over from neighboring County

Roscommon. The wedding was at St. Ann's Church in the then-Irish Mott Haven section of the Bronx near Yankee Stadium. They got married at about the same hour—noon New York time—that Japanese planes started hitting Pearl Harbor. About five in the afternoon, the unthinkable news started spreading through the reception: the United States was definitely now at war. There was bewilderment. Needless to say, the attack put a damper on the reception as the wedding party was more attuned to news on the radio than the nuptials. This was certainly a day that would live in infamy for the McDermott clan. When Tom got shot on December 7, the date took on new, tragic meaning for the McDermott family.

Tom had been born in the Bronx, but his parents moved back to his dad's hometown of Poughkeepsie when he was four. He was the second of six kids. At age seventeen, Tom moved with his family to Hyde Park, the former home of Franklin D. Roosevelt, a couple of hours north of the city. The family would go back to Brooklyn regularly to visit Tom's aunt, who couldn't come see them because she was a nun. Not just an ordinary nun, either. His aunt, known as Sister Mary of Carmel, lived in a walled oasis of prayer on Fort Hamilton Parkway in Brooklyn near Bay Ridge, the working class setting of *Saturday Night Fever*. The nuns there give themselves totally over to the spiritual life. Inside their cloistered walls they say prayers every two hours. That's half-hour prayers every two hours, twenty-four hours a day, seven days a week. As a boy, Tom found this schedule implausibly arduous. He had joked with his aunt, "Oh, c'mon, you don't really get up in the middle of the night every night. I'm sure you sleep through it sometimes."

"Tommy!" she'd cry. "Don't say such things."

The McDermotts were unwavering Catholics. Another uncle studied to become a priest. Tom's father worked on the railroad, first as a "fireman" shoveling coal into the steam engine, and later as an engineer on diesel engines.

Tom's dad used to take Tom to the courtroom to see trials. He sensed early on where his boy was headed. The whole county knew its prosecutor, Ray Baratta, Sr. When the local boy Baratta was working his way through college and law school, the conductors, admiring his struggle, would let him ride the train to New York City free, Tom's dad said. Tom also knew him as the dad of his close friend, Ray Baratta, Jr. During high school Tom would sometimes stop by the courthouse on his own to see the senior Baratta at work. He was like Gregory Peck's Atticus Finch—minus the one big case of *To Kill a Mockingbird*: a steady, low-key figure of decency.

Tom and Ray, Jr. went to nearby Marist College together. Tom graduated in 1965 and started working as a social studies teacher at a local grammar school. The next year he and several college friends shared an apartment and taught high school at Cardinal Farley Military Academy, operated by the Irish Christian Brothers in Rhinecliff, New York. Tom taught social studies and English and was the head junior varsity football coach. When the religion teacher, a priest, got sick, the brothers gave Tom that job, too. The position wasn't too much of a stretch for McDermott, given his religious background. The first day, the boys gave McDermott the traditional substitute teacher assault with their creative religious inquiries: "Hey, Mr. Mac, say you're in the back seat of a car with a girl, you're horny as hell, how far can you go? I mean really, tell me." He told the kid to shut up and got on with the class.

He loved the place, but the Vietnam War was on and he felt a duty to go, even though he wasn't gung-ho about this particular war. He enlisted in the army. He was supposed to go Fort Dix, New Jersey, for basic training, and then to officer-candidate school in Fort Benning, Georgia. With just a week to go in New Jersey, he hurt his back and spent three days in the hospital. When he got out, he had to finish his infantry training with another class, and by then his spot in officer-candidate school had been taken.

The army had a solution: he would go work in Korea for up to a year, then go to officer school, and then serve his two-year commitment. Some how the army had just signed him on for another year. He got sent down to the personnel office, where a clerk gave him the option of opting out of officer school altogether. Tom instantly agreed. Another clerk down the row overheard what was going on and asked Tom, "Where'd you say you were from?"

"Hyde Park," Tom told him.

"I'm from Kingston," the clerk said, referring to a nearby town. "Do you know Hoby Armstrong?" Armstrong was a famous area high-school football player.

"My brother, John McDermott, played football with him."

"That's my cousin," the clerk said. "Okay, you want to stay here at Fort Dix?"

"Yeah, I'd love to stay at Fort Dix."

"Okay, done."

Tom was no longer going to Korea; he was going to work in personnel with his new best friends. He worked at Fort Dix through most of 1968. In the fall, he enrolled at New York Law School on Worth Street in lower Manhattan. He commuted 180 miles roundtrip, four nights a week. He would work his shift for the army, then get a bus, train, and subway to school, where he would take classes from 6:00 to 10:00 P.M. He got back just in time for the last bus out of Trenton at midnight.

One November night, just before exams, he came back to sign in at the base and the company clerk said, "I've got bad news for you. Look up at the board." Tom's new assignment had been posted: He was going to Vietnam.

He went back to law school the next night and his torts professor announced that they were losing Tom to Vietnam. A gasp of dread went through the classroom.

His family had a big, emotional goodbye and his friend Ray Baratta, Jr. drove him to Stewart Air Force base near West Point. When they got there, they learned Tom's flight was delayed until the next day. Rather than go through another wrenching send-off, he went back to the Baratta house and stayed up all night talking with Ray Jr. and Ray Sr., who by then was a judge. "I remember so well his [Ray Sr.'s] being overcome with good wishes and the emotion of the moment," Tom said. "He said he would see me again—he knew he would—and he would think of me often."

Tom was stationed in DaNang, a teeming city with a large Marine base that fell and was evacuated just before Saigon. Again, he worked mainly in personnel, administering tests. Some of his other jobs included hopping on prop planes as a courier with documents to Saigon and guarding the base at night, where he faced rocket and mortar attacks. "It was a very fortunate assignment, to say the least," Tom recalls. "The only dangerous times were when I was guard duty out on the perimeter."

Discharged in 1969, Tom moved to New York City. He started law school at St. John's, a Catholic university then in Brooklyn, in February 1970 and got an evening job at a bank to pay for tuition. One night that spring he went out drinking with friends, including some visiting West Point cadets. Late one night as they left the Mad Hatter, then an institution on the Upper East Side, they ran into a bunch of young women, one of whom was Rosemary, and started talking. A West Point cadet assisted Tom in getting Rosemary's phone number and even pinned it to Tom's bulletin board so he wouldn't lose it. That fall Tom started a day job as a special agent with the New York–New Jersey Waterfront Commission. By 1971, Tom and Rosemary were married and living in Stuyvesant Town, the massive housing complex in lower Manhattan built for World War II veterans. Two years later they bought a house in Rosemary's hometown of Garden City and had Katie. Three years later, in 1976, Ryan was born.

When Tom graduated from law school in 1974, he became a special assistant attorney general in the New York State Special Prosecutor's Office, which was investigating corruption in the New York City criminal justice system. The lawyers worked out of the World Trade Center in its early days when it had a vacancy problem and government agencies tried to fill it.

Tom tried to follow the example of Ray Baratta, Sr.: A prosecutor should be fair and compassionate, not just out for big convictions. Tom once busted a veteran cop, near retirement, whose son had stolen one of his guns, which had ended up being used in a crime. When the cop found out, he was suicidal, not only about his drug-addled son's behavior, but because his wife might lose his pension. He told Tom he'd kill himself that night.

Tom had no stomach for prosecuting the case, but he arrested the man in order to take away his gun so he wouldn't harm himself. Then he released him, sent someone to watch over the guy, and arranged for a more lenient police internal affairs office to handle the case.

Tom could have sympathy, but not when it interfered with his mission of ridding the city of a certain kind of sleaze. The work of the Special Prosecutor's Office was the basis for the bestselling book and Academy Award–nominated movie *Prince of the City* about an elite investigative cop, Det. Robert Leuci, who went undercover to expose cops on the take. Tom worked in the Bronx bureau with Joel Cohen,[12] who led the investigation into cops substituting flour for the 112 pounds of heroin seized in the day's other famous real-life police drama, the "French Connection" case. Cohen led the prosecution of Det. Leslie Wolff (Jerry Orbach played the fictionalized character who was renamed Gus Levy in the movie),[13] and McDermott helped him. Wolff would never admit anything, McDermott said, because he didn't want his son to see him as a bad cop. In the film Orbach brags of busting a string of criminals, "and not one of them a cop,"[14] and the central theme is whether the prosecutors were overzealous in pursuing police officers instead of crooks. At the trial, Wolff's attorney also attacked Cohen and McDermott for going to extraordinary lengths to pursue cops, using murderers and drug dealers, the dregs of the earth, as witnesses. Those were the people whom crooked cops dealt with, Tom said, so they had no choice. Wolff's lawyer attacked Cohen and McDermott personally for their decision even to bring the case. Joel Cohen handled the witnesses but let Tom do the summation. Tom spoke about the mission of a prosecutor, the way he had learned the job from Ray Baratta: to do justice in good faith and not to break the law, turning the other way when a case becomes uncomfortable. Tom looked directly at the jury and told them to acquit Wolff if they thought the prosecutors had broken the law. He told them not to even bother spending five minutes in the jury room or to examine any testimony or evidence if they believed McDermott and Cohen had framed Wolff.

The normally stolid Cohen almost cried. To this day he thinks of the speech as Tom's defining moment. The jury took four days to deliberate, illustrating its faith in the prosecution, but it acquitted Wolff.[15] Interviewed later, jurors told prosecutors it wasn't fair to punish only Wolff when two other cops got off with cooperation and one committed suicide.

In 1977 McDermott moved on to the Nassau County District Attorney's office, closer to his home in Long Island, where he went after politicians on the take. He became the deputy chief of the official corruption bureau. In 1981, he left to start a private practice, but in 1983 he got an offer to work as outside counsel for a new government agency, the New York State Thoroughbred Racing Capital Investment Fund. The state started the agency because the three New York tracks were falling apart.

The New York Racing Association, a non-profit corporation made up of high society horse owners, has run racing and betting in the state since the 1950s, but the state was still squabbling with the association over who owned the tracks and who should pay for improvements. Either way, the state expected to get the three tracks, Saratoga, Belmont, and Aqueduct, back when NYRA's contract expired (in 2007), so it wanted to maintain them. It created the New York State Thoroughbred Racing Capital Investment Fund to help finance capital improvements. The fund worked out of an office, filled with horsey décor, above Penn Station.

The job wasn't glamorous, but it gave him just the independence he craved so he could take on private cases and spend time with Rosemary and the kids.

Two

A MIRACLE, A MISSION: FINDING PURPOSE IN TRAGEDY

THE SHOOTING AFTERMATH, DECEMBER 1993

The time following the shooting was a jumble of events and emotions. The news at first was that just four people had died in the shooting. James Gorycki, fifty-one, a father of four and a friendly salesman who had just been moved to a Manhattan office; Richard Nettleton, twenty-four, a young kid who liked to write, play the drums, and hang out with his family; the Filipino woman McDermott had seen with the head wound, Marita Magtoto, thirty, who had just passed the bar exam and gotten a legal job in Manhattan; and Dennis McCarthy, fifty-two, an assistant manager at Prudential Securities.[1]

The small McCarthy family had suffered grievously. Not only was its patriarch dead, but the McCarthys' only child, Kevin, twenty-six, had been shot. Dennis had stayed late that day so he could take the train home from work with his son. Earlier that fall Kevin had started working at Prudential Securities with his father and since then they'd grown close. "I think father and son are always at a bit of a distance," Kevin's mother, Carolyn McCarthy told *Newsday*. "But in the past couple of months, you could see a bond developing. To see it, father and son, I think it was beautiful. I think it was all on the train."[2] The McCarthy men were planning to put up the Christmas tree that night, but they were sitting in the rear of the car, where Ferguson started his rampage. They both were shot once in the head. Dennis fell into Kevin's lap. Now doctors gave Kevin only a 10 to 20 percent chance of living.[3] Even if he did survive, there was a good chance of paralysis on his left side. Besieged by requests to help her son, Carolyn McCarthy set up a fund for Kevin's rehabilitation.

There were other lives hanging by a thread. One belonged to Mi Kyung Kim, 27, who was a supervisor of the Columbia University math library and aspiring animation artist. Kim died the day after the shooting. She was so gentle that she had often told her younger sister of her cat, Mabi: "I don't know what I'd do if Mabi died." Now Mabi would have to make it without her. The other woman Tom had seen lying on the train floor was Amy Federici. She was twenty-seven, an interior designer at MTV and recently a widow. Only the previous July she had married and was looking forward to a bright future. Two weeks after the wedding her husband was diagnosed with pancreatic and liver cancer, and within months he was dead.[4] She was on life support and died five days after the shooting.

The three heroes on the train turned out to be young men from Garden City. George Kevin Blum, a forty-two-year-old bond trader, had been talking with Michael O'Connor, thirty-one, who worked at Goldman Sachs. O'Connor described to *Newsday* how Blum had taken charge and rushed at Ferguson: "We turned around, and we saw [Ferguson] standing in the car. And then Kevin said, 'Let's get him,' . . . I dove on top of the pile . . . I had his right arm, and the other guy [Mark McEntee, thirty-four] had his left arm." After the carnage, Blum went out to direct traffic. O'Connor shied away from being called a hero and gave all the credit to Blum.[5]

The *Today Show* called: Katie Couric wanted to interview one victim, McDermott, and one rescuer, O'Connor. Tom's daughter Katie knew O'-Connor's younger sister, so they already had a connection, and Tom agreed. He wasn't comfortable in the designated victim role, but he wanted to help honor O'Connor and the other heroes. He was not prepared for the media beast that would show up in his hospital room at 4 A.M. to lay cable.

On the air, Tom got another surprise. O'Connor called Tom the real hero of the event. He described how Tom had covered up a young woman's head with his trench coat after he had been shot and lying on the ground.

This was news to Tom. He said he just didn't remember.

Tom would learn that the human mind can play tricks on you in a traumatic event. Some details of the shooting were forever vivid and others mysteriously blacked-out. This was common mental terrain for shooting victims.

Joel Cohen, who had worked with Tom in the special state prosecutor's office, showed up at the hospital. Cohen had been on a business trip out west and saw the news of the shooting on the airport TV. Cohen thought he recognized his old friend McDermott, whom he hadn't seen in years, on a stretcher. But all around Cohen, people shrugged off the shooting as just another piece of New York mayhem

That blasé attitude shocked Tom, but he quickly realized it was common outside New York. Tom's nephew in Minneapolis described how he had sat around with colleagues on the day of the shooting, discussing how New Yorkers knew what risks they were taking. The next day, he got the news that his own uncle was one of those wild risk-taking New Yorkers. "Uncle Tommy, the reaction in our office was, 'What do those people in the subway expect when you live in a place like New York?'"

"This is a college-educated guy," McDermott emphasizes. "That Midwestern mentality was *Gee, what are you guys complaining about? You got what you deserved.* It wasn't until later that he saw anything that he could identify with. Then when he connected with an individual, it was *Oh, that's terrible.*"

People naturally concoct rationalizations as to why tragedy can't happen to them. It's in New York. Much of the nation's view of urban travel is still focused on the images of 1970s high-crime, graffiti-covered trains. Of course, in New York itself, people resorted to the explanation that the shooting didn't happen on the train they usually ride. It was the LIRR to Port Jefferson—totally different.

As the story became clearer and people learned this hadn't happened on some grungy subway car, but a suburban commuter train, some perceptions changed. Certainly there was some calculus as to the race and class of the victims that made these (mostly) white suburban commuters more important. But still Tom and Joel were amazed, as they talked over the next days and weeks, that for the rest of the country this wasn't an earth-shattering event, that not everyone was shocked by the realization that this could happen anywhere, to anyone.

Colin Ferguson, the thirty-five-year-old who shot up the train, garnered the lion's share of the public's interest as it tried to figure out what could have turned him into such a monster. In the days after the shooting the press reported that Ferguson was not anything like the typical American gun criminal—unprivileged, black, a product of the ghetto—that many had figured him for.[6][7][8][9][10] He came from an upper-class family in Jamaica. His father was a pharmaceutical company executive and he had four high-achieving brothers. He was not a destitute immigrant; he was the product of private religious schools. But when his parents both died when he was a young man, he was set adrift emotionally and wound up in America. He tried to make a life in California and then came to New York.

At first things went well. He worked, took classes, got married. Then his wife left him. After that, he started losing jobs and getting kicked out of schools. It's unclear whether mental illness started this downward spiral or vice versa. He fell off a chair at work and collected worker's compensation. He badgered the state office to extend his payments until eventually it relented. When the extension came close to running out, he started calling many times a day to hound the office to extend his payments yet again. He started accusing white students at Adelphi University, his peers, of racism.[11] A history professor tried to defend him against disciplinary charges after Ferguson repeatedly unleashed racial tirades, but Ferguson wasn't satisfied with his efforts and he turned on him, too. He accused the professor of racism, and when he went so far as to threaten the professor, the school kicked him out. One theory about the shooting is that Ferguson was really headed toward Adelphi in Garden City (which is nearby, but on another line) but somehow took the wrong train.

His only previous brush with the law was an argument on the subway the winter before. New Yorkers have silent territory disputes all the time over subway scat encroachment. This one, however, turned violent. Ferguson was splayed across more than one seat and a woman asked him to move so that she could sit. He did, but when she sat down, he began to elbow her forcefully. She called the police, and he was dragged off in handcuffs in Times Square.

Ferguson moved back to California briefly. No one is sure if the move was meant to be permanent or was just his gun-shopping trip, but it ended within a few months. You have to live in the state where you buy a gun. In California you have to wait fifteen days. Ferguson bought his gun, a Ruger 9 mm, on this California trip. He used his hotel as his address. He waited the fifteen days. The sale was legal, although the recent move and the temporary address could have raised flags, if the store clerk were interested in seeing them. And certainly any rudimentary mental background check or exam would have turned up trouble. But it wasn't as if a local sheriff was doling out licenses to those he knew and deemed okay; it was a massive, lumbering system in which all but the most provably egregious requests for guns just sailed through. Just before the killings, his landlady, who was about to kick him out because of his increasingly belligerent tirades, noticed that he had become serene and quiet.

In his pocket Ferguson had a fugue of a letter in which he tried to explain the shootings. He blamed his rage on whites. The note explained that he did not commit his crime in New York City out of deference to Mayor David Dinkins, who is black. He also listed his epic grievances with Adelphi, the worker's compensation board, and the woman from the subway dispute, but people focused on his racial rage.

The day after the shooting, Nassau County Executive Tom Gulotta, considered a possible Republican candidate for governor, said: "The person who committed these crimes is an animal. No penalty is too severe." Comparing Ferguson to an animal kicked off a racial firestorm. A group of black ministers called the animal remark "unacceptable, inexcusable, and reprehensible."[12] The Reverend Jesse Jackson entered the fray, saying the connotation was racial and demeaning. Gulotta and his defenders insisted that his use of the term "animal" had no racial overtone. Then Jackson urged Gulotta, who wouldn't apologize, to stop playing George Wallace.

To Tom, all of this was a distraction, a red herring, a way not to think about the real issue: guns. Ferguson might be crazy. He might be enraged because he was black. Or not. There were countless people like him, but what set him apart and gave him the ability to slaughter a train car of full people was the gun.

THERE BUT FOR THE GRACE OF GOD

Two days after the shooting, McDermott came home. Friends and family celebrated the fact he had not died by practically having a wake for him. They swarmed the house and filled it with food. The hubbub kept the family occupied for the next few days. On the Saturday after the shooting, the McDermotts attended the funeral of James Gorycki. They had never met Gorycki, but Tom had much in common with him. Both were in their early 50s, both had teenage children, and both also had light hair and a stocky build. In fact, they looked so much alike that on the night of the shooting, one of Gorycki's relatives saw Tom on TV, in his now famous argument with a cop and mistook him for Gorycki,[13] welcoming the news that he was okay. James's wife Joyce saw right away that the man on the stretcher wasn't her husband. After hearing the news of the shooting and knowing her husband was on that 5:33 train, she called around trying to find him and taking calls from worried friends. "I was going crazy calling all the hotlines they'd set up," she said. "And when I didn't get word from him, that made me more worried." The passing hours told her what no information officer could. By the time police officers came to her door at 10:30 P.M. to deliver the news, Joyce Gorycki already knew in her heart that her husband was dead.

Joyce describes the days surrounding her husband's wake and funeral as a "This is Your Life" episode. Everyone who had ever known the couple came to Corpus Christi Church in Mineola, a modern Catholic church made of red brick, with white pillars and a spire. Even people who didn't know them turned up. The shooting victims held a special status on Long Island; the community both revered and pitied them and their families. People understood that anyone on Long Island could have been shot by Colin Ferguson. There were so many deaths that the church had a tight funeral schedule. Joyce heard that Carolyn McCarthy wanted her husband buried there, too, but was waiting, fearful that she would need to have a double funeral if her son Kevin also died.

Tom's exuberance and relief at his own survival vanished as soon as he entered the church. Many of the wounded would feel a survivor's guilt and question why they had lived while others died. Tom's reaction was more vivid than that: in a flash, he saw himself in the coffin and Rosemary, Katie, and Ryan sitting in the first pew, where James Gorycki's family now sat. The Gorycki kids were about the same age as his own. "It was overwhelming. I felt faint. It was just so surreal, so woozy. It was hard to process that it could be me in the coffin," he said.

Tom—and other fathers who had narrowly survived on the train—thought of how close they had come not only to leaving their family behind, but to doing so without a farewell. "The suddenness, the absolute unexpectedness," he says. "The unanticipated end of life—without having that one glimmer, one or two seconds, to say goodbye."

The real tragedy for Tom would not have been dying; it would have been stranding his family. They would be the real victims. The randomness of fate. Three fifty-something fathers, who all looked pretty much alike, got on the Hicksville 5:33. Dennis McCarthy, fifty-two: dead. James Gorycki, fifty-one: dead. Tom McDermott, fifty: "miraculously" fine.

It was too much for McDermott.

THE BIRTH OF AN ACTIVIST

No one wants to believe that life is so random that a person can just get on the wrong train car and die for no reason. The religious especially want to see God's hand, even in the horrific. And if people can't see the good, they may try to force something positive out of a tragedy themselves.

Tom and Rosemary McDermott, who had both grown up Catholic and never lapsed, talked more and more with Tom's old friend Joel Cohen about what they all saw as the religious implications of Tom's survival. First there were the coincidences that put him on the early train with Ferguson. Then, he survived nearly unscathed when others around him died. Tom said he didn't feel as if he had been spared for living a decent life. Quite the opposite: "I felt the people who died were maybe better people than I was."

Joel, an observant Jew, tended to see the world through a religious lens; he would go on to write a play and biography called *Moses: A Memoir*. Together, they all started to perceive Tom's shooting and survival as a kind of miracle. The extra years of Tom's life were a gift from God, a gift that had to be used judiciously.

As if to add to their conviction, Tom's orthopedist was mystified by Tom's own "magic" bullet, which went straight through him, avoiding all his vital organs and nerves. If the trajectory were just slightly different—thrown off by milliseconds in his ducking movement—the bullet could have hit Tom's spine, heart, lungs, or a major blood vessel. Instead Tom had a sore shoulder that took a session or two of physical therapy, but that was it. No surgery. He didn't even need stitches.

This is a miracle, Joel would say. Sometimes, in fact, he would just call up and leave an answering machine message: "This is a miracle. You've got to use it."

Tom started to go out to his backyard and pace at night, trying to figure out just how to use his gift of extra years. This was not the same as surviving a car accident or a natural disaster, he thought to himself. He had faced a man-made evil on that train. Or, as he was beginning to feel, he had faced two monsters. One was Colin Ferguson, who was already locked up and conquered. The forces that allowed Ferguson to get that gun were the other. It was a monster that was still living—and still killing.

All of Long Island shared Tom's dilemma as people struggled to find a reason for the shooting—and something or someone to blame.

The community broke into two camps. One side blamed Ferguson and his insane racial hatred. Its adherents wanted to put Ferguson to death to teach others a lesson. McDermott quickly dismissed Ferguson as crazy and figured that because we all know there are going to be crazy people, we had better not let everybody have guns. He gravitated toward the other side, which blamed the monstrous forces of American gun culture, gun politics, and the gun industry that made it so easy for this man to get a Ruger, bullets designed to open on impact to maximize injuries, and an extra large clip.

The radical left and the radical right both focused on race as a cause. The left blamed the racism Ferguson had encountered in his life. The right thought he was just another crazy black man. Ferguson's crimes, however, were much like his background: more typical of whites than blacks. Almost all mass murderers are whites. And most murderers target their own race and socioeconomic group.

For McDermott, there was another racial aspect. Like most Americans, he hadn't paid much attention to gun violence. Maybe that was because its victims tended to be poor black teenage boys.

The NAACP would later find black teens sixteen times as likely to die from gunshots than white youth.[14] And Tom didn't know it then, but the idea that Americans shouldn't worry about guns because so many shooting victims are black has been discussed by gun rights activists, even if they don't say it too loudly in public.

NRA board of directors member Jeff Cooper wrote in *Guns & Ammo* in 1991 that "the consensus is that no more than five to ten people in a hundred who die by gunfire in Los Angeles are any loss to society. . . . It would seem a valid social service to keep them well-supplied with ammunition."[15] [16] Pro-gun academic John Lott wrote, "we cannot ignore the unfortunate fact that crime (particularly violent crime, and especially murder) is disproportionately committed against blacks by blacks."[17] Another NRA board member, Rep. Barbara Cubin (R-WY), would object to a gun control bill: "My sons are twenty-five and thirty. They are blond-haired and blue-eyed. One amendment today said we could not sell guns to anybody under drug treatment. So does that mean if you go into a black community, you cannot sell a gun to any black person, or does that mean because my. . . ."[18] Then she was interrupted.

Whether Tom heard the rhetoric directly or not, it had seeped into the public consciousness as an excuse not to worry about guns. Tom McDermott saw now that if it could happen to him, despite all his hard work and decent living, it could happen to any American. In 1993 alone there were 39,358 Americans killed by guns.[19] If December 7, 1993, was typical, then the six deaths on the Long Island Railroad were just a sliver of 107 firearm deaths expected to occur that day in America. According to the Centers for Disease Control, another 104,000 people were injured by firearms that year. So Tom was one of about 285 Americans injured that day by a gun. In 1993, the U.S. homicide rate was 9.9 for every 100,000 people: 7 of those 9.9 were killed with a gun. That same year the homicide rate in Japan was 0.62 and the gun homicide rate was 0.02. That means in America seventy people per million would be murdered with a gun while in Japan it would only be six. In 1994 France had a homicide rate of 1.12 and a gun homicide rate of 0.44; Germany had 1.17 and 0.22.[20] The reason this shooting got so much attention was that it happened to white suburban commuters in what was supposed to be a safe community in Long Island.

The suburbs of Nassau County are just the sort of place where, after a mass killing, people say that they never thought it could happen here. Long Island is literally an island, which includes the New York City boroughs of Brooklyn and Queens and then suburbs beyond them to the east. Suburban Long Island is divided east to west into two counties, Nassau, the Republican county close to the city, and Suffolk, the less densely populated (and also Republican) outreaches. A glacial ridge also divides it from north to south. Sometimes the North Shore, home of Fitzgerald's Jay Gatsby in the novel's invented East Egg and the real-life modern affluence of Great Neck, looks askance at the South Shore, where the "Lawn Guyland" accent prevails. The year before the LIRR shootings, the big national crime story and all-around cultural joke was Amy ("The Long Island Lolita") Fisher's shooting of her lover Joey Buttafuoco's wife, Mary Jo, in South Shore's Massapequa. The Ferguson mass killing took place in northern Nassau, where most of the victims lived. The people there are neither extremely rich nor extremely Republican, but the county has been solidly in GOP hands for years. Even Democrats here tend toward social conservatism.

All of Long Island felt the shooting as a violation. It enraged these ordinary Americans, made them feel threatened in their supposedly safe neighborhood, made them realize it could happen here and it could happen anywhere in America. But for all the shock, there was no innocence about guns left to be lost in 1993. Only seven years earlier, postman Patrick Henry Sherrill killed fourteen in an Oklahoma post office, part of a wave of mail carrier homicidal outbursts that inspired the phrase "going postal."[21] James Oliver Huberty murdered twenty-one in a McDonald's in San Ysidro, California, in 1984.[22] On the other side of New York City in New Rochelle, the fictional home of *The Dick Van Dyke Show*'s Rob and Laura Petrie, neo-Nazi Frederick Cowan gunned down five, including police officer Allen McLeod, on Valentine's Day, 1977.[23] [24] In 1966 Charles Whitman had quickly killed fourteen people from atop a University of Texas tower; a fifteenth died in 2001 after decades of surgery and dialysis.[25]

These mass gun murders are inevitably portrayed as an aberration. In its coverage of the Sherrill killings, *Time* wrote, "It is a phenomenon peculiar to the late twentieth century. a single twisted soul slaughtering near or total strangers, acting on a vague, incomprehensible motive." Some argue that Whitman was the founder of the shooting rampage trend. In truth, mass shootings have been going on much longer; it's just that the weapons haven't been so effective.

For as long as guns have been around, people have been shooting their family members, begrudged neighbors, and complete strangers. Smaller capacity (fewer bullets), lower caliber (smaller bullets), and slower guns had lower body counts, but they were still mass shootings. Newspaper accounts from as early as the nineteenth century show similar shooting sprees.[26] [27] In 1896 the *New York Times* judged that an unemployed man shooting six people then himself to death to warrant only four paragraphs of notice.[28] The early mass shootings tended to involve family, but public shootings were common enough that in 1889 the *Washington Post* devoted only one paragraph to the story headlined "Slain by Drunken Fiend, A Tragedy in Minnesota in Which Four Persons Were Slaughtered."[29] The brief reports often blame alcohol instead of mental illness. Criminologists distinguish between serial murders, a series of individual killings that take place over a stretch of time, and mass murders, which are accomplished all at once. Serial killings date back ages, but mass killings, in which the killer has to be able to overpower a crowd, are more novel because they require either a high-capacity gun or a bomb.

The American mass murder came into the public consciousness with Howard Unruh in Camden, New Jersey, in 1949. He shot twenty-six people, killing half of them. Since then, mass murders have become more commonplace. Noted criminologist James Fox of Northeastern University says that while mass murders with weapons other than guns have gone up a little in the late twentieth century, mass murders with guns have sky-rocketed. The easy availability of guns is what caused the rise in mass murders, he notes.[30] The death toll, if not the number of shooting incidents, has gone up dramatically.

When these incidents happen they are shocking and widely reported. Public attention fades quickly—until the next mass shooting. The media and public treat each mass shooting incident as a new and startling event. The truth is more disturbing: The public simply forgets about long-ago horrors. And it ignores the staggering body count of more typical, less spectacular shootings, in which the typical victim is a black teenage boy.

As Tom told Joel of his unformed but growing sense of calling to do something about guns, Joel saw the mission-driven Tom he had known as a young prosecutor return. Tom had spoken simply and genuinely in the courtroom about doing what was right that day. Now he was starting to act the same way.

It was as if Tom had taken a daddy-track career path: The impassioned young prosecutor had taken time off to raise his family, but now that they were grown, he was shifting to the outside world again. Tom the young prosecutor was back. However, this time his quest couldn't be his full-time job. Instead he would have his "day job" to support his family and then he would have his mission, devoting his life's work—really a separate career's worth of work—to his private gun project.

Rosemary and Tom were centrist Democrats. They were both law-and-order types. They had no strong feelings on the gun issue before the shooting. Rosemary grew up with guns. Her father was an FBI agent who taught the kids to respect guns and leave them alone. Rosemary's brother became an FBI agent, too. So Rosemary was used to the men in her life carrying guns. Tom had even carried a gun for a couple of jobs, once as a park policeman and then again at the waterfront commission. And of course, he'd used guns in the army.

The McDermotts never hated guns or gun owners. They just never gave them much thought. But now they found out that their whole future could have been stolen by one. And they suddenly wanted to warn people about guns, even as Tom knew he had much to learn himself first. First he needed to find out what he was up against.

There was no one clear path to take. There were all kinds of gun control groups—support groups, victims' rights group—but there was no single organization to join the way the NRA served pro–gun rights adherents. If there had been, it would have been a powerful force. One 1994 report noted that a half-million Americans had died from firearms injuries since 1960.[31] If just one or two survivors of each of those dead Americans had banded together, they would be a major lobbying group. Add to them all the millions who had been injured and their friends and family, and the organization of shooting victims would easily overpower the NRA.

But it didn't work like that. Previous shooting survivors would reach out to Tom McDermott informally; they would teach him what they had learned themselves. While a few of them stuck around for years, most tired of the emotionally grueling topic. The newer ones enmeshed themselves in learning about the cultural, legal, and financial beast they were fighting. It wasn't as if the Learning Annex offered a Gun Control Advocate's class.

Was the problem with gun laws? Maybe Americans and their lawmakers just didn't understand that guns were sold so cheaply and easily that any American could end up shot dead, just like those people on the train. The half-million Americans killed by guns effectively disappeared from the political discussion. Tom would have to go in their place to town halls, state capitols, and even the U.S. Capitol to try to persuade them. He would have to speak for the dead.

Did the Second Amendment really guarantee everyone the right to own a gun? He had always heard of the Constitutional right to guns, but what was that other part of the amendment, the part about a well-regulated militia? He vowed to find out.

Was it really all about the National Rifle Association? Tom didn't know much about the gun issue in America, but he had, of course, heard of the NRA; he lived on Long Island, not on the Galapagos Islands. What was its purpose really? How did one little group with a largely rural and Southern membership dictate gun laws that got people killed in Northern cities? Were they really as powerful as people made them out to be? Were they really the main obstacle in his path?

Was it just money? Did the NRA have that much money? Were guns big business anymore? How could anyone make money selling low-quality handguns that sold for less than $100, whose low price ensured their high popularity among the urban poor? These guns, nicknamed Saturday Night Specials by Detroit cops to describe the cheap handguns impetuous Detroiters picked up in Toledo and with which they settled a score on a Saturday night, may not have caused the deaths Tom witnessed on the train, but they had certainly caused many others.

The impulse of any investigator, especially one trained in financial fraud like Tom, was to follow the money. Somebody had to be profiting from all the extra guns sold on the street. He needed to figure out who and how. Did the solution to the gun problem lie in the courts? Tom had heard people were actually suing gun companies, trying to make them pay for the damage their products caused. At this point, even suing tobacco makers was considered far-fetched, greedy. But if the answer was in the courts, where Tom felt most comfortable, then he was better prepared than most to find how to make the courts solve the gun problem.

This was his new purpose, the reason he and Rosemary believed Tom had been spared. At first he was possessed only of a vague sense of injustice. He was facing an amorphous beast: There were too many guns on America's streets, guns that were too powerful and that found their way into the wrong hands too quickly and too easily. The enemy was a three-headed monster: American gun culture, gun control politics, and the gun industry. Which part should he attack? He needed to find this beast's vulnerability.

What had started off as a 55-minute train ride would become a decade-long quest to do something, do anything about guns. It would become Tom McDermott's mission in life.

Three

WALKING VICTIM IMPACT STATEMENT: SPEAKING OUT

THIS WEEK WITH DAVID BRINKELY, DECEMBER 12, 1993

Tom McDermott turned down most media requests, but then producers from David Brinkley's show called. They wanted him for the Sunday after the shooting, December 12. Brinkley, the éminence grise of American TV news who had gotten his start in radio, had been Tom's favorite reporter since he was a kid, so he agreed. Even though the issue was new to him, he hoped to talk about guns.

Brinkley taped his show in Washington, D.C., but McDermott would appear in New York via satellite. He went into the city early that morning. The producers put him in a dark booth. Off to the side and through a window, he could see the other guest but not hear him. He could hear Brinkley's voice in his earpiece. When a red light went on in the booth, that meant it was McDermott's turn to speak. If guests were allowed to see and hear Brinkley on a monitor, a producer explained, they would instinctively speak to the monitor instead of to the camera.

Brinkley introduced McDermott and asked: "Aside from being lucky to be alive and happy to be alive, what thoughts do you have about this event now?"[1]

McDermott was already getting used to—and weary of—what people wanted to hear: a story of the massacre, what it felt like to have your suburban commuter train turned into a battlefield. He wanted his appearance to speak to something more than that.

He said, "Well, David, the gratitude that I feel, of course, for being spared by God and the gratitude that my family feels, is hard to describe . . . . [It] has caused me to not only look at my life in a different perspective but try to make some sense—or I'm going to attempt to try to make some sense out of this entire episode."

He was groping for meaning—and would for years—but Brinkley wanted an answer now and prodded, "Mr. McDermott, it does seem, without being too excitable, it does seem to a great many people that our country is becoming increasingly dangerous. Does it seem so to you, and do you have any thoughts about that, any answers?"

McDermott saw this statement as an opening, but he tried to stay focused: "Well, my thoughts are I concur completely. Here we had eighty passengers, innocent people having finished a day's work, that, in the flash of an eye, a gunman presents himself, as I later learned, has over one hundred rounds of ammunition in his possession, but in a very brief period, David, of three minutes or so, between two train stations, holds eighty passengers in absolute terror, and those rounds that he got off during that brief period of time seemed like an eternity."

Tom thought Brinkley was trying to control the interview and end all talk of gun control when Brinkley responded: "They talk of gun control. This man had abided by all the laws. He bought the gun legally, waited for the required legal waiting period, and then began shooting."

McDermott was angry at the easy availability of massive firepower. He imagined how different the shooting would have turned out, how many lives would have been saved, if Ferguson was able to only obtain a ten-round clip instead of one that held fifteen bullets. He responded: "Yes, I was quite surprised to learn of that. . . . And the irony of that, David, to me is that I dare say whether it were a thirty-day period that the Brady bill, I think, originally contemplated, or a sixty-day, if it even were a six-month period I don't think that that is where the focus should be. And my focus— my own individual focus right now—is on the gun itself."

Brinkley quickly ended the interview: "Well, that is a very difficult controversy yet to be settled, and we thank you for coming in and talking with us today, and good luck to you."

"Thank you very much." Feeling dismissed, McDermott was left alone in the darkened sound booth. "I felt such a kick in the stomach, a disappointment, a futility. There were no advance questions given to me. I thought I was there to address what my concern was, the fifteen-round clip. He devoted his questions to the human element, the sorrow, the death, the combat." McDermott stewed, nursing a growing sense that he was there to speak for the people who had not made it off that train. Next time he would do better.

He went home, went to church, and watched the Sunday morning news shows with Rosemary. The Long Island Railroad shootings were a main topic. He saw Brinkley ask him whether "our country is becoming increasingly dangerous." Well, of course it seemed more dangerous. And the reason, glaringly evident to the McDermotts, was how easy it is to get guns. Before the shooting, he never thought about how easy it would be for someone as obviously disturbed as Ferguson to get a devastatingly powerful gun. While Tom McDermott was busy raising his family, the country had changed. America had become infatuated with guns, even if that meant letting anyone have any gun he or she wanted. Some people needed guns, sure. He had carried one himself. But why a gun like the one Ferguson had? Was America that different from the one he grew up in, where buying and owning a gun was an awesome responsibility? Was it the instant gratification and fun of shooting that overpowered people's awareness of the consequences?

As they watched, the McDermotts saw what other people were saying about the incident. Tom and Rosemary saw Sen. Alan Simpson, a Republican from Wyoming, appear a few segments after Tom's interview. Tom found his tone surly and dismissive. When Sam Donaldson asked him about voting against the Brady bill, Senator Simpson said, gesturing as if he were aiming a long gun from his shoulder, "Yes, I did. I come from Wyoming, where gun control is how steady you hold your rifle. That's an ethic of our land and in our part of the country, and that's the way it is."

McDermott leapt off the couch and yelled, "You sonofabitch!" He couldn't believe a senator joking about guns in an interview that was supposed to be about the Long Island Railroad shooting. This was not a public policy debate at Harvard; real Americans were still in the hospital barely hanging onto their lives thanks to this cowboy attitude about guns. McDermott found the senator's stance both ignorant and offensive, but he began to see why federal gun laws were somehow foreclosed from change. "If I ever meet Simpson, I'm gonna tell him just how disgusted I am, that a United States Senator could act that way, think that way. . . ." Tom McDermott didn't realize it, but he was already starting to plan his career as an anti-gun activist. He was surprised how off-track the country had gotten on guns and felt maybe the bullet wound in his shoulder gave him the credibility, if not the obligation, to say something about it. He had never cared much about the NRA, the Second Amendment, the gun industry, the battles over gun control, but, like the lawyer he was, gearing up to make a case in court, he knew would have to learn everything about them to find his opponent's weakness. He barely heard New York Rep. Charles Schumer, from nearby Brooklyn, answer Simpson: a Schumer proposal would have stopped Ferguson by looking for warning signs, like Ferguson's temporary I.D. or his hotel address.

The technicalities of what to do were unimportant, but he knew he wanted to help do something. Since he was used to persuading juries, he figured public speaking would be a way to contribute. He had what he considered a successful life, the American dream—wife, kids, a satisfying job—but it had all been nearly stolen. If people could understand how much they were risking for guns, how close he had come to losing his life, how much in jeopardy any American's life was, maybe, just maybe, the country could start being more sensible about guns.

GUN CONTROL ADVOCATES REACH OUT

Tom wasn't the only one offended by Sen. Alan Simpson's cowboy bravura on the Brinkley show. Less than ten miles away from Garden City, in the tonier suburb of Great Neck, a fledgling gun control activist, Michelle Schimel, a poised, well-dressed blonde thirty-six-year-old mother of two boys, had the same reaction as Tom had.[2] Some news show hours or days later had actually split the screen, featuring Simpson on one side and McDermott on the other. Tom was wearing a sling and talked about how the shooting had changed his life and how he would do something about guns. She jumped up, threw some insults at Simpson, and then pointed at Tom on the screen and told her husband: "See this guy here? He's the one. He's going to be my friend. I'm going to get to know him and we're going to work together."

This, Michelle admits, was her own bit of bravado. "I was already a little involved, writing letters, screaming at people, not knowing where to begin," she says. "Then I thought, 'This guy is never going to get to know me. He's already on TV.'"

Most big gun control activists had either been shot themselves or knew someone who had been. Michelle was different. She got involved just out of the sense that she or her family could be shooting victims. The Long Island Railroad shooting was the catalyst. She had always been an activist, channeling her involvement through her synagogue, Temple Beth El.

On Tuesday, December 7, the day of the shooting, she had gone with her rabbi to a Long Island interfaith conference on local issues. The Catholics opposed abortion; most others did not. A debate went on, without anyone agreeing on much. Michelle, the only woman and the only lay person there, finally stood up and timidly told the group that it should focus on gun control. One of the men countered that guns were a city problem. "The suburbs are no longer the sanctuary. It's coming our way," she said, before sinking back to her seat. She went home, heard the news on the radio about the shooting, and cried on her kitchen floor for two hours before her husband came home, so sorry to be so right.

If that's not a sign, what is? Michelle thought. She had already told her rabbi that gun control would be her mission.

"Okay, okay, take us with you," he told her.

So when she saw Tom on TV that Sunday afternoon, she wrote him a letter asking if he'd speak at her synagogue.

Tom meanwhile was trying to figure out what he would do next. After watching the Brinkley debacle, he turned to the Sunday papers. An op-ed piece in the *New York Times* intrigued him. A fellow victim of gun violence, Katina Johnstone, had a column that day.[3] In 1992 Johnstone's husband, David, was shot on a business trip to San Francisco. Three teenagers tried to rob him and ended up shooting him in the spine. He was back in New York, getting ready for his life as a quadriplegic husband and father when a blood clot finished him off. Since then, Katina had also been searching for an outlet for her anger about guns.

She had written to Richard Haymaker, the host father of the Japanese student Yoshihiro Hattori, who was dressed like John Travolta for a Halloween party when a wary Louisiana homeowner shot him to death on October 17, 1992. The two were starting to plan what would become the Silent March, a parade of empty shoes to represent the number of Americans shot dead in a typical year.[4] According to the Centers for Disease Control, in the decade leading up to the Ferguson shooting, 350,773 people in America died from gunshot wounds.[5]

But the number of American dead, 35,000 each year, was an abstraction to most people until they saw the display of vacant shoes.[6] Johnstone and Haymaker collected donations of shoes and set them up on community commons around the country. They separated those that came from actual victims and treated them with particular care. The sight overwhelmed people.

The day before the LIRR shooting, Johnstone had appeared before a House committee on the financial costs of firearms violence. After the LIRR shooting, she sent her testimony to the *New York Times* op-ed page. When Tom saw it, he called her up. Johnstone was amazed at how naïve he was about the state of American gun laws and how much he had to learn, but realized she'd been the same way just one long year before. In fact, she was continually amazed how much she had to learn. No wonder people avoided the issue. "Our first conversation all we talked about was guns, guns, guns," Johnstone recalls. "He was shocked."

Tom obsessed over the idea that Ferguson would not have been able to slaughter so many people had he carried the normal ten-round clip. How many bullets would he have been able to get off? Only twenty instead of thirty? Would someone have been able to tackle him sooner? Would some of the six people be alive? McDermott kept asking himself these questions. The extra-large clip made the gun simply a killing machine. What legitimate purpose could it serve? Certainly not hunting. The more he obsessed, the angrier he became at politicians loyal to the National Rifle Association instead of their fellow citizens.

Inspired by Johnstone, McDermott wrote his own op-ed column for the *New York Times*, which ran the following Sunday.[7]

Garden City, L.I.—On Tuesday, Dec. 7, a man stared blankly at me in car No. 3 of the 5:33 Long Island Rail Road train out of Penn Station. With a dazed look in his eyes, he fired at me from point blank range. The Lord shone His countenance on me that day: I was spared with only bullet wounds to my shoulder. . . .

Colin Ferguson, whatever a jury will say about him, was a crackpot with a gun in hand. No matter the verdict, no one can credibly deny that we, the American people, put that gun in his hand.

Staring down the barrel of a gun radicalizes. Before, like many people of good will, I was a lukewarm supporter of handgun control. Now I am a radical—a radical for the safety of us all, black and white. Guns and bullets know no colors, no ethnicity.

. . . If this matter is left wholly to the politicians, and if past is prologue—the kind of past that left James Brady paralyzed—the six casualties on that 5:33 will have died in vain.

Why did it take so long to pass the Brady Bill (which, sadly, at the end of the day was pretty toothless)? Why didn't Ronald Reagan, the most popular President in recent memory, support tougher gun control laws immediately after the thwarted attempt on his life? Why did he voice support only after leaving office? In an acronym: N.R.A.

Tom knew almost nothing of the National Rifle Association at this point, besides its prevalent image as a wealthy, powerful force, fighting to preserve the Second Amendment. But Tom would soon get to know the NRA rather well, up close and personal.

YOUNG ISRAEL SYNAGOGUE, DECEMBER 20, 1993

Joel Cohen, McDermott's former colleague in the Special Prosecutors Office, invited McDermott to talk about the shooting at the Young Israel Synagogue in Greenwich Village on December 20, the day after the op-ed ran, Cohen was nervous about having Tom speak so quickly after the trauma. "Is this guy going to be okay?" he wondered.

Tom was an odd fit for this temple. The Orthodox congregation had never had a gentile speaker before. Tom had never seen anything like this: the women in the balcony, the altar like a stage, the bearded rabbi.

Finally McDermott got up to speak to the crowd of 150. He talked about guns and his brush with death. He told the crowd how he had felt on the train. "Imagining, if I never spoke to my son Ryan again, I thought it would be even more of a tragedy, to leave him while we're in this stupid fight." He realized that before the shooting, he had lost sight of the big picture. Now, he said, he worried that the public, the community, the politicians were also missing the big picture by concentrating on the drama and ignoring the collective responsibility to get dangerous guns off the street.

He went on for a half an hour. When he stopped, the congregation sat silent.

Oh, my goodness, Tom thought: *nothing.*

He attended the social hour afterward, though he figured no one wanted to talk to him. He was surprised to realize what an effect he'd had. Men and women asked him questions, not just about the emotional trauma of being a shooting victim but about guns. They wanted to know what to do. They wanted him to speak more.

"It was a great ecumenical moment; we're all in the same boat," Cohen recalls. "They didn't know what to do for him . . . they were hoarding him, he was just so popular there. People still ask about him."

Cohen and McDermott wrote an article for the *New York Law Journal* asking why lawyers weren't doing more to push for stronger gun laws.

BLACK AND WHITE

Tom was starting to get some reaction from saying the issue was guns, not race.

Ever since his appearance with David Brinkley, his family had started to get messages on the answering machine from people around the country. Some said they were NRA members. They were angry because to them, there was no gun issue in America. The callers seem unconcerned that Tom was their fellow American and that he was one of too many who had been shot. Their only concern about guns was that people like Tom considered more restrictive laws, which in their minds inevitably lead to the confiscation of all guns. They were furious that Tom would blame deaths on the train on the size of Ferguson's clip. To them, Ferguson was just a crazy black guy who bore 100 percent of the blame.

He'd get messages on his family answering machine saying things like "That nigger bastard should've blown your fucking brains out." Others told him, "You deserved to die on that train" and "You're a flunky for the left wing." More than a few wished that the entire McDermott family would burn. After a while, he just listened to the first few words, got the gist of it, and hit Delete. A few calls got to him. One caller said he would figure out where Tom's office was. Another got young Ryan McDermott on the phone. Dismissing the callers as crackpots, McDermott never bothered the police with them, and after a few weeks the messages stopped.

"I didn't want to waste the FBI's time with these bunch of jerks," Tom says. "That would just give them satisfaction."

Race was an issue in the shooting for both those on the far right and the far left. Legendary civil rights lawyer William Kuntsler and his partner Ron Kuby announced they would defend Ferguson using a "black rage" defense. Kunstler had built a career around defending pariah clients, especially if there were a racial element. He'd been counsel for the Chicago Seven; Qubilah Shabazz, Malcolm X's daughter who was accused of plotting to kill Louis Farrakhan; and Siddiq Ibrahim Siddiq Ali and Ibrahim A. El-Gabrowny, who were linked to the first World Trade Center bombing.[8] They tried to mount a traditional insanity defense but claimed that black rage had triggered the insanity and then the massacre, likening black rage to battered women's syndrome. In a letter to the *New York Times,* Kunstler and Kuby cited one legal poll that found that two-thirds of blacks and half of whites saw validity in their claims.[9]

VICTIMS GROUP

Aside from all the political dilemmas, the train passengers had to cope with the trauma that typically follows a violent crime. Because so many of the victims were from Tom's hometown of Garden City, the local non-denominational Community Church, two blocks from Tom's house, hosted the victims' group.

The first session was largely organizational. The large group that met in the main church included anybody who had been on the LIRR 5:33. Grief counselors assessed each person's psychological damage in rooms to the side and sent some off to individual counseling. They planned to divide the group up into much smaller groups depending on when it was convenient for people to meet.

When the therapy started, it took the form trauma experts have found most useful: Victims simply told their stories. Because they shared this experience, they were able to compare notes and re-create the shooting.

They learned from news accounts that Ferguson had boarded the train at Jamaica, a big transfer station in Queens. He carried a duffel bag that contained his Ruger pistol, an extra-large clip specially designed to hold fifteen bullets (to cut down on reloading time) and more than one hundred "Black Talon" hollow point bullets.[10]

He sat quietly in the very back seat and paid the conductor for his ticket. Just after 6:00 he stood up with his duffel bag and began his rampage by shooting Maryanne Phillips, the woman sitting across the aisle from him. Because the passengers in the back of the train were facing forward and the others were fleeing from Ferguson, only Tom McDermott and Maryanne Phillips actually saw him shooting some of the people. The two became the main sources of information. Everyone wanted to know: "Did you see me before I was shot?" "Did you see me after I was shot?" "Did you see me get shot?"

"People were groping, looking for answers," Tom says. "We were trying to run their recollection of events past the room, to see if there was any connection to reality."

Some stories matched the communal account, while some did not. The man who had shoved his way over Tom's seatmates appeared at only one meeting. "He gave a version different than what happened, so I asked him to reconsider what he had just said, which was that he had attempted to knock the gun out of Ferguson's hand or strike him, without success. And that Ferguson may have even had two guns." Tom didn't tell the man he was wrong or to shut up. Tom just told the man his own, different version of events.

The man never came back to the group.

Tom heard again the story of how he had sheltered a young woman under his trench coat. Still, he remembered nothing about that. No woman ever turned up remembering that he had saved her, either. It remained to him a foggy story, like one on undeveloped film, one he was not sure he believed.

He found the woman whom he had seen in the rear section of the train, miraculously unharmed, yet shaking and chanting, "God help us." He told her he did believe it something of a miracle that she wasn't shot. She didn't remember the chanting or seeing Tom at all.

The human brain usually remembers emotionally charged events more vividly than banal ones, but the members of the victims' group all discovered how fragile and faulty their memory of this life-changing event was.

Once all the shooting victims finally pieced together their communal truth about what had happened on the train, they argued over what to do next or even whether they should meet again. Tom immediately worried that if the group divided up, its power—both to heal each other and to effect political change—would slip away. He wanted the entire crowd to work together, to stay bound together. The shooting had changed his life and he didn't see why this group should carve itself up according to their schedules. Mass killings in America were becoming routine. Tom knew that if he didn't work to make people remember, they would just as soon forget the LIRR shooting, the way they had let so many other horrific killings slip to the back of their minds.

A wide swath of the community had been affected: housewives, businessmen, lawyers. Tom wanted the group to unite against guns. The idea of civilians owning combat-style weapons was currently being tried—if not in a real court then in the court of public opinion—and he wanted this all-American, average suburban group to be Exhibit A. Their very ordinariness gave them a special power here: No one could rationally say the passengers deserved it or had put themselves in harm's way. Tom thought a fitting memorial to the people who died on the train would be to do something to prevent, or at least reduce the chances of, a similar massacre.

Not all the victims agreed. Some didn't even want to be part of the group. A Japanese company advised one of its employees who'd been hit not to speak out. Fellow LIRR widows Joyce Gorycki and Carolyn McCarthy spent time together, constituting an informal bereavement group. The victims couldn't agree on what political reform they wanted to see. Some felt that the problem was too-lenient prison sentences. One told Tom, "Hey, what else can you expect when you don't lock up criminals and throw away the key?"

Lucy Friedman, then director of Victim Services (now called Safe Horizon), the country's largest victim advocacy group, wrote a 1998 paper for the Department of Justice on how fighting for a cause helps victims overcome much of the emotional damage of crime.[11] Crime victims commonly feel angry, powerless, isolated, and depressed. They find ways to blame themselves for what happened. Many victims follow a pattern to recovery. First they are overcome with emotions, mainly rage, and they want whoever consigned them to victimhood to be severely punished. Only later do some—and only some—accept what's happened and try to force something positive out of the tragedy, either by helping other victims or by trying to prevent similar crimes. Her paper "From Pain to Power: Crime Victims Take Action" centers on two victims, the father of a shooting victim and Tom McDermott.

"What was different about Tom is, with most victims there is this incredible evolution from being emotional and passionate, to being more dispassionate and analytical. A lot of them are motivated to be more effective speakers and you can't do that; nobody wants to listen if it's all about your pain," Friedman said. "With Tom I never saw the irrational. He was always analytical."

McDermott didn't follow the typical pattern of activist crime victims at all. First of all, those who become involved are typically women. The theory is that women are more comfortable with their emotions and more apt to want to nurture others. Second, McDermott never succumbed to the urge for vengeance. His anger from the start was deflected from Ferguson because Ferguson was insane. Friedman hadn't seen someone so rational right from the start.

Tom looked with admiration at Amy Federici's parents. Federici, a twenty-seven-year-old Fashion Institute of Technology student, was the last person who died. Federici's parents, Arlene and Jack Locicero, donated her organs and saved several lives. Every Mother's Day, one recipient sends them flowers with a card that reads, "Love, from Amy's heart." The Lociceros have since become spokespeople for organ donation.[12]

No one has the obligation to turn personal tragedy into a public bene-fit, and few have that capacity. But Tom tried to pull the others along with him. Some of the shooting victims clearly fell into the camp that favored the death penalty over gun control. Barker said he respected Gulotta, the county politician who'd made the "animal remark."[13] Tom thought fellow passenger Robert Giugliano, who was shot through the arm and chest, was going too far when he talked about taking vengeance on Ferguson person-ally. Tom thought Giugliano was "off the reservation."

Since Tom didn't see Giugliano in his group, he looked him up in the phone book to try to talk him out of speaking that way in public. Tom asked him to tone his language down. His plea did not go over well. Tom recalls that Giugliano told him that he would say whatever was on his mind, however he wanted, whenever he wanted. Then he stopped return-ing Tom's calls.

Michael O'Connor, one of the three who subdued Ferguson, was more receptive to Tom's lead. O'Connor would call Tom to talk about his calls from reporters. "If they're only discussing the fact that he's black," Tom said, "that's what we've gotta stay away from. We can't let ourselves be victims again. We've gotta keep this contained, from getting to become a lynch mob."

The death penalty issue had been simmering for decades in New York. The legislature would pass bills, only to be vetoed by Governor Mario Cuomo and his predecessor Hugh Carey. Ferguson's crime was just the sort of monstrous act that would renew debate about bringing back the death penalty to New York. Tom favored the death penalty, but he thought the shooting should have more meaning than ensuring the quick death of a handful of murderers who would be locked up for life anyway.

Tom, using his lawyerly powers of persuasion, steered the group to-ward a discussion about guns. To him, working toward a goal, forcing a positive outcome from the tragedy, was his therapy. One version of the as-sault weapons ban under debate in Congress would have done just what he wanted: lowered the number of bullets in a clip from fifteen to ten. Tom ar-gued that the group ought to invite their own local Republican congress-man, David Levy, who had opposed the assault weapons ban, to meet the group. "He ought to know our concerns and what we felt about guns."

Tom called the office himself and made the request.

"Can we send a legislative aide? Congressman Levy is too busy the next few weeks," an aide responded.

"That won't suffice," McDermott said. "Where does he live? We'll just have ten to twenty of the Long Island Railroad shooting victims hold a can-dlelight vigil outside his house."

The stunned aide asked him to repeat himself, then got off the phone. The Republican Congressman, who backed the NRA even though his district didn't, must have envisioned the public relations nightmare that would ensue if he ignored the Long Island Railroad shooting victims. Twenty minutes later, Levy himself called back, saying he understood McDermott's urgency. He would meet with the group in two weeks.

HITTING THE BOOKS, 1994: THE SECOND AMENDMENT

Benjamin Franklin 1776 letter to Gen. Charles Lee on bows and arrows: "These were good weapons, not wisely laid aside. . . . He can discharge four arrows in the time of charging and discharging one bullet . . . His object is not taken from his view by the smoke of his own side. . . . Bows and arrows are more easily provided every where than muskets and ammunition."
—*Works of Benjamin Franklin,*
by Jared Sparks (Boston 1839), vol. 8, p. 171

To prepare specifically for the victims' group meeting with Levy, and in general for his advocacy work ahead, Tom decided to research the current state of gun laws. What sort of law should he push for? As quixotic as the idea sounded, he wondered if he should start a movement to repeal the Second Amendment.

First he needed to find out what he was up against. So Tom headed to the Hofstra Law Library to research the Second Amendment.

On first glance, the Second Amendment appears straightforward enough: "A well regulated Militia, being necessary to the security of a free State, the right of the people to keep and bear Arms, shall not be infringed." Back when the Founders wrote the Bill of Rights, patriots weren't so enthusiastic about guns and the militia as contemporary NRA members. Guns were expensive, unreliable, and in short supply. The Founders' notion of arms bears no relation to what's on the streets of America today. The convenient handgun wouldn't become more commonplace for a century after the Revolutionary War. And Revolutionary War soldiers were notoriously lousy shots. It wasn't their fault. British Major George Hanger described the condition of fighting in the Revolutionary War: "A soldier's musket, if not exceedingly ill-bored . . . will strike the figure of a man at eighty yards; it may even at 100; but a soldier must be very unfortunate indeed who shall be wounded . . . at 150 yards, . . . at 200 yards with a common musket, you may just as well fire at the moon and have the same hopes of hitting your object. . . ."[14]

Americans fought for their freedom with the British Brown Bess and the French Charleville. Both were muskets, sometimes up to the unwieldy length of six feet, and both had to be loaded from the muzzle—that is, where the bullet comes out.[15] The Continental Army was forever scrounging for guns, gunsmiths, and iron and worrying over preserving its powder supply. The famous Bunker Hill admonition, "Don't fire till you see the whites of their eyes," was really intended to save gunpowder. Military strategy was more formal then, consisting largely of battle by appointment. Long lines of troops would stand shoulder to shoulder. A cannon would go off, followed by volleys of musket. Finally, there was a charge, ending in hand-to-hand combat. Out would come the bayonets. Soldiers would use their guns more like cudgels.

Since the sixteenth century, gunsmiths had been rifling guns—engraving two to five lines down the length of the barrel. These lands and grooves twist and grab onto the bullet and spin it the way a quarterback spins a football. This was a remarkable improvement over the smooth bore musket, in which a ball of lead would tumble unpredictably out of the barrel. Rifles existed and were recognized as superior. But hardly anyone could afford them, any more than the average American can conveniently afford a plasma TV. Military planners stubbornly held onto their muskets even though they knew rifles were more accurate.

Ben Franklin thought the gun so impractical he recommended arming troops with bows and arrows. Others used axes, pikes, spears, and knives. The preeminent gun historian William Wellington Greener wrote in *The Gun and Its Development,* which was first published in 1881, that the supporters of the bow and gun held frequent contests, and as late as 1792 the bow usually won.[16]

At the time, citizens debated whether to have a standing professional army or volunteers. The militia won a few famous battles early in the Revolution, but its reputation deteriorated after that. "By the summer of 1776 Congress was well on its way toward creating a military establishment that placed a premium on military expertise, avoided the use of militiamen whenever possible," wrote Lawrence Telbert Cress in *Citizens in Arms: The Army and the Militia Society of the War of 1812.*[17] But when the Bill of Rights was ratified in December 1791, the militia made a comeback, thanks to anti-federalists' fear of a standing, professional army[18]—like the one we count on today.

The Virginia legislature, for example, spelled it out: "That a well regulated militia, composed of the body of the people, trained to arms, is the proper, natural and safe defense of a free state; that standing armies, in times of peace, should be avoided, as dangerous to liberty; and that in all cases the military should be under strict subordination to, and governed by, the civil power."[19]

The Second Amendment spoke more about the militia than it did about arms. But once the amendment was written, the two have been intertwined in American debate.

Some claim their de facto membership in the militia allows them the right to unfettered access to firearms as part of a militia that is forever poised to rebel against federal tyranny. A 1792 law placed the militia under loose federal control, making it a requirement for all "free, able-bodied white male citizens." It also required them to buy "a good musket or fire-lock, a sufficient bayonet and belt, two spare flints, and a knapsack, a pouch, with a box therein, to contain not less than twenty four cartridges, suited to the bore of his musket or firelock, each cartridge to contain a proper quantity of powder and ball; or with a good rifle, knapsack, shot-pouch, and power-horn, twenty balls suited to the bore of his rifle." And officers needed "a sword or hanger, and espontoon [long spear]."[20]

The wording also makes clear these guys weren't supposed to be over-throwing anybody. The president called out the militia and could send it to put down insurrections; it wasn't up to militia members to pick which side they'd be on.

Those who claim that it would be a "dereliction of duty" as an Amer-ican not to own a gun because of militia requirements would do well to check the supply list. Even then, the supplies were hard to come by. The states were required to have a militia for federal disposal, but Northern states were more diligent. Congress debated paying for supplies, but that annoyed the states that had already bought their weapons. Gradually mili-tia regulations slipped everywhere.[21]

In turn, someone invented the term "unorganized militia" as a beard to help cover the men shirking their militia drills. Citizens could claim they were still part of a militia, just an unorganized one, according to research by historian Mark Pitcavage, a historian at the Anti-Defamation League. Industrialization was a natural time for the citizen soldier to go out of busi-ness. In early America, citizens were called on to do just about everything. Those beleaguered early Americans had countless jobs: They were citizen soldiers, citizen police officers, citizen fire fighters, and citizen road labor-ers as well, with local governments often pressing farmers to do roadwork one day a month. But the Industrial Revolution was making sure Ameri-cans had just one crappy job, not twenty-seven.

Military historian Jerry Cooper calls it "tempting to make fun of the uniformed militia. Their outlandish uniforms, wholly unfit for field ser-vice. . . ." Mid-century immigrants formed private, local, ethnic militias. Germans brought to America their fondness for shooting and the system-atic military practice, a new innovation from Prussia, later part of Ger-many. Many were more social than martial, but Nativists were not pleased and formed their own militias. In 1879, Illinois passed a law to curb these wayward private armies. Herman Presser led his group of German anar-chists, *Lehr und Wehr Verein,*[22] who were gearing up for an anti-capitalist revolution, on a march across Chicago with forty riflemen in 1897.[23] Presser fought the law to the Supreme Court, arguing that the Second Amendment gave him the right to have his gun and his militia. In 1886, one of the first landmark gun cases, *Presser v. Illinois*[24] held that a state could disallow specific militias. In a slap at self-appointed militias, the court said a group couldn't just form a club of rowdy friends and claim it was a militia enjoying the special protection of the Constitution.

Tom then had to find what the Supreme Court had been saying about the Second Amendment and guns. He found only two big Supreme Court decisions, both involving men named Miller. Neither was a gun rights theorist; both used guns in crimes.

In *Miller v. Texas* (1894),[25] the Supreme Court affirmed that states had the right to pass gun laws. Police had arrested Miller basically for being a white man living with a black woman.[26] After he was released he stood in front of his house handling guns and saying, "I will kill the first son-of a bitch of a policeman that attempts to arrest me." Texas law at the time was far stricter than today: People could carry guns only if they feared an immediate attack. So the police tried to arrest him for illegal gun carrying and, as threatened, he shot one. He was convicted of murder but then appealed to the Supreme Court that the gun law violated the Second Amendment. The Supreme Court said Texas's law was fine.

The next big Supreme Court case, *U.S. v. Miller* (1939),[27] addressed the constitutionality of a federal gun statute. Jack Miller and Frank Layton brought a sawed-off twelve-gauge shotgun from Arkansas to Oklahoma in violation of the National Firearms Act, which subjected those and other dangerous guns to a prohibitive $200 tax. Miller argued that the Second Amendment trumped the national gun law. The Supreme Court, in a brief decision made after Miller had died, said Miller's activity wasn't protected by the Second Amendment because neither he nor his shotgun were part of any well-regulated militia: "The Court can not take judicial notice that a shotgun having a barrel less than 18 inches long has today any reasonable relation to the preservation or efficiency of a well regulated militia; and therefore can not say that the Second Amendment guarantees to the citizen the right to keep and bear such a weapon. 26 F. Supp. 1002, reversed."

After reading those cases, Tom was amazed that he'd ever thought the Second Amendment gave each individual a right to have a gun. He wasn't alone, of course. Former Supreme Court Chief Justice Warren Burger, a Nixon appointee and a solid conservative, said that it "has been the subject of one of the greatest pieces of fraud, I repeat the word 'fraud,' on the American public by special interest groups that I have ever seen in my lifetime." He referred, of course, to the National Rifle Association.

Burger also wrote a piece for *Parade Magazine*[28] that appeared on January 14, 1990, crystallizing the arguments and indicating that the United States had outgrown the Second Amendment. He wrote: "People of that day were apprehensive about the new 'monster' national government presented to them, and this helps explain the language and purpose of the Second Amendment . . . [which] grew out of the deep-seated fear of a 'national' or 'standing' army. The same First Congress that approved the right to keep and bear arms also limited the national army to 840 men. . . .

"In the 1789 debate in Congress on James Madison's proposed Bill of Rights, Elbridge Gerry argued that a state militia was necessary: 'to prevent the establishment of a standing army, the bane of liberty. . . . '"

McDermott was fascinated. He had followed Burger's decisions for decades, but never expected to find this. "Here's this preeminently conservative guy who should be an NRA board member and he's saying they've perpetrated this fraud."

Later, in 1995, U.S. News and World Report[29] found that three out of four Americans think, "The Constitution guarantees you the right to own a gun." But no amount of debunking in the national popular press seemed to dissuade the American public. Where did everyone get the idea that the Constitution guarantees each individual the right to a gun? Tom had no doubt: The NRA. Former NRA President Charlton Heston called the Second Amendment "the eternal bodyguard" and measured it more important than the First Amendment. "To make sure we have the means to secure our freedoms, the Founders enshrined their vision in the Second Amendment," said NRA Executive Vice President Wayne LaPierre.[30]

Before McDermott started his research, he thought he might join a battle to repeal the Second Amendment. Now he felt he didn't even need to. The Supreme Court and history were on his side. "From that point on," he says, "at every opportunity I reminded the listeners in whatever group of the cruel hoax that the NRA is in its interpretation of the Second Amendment."

Four

MCDERMOTT VS. THE NRA: THE FIGHT FOR LOCAL, STATE, AND FEDERAL GUN LAWS

THE LONG ISLAND CONGRESSMAN

When Congressman Levy came to the Garden City Community Church to address the LIRR 5:33 victims' group, he began with a prepared talk on why he was against gun control. Then Tom McDermott started asking questions about Levy's views on the proposed assault weapons ban. Levy didn't answer. McDermott said he understood. Just two months before, he neither knew nor cared about the gun issue himself. He asked Levy if he wouldn't mind doing his homework over the next month and coming back to articulate his full position.

"Well . . ." Levy stammered. "What do you want my position to be?," Tom recalled.

McDermott later felt sheepish about ambushing Levy with his new-found knowledge of the Second Amendment, the NRA, and gun laws. "Two months before I didn't know any of this, either. I didn't intentionally seek to embarrass him, but it made it appear that he did not have a firm basis for his opinions. He said he would revisit the issue and seek legal opinions to analyze this subject. He committed to the group."

McDermott was starting to see the power of his voice. He got Levy to take the issue seriously. That spring Levy, like all Long Island legislators, would end up voting in favor of the assault weapons ban. Just by being a

Long Island Railroad shooting victim, Tom could get people to listen to him. He was officially a stakeholder in the issue.

Normally, in the gun debate, the only people who seemed to know what they were talking about, the only people who could say, H*ey, this gun law will definitely affect me* were in the pro-gun camp. Other people, for instance, mothers of city teenagers, could say that a gun might one day affect them. But the threat was usually too abstract—either for the mothers to get motivated to fight or for people to take them seriously as people whom the laws would touch. (This was, after all, years before the 2000 kick off of the Million Mom March.) With his knowledge and his status as a shooting victim, Tom could command people's attention.

He didn't want to go around talking about the shooting forever. With just a few months of research, he had changed his whole view of gun laws. He couldn't believe how ignorant he had been, how naïve the general public still was. He felt he could really make a difference, just by explaining, just by teaching.

The victims' group went on for months as more victims were released from the hospital or otherwise surfaced and wandered in for care. After the meeting with Levy, though, Tom drifted away from the original shooting victims' group. He felt that he had told the other people all he could and now the experience was just getting repetitive.

Instead of talking to his fellow shooting victims, who were pretty well with him in calling for stricter gun laws, he wanted to reach out to other people.

CAROLYN MCCARTHY

One victim Tom hadn't met at the groups was Carolyn McCarthy of Mineola. Ferguson shot and killed Dennis McCarthy, 52, Carolyn's husband, and her son Kevin, 26, remained in North Shore University Hospital in Manhasset. Not until a week after the shooting, when doctors removed a respirator, was Kevin able to speak. That's when his mother finally told him, on the day of the funeral, that his father was dead.[1] Kevin was one of the most gravely injured passengers, and it was considered a wonder that he survived his head wounds.

Catholics give mass cards to commemorate the fact that a church will say prayers for someone. Tom dropped by Carolyn's house with a mass card from the Sisters Adorers of the Precious Blood. This card offered not just one mass, but perpetual masses. The church had special meaning for Tom; it was his aunt's convent that he'd visited as a boy. Tom left the mass card with a note: "If you would like to talk, give me a call."

Carolyn did call. And they started talking. Both Irish Catholics, both socially conservative, both infuriated by the threat of guns to their families, they hit it off. By this time Carolyn's son was back from the hospital, but still undergoing therapy and successive surgeries. Much of the media attention had focused on Carolyn and her unbearable tragedy. Tom asked if there was any way she could find time in the midst of this to work on the gun issue. "I just thought she would be a terrific asset to spread the message that this could happen to anyone."

They were both appearing at churches. Every once in a while they went together, such as to a conference of churches in Uniondale. They appeared once with a fellow Catholic advocate, Sister Helen Prejean. McDermott calls her "Sister Dead Man Walking." She's the nun who works on Louisiana's death row. She wrote a best-selling book of that name on the death penalty, and Susan Sarandon played her in the movie. Working with other Catholics, Tom's support of the death penalty eroded. It was like the old Catholic Church of the 1960s, concerned about working people and economic justice instead of sex and abortion.

ALBANY

Some of McCarthy and McDermott's earliest forays together were to Albany, where legislators were considering a state ban on assault weapons. Congress was also mulling a federal ban, but the proposed New York law was considered both more stringent and more likely. The federal law wanted to ban only nineteen specific assault weapons, but New York wanted to get rid of all military-style assault guns.[2] (It's worth noting that fully automatic guns, like machine guns, were already effectively banned.)

Tom and Carolyn would witness in Albany just how challenging it could be to take on the gun lobby. They would take the train up with other fledgling gun control activists like Michelle Schimel and Katina Johnstone, all freshly minted advocates. It was as if they were freshmen attending classes together. The school, however, was almost completely self-study; they had to learn from each other. They didn't even have a set of upper classmen to teach them the ropes. Gun control advocates tend to have a short span of ardent activism. No one really understood why, although perhaps those who started from grief reached a point from which they needed to move on.

When Tom got to Governor Cuomo's office he saw Jim Brady, who had been nearly killed and partly paralyzed by a bullet meant for Ronald Reagan. He was again hit with a flash of seeing how his life could have turned out because of a gun. Brady's wife Sarah spoke, then Tom went on.

Tom had anxiously typed up a speech to give in Cuomo's office that January, but he found himself speaking emotionally, extemporaneously, on gun laws: "I am here to tell you that it can happen to anyone, anytime and anyplace . . . . I rejoice that the grave did not close on me and the eighteen others who were shot while riding home on the 5:33 as it did for six of my fellow passengers. Those first fifteen rounds got off in less than a minute before I could even see the shooter."[3]

He got a standing ovation. Afterward Cuomo himself pulled him aside to compliment and thank him. Cuomo's press secretary asked if he could come back. By all measures, McDermott had succeeded.

Yet nothing happened in the legislature.

He came back again, two weeks later.

"I came here two weeks ago and you received me warmly, but then did nothing. If you don't pass the assault weapons ban," Tom warned the legislators, "there may be another shooting like the one I survived. And if that happens, there will be a funeral dirge that would be heard in the Capitol that will be deafening and will not be silenced."

The governor again followed Tom, and Tom was gratified he picked up on his words. Again, he felt he had succeeded beyond his expectations, but again, there was no result.

The third time back, McCarthy and McDermott met with state Senate Majority Leader Ralph Marino, who was from Long Island. He was a practical politician; when the state assault weapons bill came up for a vote, he explained to Carolyn and Tom that it was paired with another bill, and it was more important to Marino that the second bill not pass.

Carolyn instinctively asked, "Why couldn't you just cut the legislation in half? Vote on one half in the morning, one half in the afternoon?" She wasn't thinking of all the Albany machinations behind the arrangement, of course.

Tom saw Marino suppress a snicker as he explained that couldn't be done.

"Although that seems a surefire resolution, it's not done that way in Albany," he said. "Don't worry about it."

"I'll make it my business that the law passes, even if it means coming back up to Albany again and again and again," McCarthy said.

Carolyn McCarthy and Tom McDermott would often speak as a team. Carolyn would start by making an emotional appeal. Tom would follow up with his recollection of the shooting and then go into hard analysis: statistics about shootings, the history of the NRA, the case for stronger gun laws. Carolyn would openly admit that she didn't know much about the gun business or gun politics but that she knew that a gun with a large number of bullets took away her husband and severely injured her son and that those guns shouldn't be in the hands of civilians.

"My family has been hit very hard since the December seventh tragedy. . . . I see no human reason to have the amount of clips that are used in some of these automatic assault weapons," she said at a March 8, 1994, press conference in Albany.[4]

"Just imagine the size of this room was the size of car number three," Tom said that day. "I want you to imagine a man coming in right from the back of that room opening fire, killing six of us and wounding nineteen in less than two minutes. There is no legitimate reason why a fifteen [round] clip for a pistol should be allowed." Once he had the crowd's attention, Tom would talk about the Second Amendment and the lackluster state of federal gun enforcement. The feds had caved under the pressure of the NRA, so that left the job of protecting Americans from guns to the states. He'd give the example of the number of licensed gun dealers. For decades, federal regulators had known that many people were getting dealer licenses so they could order guns by mail. It had been a weak, faint-hearted effort to bring the resources of the federal government to bear on the problem, which Tom attributed to the NRA. He'd point out that the number of gun dealers in the country now exceeded the number of gas stations. The marketplace was so unregulated that once someone got a license, he would be troubled with an inspection once every five years, at most.

What impressed Lucy Friedman of Victim Services,[5] the support and crime prevention group, about Tom was that within a matter of months, he seemed already to know what many crime victims don't learn for years: If they talk only about emotions, they will be unbearable for people to listen to. To accomplish what they want, to be effective, they have to become detached.

Tom's son Ryan and his high school classmates went door to door and camped out at shopping malls to gather 22,000 signatures for a petition supporting the assault weapons ban. New Yorkers Against Gun Violence took them to State Senator Marino's office. "When we delivered the boxes by hand truck, he was completely taken aback by the number of petitions," recalls Tom. When the group later asked for them back to send out mailings, however, Marino's office said the petitions could not be found.

GREAT NECK: MEETING THE NRA FACE TO FACE, MARCH 16, 1994

Tom was also working on the local front. A town right on Long Island considering a fairly insignificant bit of local zoning code gave him his first glimpse of how fierce the NRA would fight any rule whatsoever.

Tom had called up Michelle Schimel, the fledgling Great Neck gun control activist, as soon as he got her letter. They were working on a Temple event when Michelle got word that Great Neck was considering letting a gun shop open in town.

Like so many components of any gun debate, real information was fuzzy and hard to pin down. Michelle couldn't find out where the gun shop was supposed to go, what kind of gun store it would be, who was proposing it, or even if anyone was proposing one at all. Even years later, these basic facts remain unclear.

Michelle was worried that the Long Island Railroad would bring gun shoppers to Great Neck, where such a store would be, to say the least, out of character. Great Neck is not far from where Fitzgerald's Great Gatsby lived in the novel and where many Wall Street traders live for real. A drab downtown quickly recedes into a posh residential district as one nears the water. Great Neck has several political fiefdoms, and one is the Village of Great Neck Plaza, home to 6,000 people and one-third of a square mile of land. It was only this little village that had decided it wasn't interested in having a gun shop.

The controversy started when someone considered opening a massage parlor—the nemesis of all suburban vice cops—and the village trustees decided they better update the zoning codes to ban the types of businesses they didn't want. Great Neck had thwarted the parlor on a technicality, but officials wanted to have stronger protection next time. As long as they were writing a code to keep out massage parlors, they made up a list of other undesirables: purveyors of explosives like gasoline; pawn shops; junk yards; car washes; animal shelters and kennels; and sellers of gunpowder or firearms.

When Jerry Preiser, a resident of Great Neck (but not Great Neck Plaza), got wind of the gun store ban, he marched into a trustees meeting on March 16, 1994. As president of the New York State Rifle and Pistol Clubs, Preiser was used to making news for things like offering rewards to crime victims who kill their assailants[6] or giving an award and cash to subway vigilante Bernie Goetz.[7] "I find it interesting that on the very evening you've taken an oath . . . to defend the Constitution, part and parcel of the Constitution of course would be the Bill of Rights' Second Amendment, which is the right to bear and keep arms," he said, according to the official transcript. "You're considering the banning of what has literally, for a hundred years or more, been a legitimate type of business that caters to strictly licensed individuals. And you'd be amazed how many well-to-do licensed individuals are in this town. . . ."[8]

The mayor, Robert J. Rosegarten, seeing he had a situation on his hands, said, "Uh-oh."

Preiser continued, " . . . that own legitimate sporting arms for skeet, for trap, for legitimate target shooting, for hunting and what-have-you. My fear is because of the rash of media plight that have been going on, you may be drifting towards essentially a political statement rather than a look at the clear issues here."

"I have to also, ladies and gentlemen, serve notice on you, if in fact you . . . and we have several volunteer attorneys here with us this evening in tandem with the National Rifle Association, we would challenge it in court."

One of the trustees asked, "Without making a political statement, I have a question. The Fourth Amendment addresses the right to bear arms—"

"Second," interrupted Preiser.

"Does it address the right to sell arms?" Rosen asked.

"Keep and bear, I think it's almost—" Preiser started, but the mayor interrupted and made him answer directly. "No, it doesn't," he said.

They continued discussing where the nearest gun store was (*in the next town over*) and if there had ever been one in Great Neck (*no*).

Preiser finished the discussion with a flourish. "And in closing I'd like to say, should the ordinance be passed, the National Rifle Association, the New York State Rifle and Pistol Association and the Federation of New York State Rifle and Pistol Clubs will have no choice but to challenge this in the courts of the state of New York. And, if need be, federal court."

Preiser stopped just short of literally throwing down a gauntlet and saying, "Good day, sirs!"

The village knew it was in for a nasty fight. That's when Michelle called Tom again to speak at the next hearing a few weeks later. They walked into the auditorium, normally empty and drowsy with the minutiae of zoning laws, and found it tense and packed with gun supporters eager to express their anger. Tom and Michelle were stunned by how many people had turned out. They had read and heard so much about the National Rifle Association, but this was the first time they got to see its actual members.

"For the first time I encountered a well-organized opposition," Tom says. "They were in one section of the auditorium. They were boisterous and condemning. There was one who was a leader of a gun club that was very adamant." In the 1980s the NRA ran an ad campaign featuring pictures of women and minorities with the caption, "I am the NRA" to dispel the popular notion that the organization was just a bunch of middle-aged white guys. The NRA members who showed up on Long Island, however, *were* a bunch of middle-aged white guys. What united the NRA members nationwide more than demographics were the arguments they would make—quite effectively—at meetings just like this one all around the country. Tom noticed that each time the NRA members mentioned the prospect of a lawsuit from the NRA, the trustees would visibly tense up, fearing a long, expensive legal battle their taxpayers would not want to finance. "It's a lot of blowhard threats without any legal basis. The louder one spoke," Tom says, "the more attention that person got."

What Michelle, Tom, and the trustees couldn't see then was that these men were not locals but the same cast of characters that would show up at nearly every gun debate in the area. "They were like a little boy scout troop that traveled around together," Michelle says. More than that, their statements were straight out of the NRA playbook, baffling arguments used around the country for such occasions, featuring anecdotal evidence, a narrow view of history, and pseudo-science. All of it was an elaborate form of harassment to make the message clear to the trustees: If you try to do anything with guns, a group of angry men will hound you, berate you, and bury you under legal arguments, however specious.

One told a story of how he had saved a woman from being raped at gunpoint. One raised the Second Amendment and informed the trustees that because of the Uniform Militia Act of 1903, every able-bodied American male was part of a well-regulated militia. In truth, the 1903 Dick Act—named for Sen. Charles Dick of Ohio and a name the NRA does not widely promote—brought the unwieldy state and independent militia system into the National Guard.[9]

A stern-looking engineer named Howard Last, sporting a beard and comb-over and wearing an ill-fitting sports jacket over an Izod shirt, became the star of the show when he tried to convince the town that bakeries were more dangerous than gun shops. He testified that the National Electrical Code "does not consider ammunition or powder hazardous at all. Okay? It does consider a lot of other things hazardous. It considers, for one thing, obviously, gasoline, LPG, liquefied propane gas, natural gas, methane, industrial chemicals. It lists other things. Among them flour, corn, cotton seeds, pecan nut shells, walnut shells, almond shells, soy flour, sugar. These are all common items which I guess you'll find in any bakery, food store or restaurant. These are considered hazardous by the National Electric [sic] Code while ammunition and powder are not. If you're thinking of doing anything about prohibiting ammunition and powder, you should consider going after restaurants, because they hold flour. Grocery stores, supermarkets hold flour. . . ."

"The most hazardous material on the list is gasoline. Ninety-nine percent of the vehicles in Great Neck are powered by gasoline . . . you have cars and trucks going right in front of here every single day. You want to go after ammunition, you have to go after cars and trucks. They are more dangerous. . . . The World Trade Center bombers used fertilizer [in the 1993 truck bombing]. Are we to ban fertilizer? Anyone who has a yard in the peninsula has fertilizer in their garage. Are you supposed to tell them to get rid of fertilizer? . . . If you go after ammunition, you have to ban these items, also. You will have to shut down this village."

By now the crowd was dumbstruck at the surreal turn of the arguments. Some recovered enough to say that flour was safe when properly stored. When Tom stepped up to the microphone and stared speaking in a quiet, clear and calm voice, the crowd quieted immediately, Michelle remembers. Considering his role in the nation's most dramatic recent gun shooting, Tom was low-keyed. He acted like a lawyer, making a straight-forward case, citing various court precedents to show the trustees that they had nothing to fear from the NRA bullying.

The conservative predisposition for local control gets tested when lib-eral cities or even middle of the road small towns pass laws conservatives don't like. Then conservatives like state and federal laws (or their interpre-tation of them) just fine. The most famous gun cases about whether a small town had a right to make its own gun laws was from Morton Grove, Illi-nois, a nondescript middle-class suburb northwest of Chicago. Morton Grove banned handguns in 1981. The NRA sued in state and federal court. The Illinois court threw out the suit, noting that Illinois's constitution says the right to bear arms is subject to police power.[10] A federal appeals court ruled that "the right to keep and bear handguns is not guaranteed by the Second Amendment" And the Supreme Court declined the case.

In the mid-1990s the NRA would try repeatedly to pressure Illinois to do away with local control altogether on the gun issue, using the tactic of a state "pre-emption" law.[11] The laws, which have been used to wipe out pro-gay, anti-tobacco, and anti-gun laws, are a way to move jurisdiction from liberal city governments to the state level, where legislators tend to be more conservative, rural, and sympathetic. The cost is the conservative goal of local control.

Tom assured the trustees that if they enacted the law, they were in no real legal danger. An NRA lawsuit would be a nuisance but a legal long-shot, at best. Tom dismissed the arguments about the flour and the threat caused by the local bakery with a legal argument. "What the board should address or concern itself with, most respectfully, is that if the board were talking about including a . . . dynamite manufacturing plant, that product itself, in and of itself, is an inherently dangerous product when used in the method for which it was manufactured," Tom said. "A gun is the very, very identical product."

Tom pointed out that gun manufacturers put themselves in a separate category of products from flour, gas, and any other consumer product. As Tom would become all too aware, gun makers have defended themselves in court against shooting victims by saying that their products do just what they are supposed to do: hurt and kill people. "The manufacturers adver-tise their weapons . . . that 'this weapon is designed to kill. If used properly, it will kill.' They represent that. They do so to the extent that there is no li-ability against the manufacturer of such a product when it is used to kill."

Tom mentioned only at the end of his speech why he cared about guns.

"On a personal note, I can tell you as one of the shooting victims of the 5:33 what an instrument can do and what it did do. In less than three min-utes it took the lives of six people, wounded nineteen others. In less than three minutes. One man, one gun, thirty rounds. That's what that instrument can do and did do. I ask the board most respectfully to consider the instrument."

The NRA members put no value on Tom's experience. They cautioned against being influenced by the political "whims" of a post-Ferguson-shooting Long Island. They argued that Tom shouldn't be granted any special notice just because he'd been shot. One NRA stalwart remarked that he'd been shot once, too.

In the next and final hearing, on May 18, 1994,[12] the NRA trotted out another of its standard yet stunning arguments: the Nazis liked gun control, so if you like gun control, you might be a Nazi. It was a dangerous note to sound in largely Jewish Great Neck.

Robert Ishkanian, the owner of Edelman's Sporting Goods in Farming-dale, twenty miles from Great Neck, was the first to play the Nazi-Jew card. Even though having more gun shops would hurt his business, he still didn't want Great Neck to ban gun shops, just on principle.

I want to leave you with one little story. I can't think of anything more fitting. When I saw this a couple years ago, I had no idea I was going to be standing here before a board today. And a chill went up my spine. Literally, a chill went up my spine when I heard the town of Great Neck was trying to do what they're doing.

Have any of you heard of a place called Yerushalayim? [the Hebrew pronunciation of Jerusalem] . . . I've been to Israel nine times in the last 10 years. I stopped at Yerushalayim. That's the Holocaust [museum]. It's the kind of place that you can't hardly come out of without crying. . . . They have bars of soap made out of people. They have hair—making pocketbooks out of hair. They have displays as to what the Nazis did to the Jews during the Second World War. It's awesome.

In that display there is a section that deals in particular with guns. Since I'm in the gun business. . . . I paid particular attention to that. And again a chill went up my spine when I thought about saying this today. But I can't think of a better example. I guess I got to say it.

There is a display there of a letter written by a little short man with a mustache, Hitler. In 1937 he wrote a letter to the town fathers in a town called Oberstdorf, Germany. It seems in 1937 part of Hitler's master plan was to ban firearms and to keep firearms out of the hands of the populace. He had a resolution that went something like: From today on we're not going to allow the population to buy, sell, have, handle guns. And only the Nazis and the Gestapo would be allowed to have them. Sociologically this was a real problem in Germany. Germans are hunters. Europeans are hunters. The Black Forest. Companies like Mauser, Sauer and Walther, these are all German companies. It was not a popular thing to do. The German people went crazy. They wanted their guns. This little town of Oberst-dorf . . . got together and decided they were going to be the first of the towns to go along with Hitler's proposal. . . . And there was a letter there from Hitler addressed to this town. That was the best part of the display. Thanking the town and the mayor of the town for being so forthright and being so progressive in his thinking. And under that it said six years later twenty-two thousand Jews were killed from the city of Oberstdorf.

That was the NRA's point that evening: gun control had gotten Jews killed in World War II. And if Long Island enacted gun control, the same thing could happen here.

"To me, this says it. That was fifty-seven years ago. I would hate to think fifty-seven years from now . . . that the town of Great Neck will be put in the same place, and that there will be a Holocaust on Long Island," Ishkanian concluded.

Tom could not believe what he was hearing and seeing in these government meetings. Residents, if they were concerned at all, showed up in favor of the ban. But the board was overwhelmed by the NRA, its show of force and its irrelevant, shape-shifting arguments. That's how it was done; that's how the NRA won battles. "The comments were so . . . not sharp, but wild, almost ridiculous as far as those warning of the apocalypse coming to Great Neck if a gun shop was precluded," Tom said. "If you get into an argument with them, you better be prepared to discuss anything from A to Z on the gun issue or they will chop you up with their misrepresentations."

The issue ended in an anti-climactic draw. The NRA and gun control advocates kept calling the town to find out the date of the next meeting, but nothing ever happened. For the rest of the year the only activity was a flurry of letters in the newspaper over the issue.

The NRA won one part of the battle: the trustees, apparently intimidated, never got around to passing a law to keep the gun stores out. On the other hand, no gun store ever tried to move in.

Months later a man approached Michelle to tell her the gun store was not just theoretical, that he had been hoping to open one. "You allow lingerie in town, let kids see that in the windows, how can you do that without letting in a gun store?" he snarled.

"Well," she said, "I've never been shot by a nightgown."

STORMTROOPERS AT THE TEMPLE

Michelle put together that gun control panel for her temple a few months later. She invited G. Oliver Koppell, then New York State Attorney General; Great Neck's Congressman Gary Ackerman, and Tom McDermott for a Friday evening Shabbat talk.

Somehow the NRA got wind of the talk and decided to show up. While temple members dressed up for Shabbat services, the NRA members wore hunting clothes, stood blocking the steps, and handed out literature with swastikas. Their argument again was that the Nazis used gun control, so anyone who made guns harder to buy was emulating the Nazis.

Michelle and Tom hadn't talked for months, but they took up their battle right where they left off. "Tom has this way, he'll disappear," Michelle says, "but just when you need him, he'll show up." Tom was late, and when he got there Michelle ran up to him in the vestibule, distraught. "Did you see what they're doing to my temple?" she asked, worried that the NRA members would intimidate everyone away.

"It's okay, it's okay," Tom said, projecting confidence. "This is perfect. Now people will see what we're up against. This is just what we want." But Tom said later he didn't want Michelle to see how upset he was. "They were going out and using someone's worst fear," he says. "It was so inappropriate and so callous."

Intellectual arguments could wait. Right now he had to take care of the thugs on the steps. He went outside with another guy and told the NRA members to "get the fuck off the steps so that people could come in." Once inside, Tom first recounted the shooting, step by step, shot by shot, and suddenly the room became quiet, except for sobs, Michelle remembers. Then Tom decided to use the men in hunting clothes that had come to intimidate them as props. He told the group: "The NRA has enormous power in our country. Before the shooting in December, 1993, I had no idea the influence the NRA had over Congress . . . . We New Yorkers can be oblivious to culture on the other side of the Hudson River, but outside of New York, this NRA is a monster power, a power with only one issue and one concern. You may never beat them financially or with numbers of members, but at least they should be exposed for what they are."

THE NAZIS AND GUN CONTROL

Nazi fascism is supposed to be the antithesis of American principles of freedom and democracy. When the NRA equates gun control with Nazis, it is trying to inflame and distract. When it hands out flyers with swastikas at a Great Neck temple, it's one step above the Nazis marching in Skokie.

The Nazi analogy brands gun law activists as anti-American traitors. It strikes fear into listeners because the citation of history gives it the ring of truth. Try to explain it away and you risk looking like a Nazi sympathizer, or worse.

The NRA is apt to insert the argument into just about any debate on gun issues and encourage its members to do the same. In August 1999, the

NRA's *American Rifleman* ran a discussion on "Nazi Repression of Firearm Owners" by Stephen P. Halbrook, Ph.D., J.D.[13]

"It would be instructive at this time to recall why the American citizenry and Congress have historically opposed the registration of firearms," Halbrook wrote. "The reason is plain. Registration makes it easy for a tyrannical government to confiscate firearms and make prey of its subjects. Denying this historical fact is no more justified than denying that the Holocaust occurred or that the Nazis murdered millions of unarmed people."

Halbrook went through the various Nazi gun control laws. In 1938, the Nazis took away guns from Jews. In 1940, the Nazis invaded Holland and gave the Dutch twenty-four hours to turn in their guns. They later did the same after invading France, Belgium, Czechoslovakia, and Poland.

Halbrook never cited evidence that Nazis confiscated guns from Germans. Hitler took guns away from conquered foreigners (or people he believed were foreigners). We may question Nazi thinking that non-Aryans were enemies, but nations have been taking arms from the conquered for ages, right up to the recent U.S. wars in Afghanistan and Iraq.

After assassinations in 1921, the Weimar Republic restricted gun ownership, but in 1928 they changed the rules and allowed guns to be owned as long as they were registered. In 1938, Hitler passed laws on who could own guns and started to enforce the previous laws against people he didn't like. The Hitler gun laws actually brought more gun freedom to people Hitler regarded as Germans.[14]

Meanwhile, the Nazis, far from disarming citizens, spent the war dreaming up new guns and preparing to hand out the guns they confiscated from everybody else to the *Deutscher Volkssturm,* their ragtag militia, made up of every German male from 16 to 60.[15] Nazis hoped sheer ardor—and fear of racial annihilation—would enable this modern militia to overcome what it lacked in training and equipment. They excluded Jews, of course, on the grounds they were "racially inferior" or "unworthy to bear arms."[16]

Gun historians regard Nazis as gun enthusiasts and innovators.[17] They spent World War II continually developing ever better guns, so many prototypes they couldn't make them all. They wanted guns that were more powerful, faster, cheaper, easier to make. In the final days of the Third Reich, the Germans pioneered the mass, cheap metal alloy handgun, according to Whit Collins,[18] firearms historian and a former senior editor of *Guns and Ammo Magazine* who has become a critic of the industry. Steel was scarce for everyone, so all sides used some alloys for different gun parts. "By the time the Germans understood the invasion was coming, they were down to using zinc for the frame," Collins says. Some think the Nazis used slave labor to mass produce the cheap guns;

others think they never got that far. The Nazis also planned to give the guns to the *Volkssturm*, the German militia.

The *Volkssturm* were the last gasp of a dying power. Yet they had the same weaknesses as past militias. The *Volkssturm* provides a rare glimpse into how a militia might fare against a modern Western army. It was, even according to those who romanticize the vain struggle of the *Volkssturm*, a complete failure. Here's what ADEQ Historical Research, which promotes re-enactments of Nazi battles, has to say about the *Volkssturm*: "The fighting ability of these Volkssturm units was practically nil. Lack of adequate weapons, ammunition and time for proper training, with units receiving only a few days and with some only a few hours instruction had its effect on morale. The desertion rate was high. . . . Fanatics did exist within the ranks and these tended to be members of the Hitler Youth. Enthusiasm for the Volkssturm was almost non-existent even amongst the Volkssturm themselves and especially from the regular troops and the civilian population."

Ken Stern, the American Jewish Committee's expert on anti-Semitism and hate groups, has heard the Nazi gun control argument again and again.[19] "I find that inherently offensive," he says. "What it's intended to do is equate situations in the U.S. government with that of Nazi Germany. And it suggests that it was for the [citizen's] lack of ability to get guns, that Nazis were able to get into power." There's no proof, he notes. The Nazis were popularly elected. And the German population went along with what they did. When the Nazis did round up the Jews, they didn't tell them they were going on trains to gas chambers, and the Jews, having no guns, simply went along. The Nazis always had some elaborate ruse—they were sending the Jews to a work camp to ease overcrowding, they were giving them showers.

THE NRA AS PART OF THE MILITARY

In Tom McDermott's opinion the NRA would do or say anything to further its position. The NRA had implicitly compared a temple of progressive Jews to Nazis. It had succeeded in killing a town ordinance banning gun stores by claiming bakeries were the real danger and that everyone in town should carry a gun because each person was part of the national defense militia system. Tom expected battles, but all of these tactics caught him off guard. He vowed to figure out the NRA, where it came from, and how it maintained its power over gun politics. He had to know its history and its tactics better than its members if he hoped to be able to counteract the NRA's A-to-Z menagerie of arguments.

One of the many ironies to be found in the history of the National Rifle Association is that its primary founder ridiculed state rights and militias, two popular arguments that the NRA regularly posits today in an effort to defeat the kind of gun laws Tom McDermott had started to lobby for. William Conant Church, a military journalist and advocate for a well-trained federal army, helped start the NRA in an effort to teach marksmanship.

He started off as a New York City reporter. In 1860 he took over as publisher of the *New York Sun,* then the second biggest American newspaper, after its legendary editor Moses Beach retired. Church battled religious conservatives who tried to make the secular *Sun* their mouthpiece and struck a deal to leave the *Sun*'s offices, across from City Hall, to become a foreign correspondent.[20] [21]

When the Civil War broke out, he returned home. He wasn't an ardent abolitionist, but he believed that the Confederates were betraying the Union. Church switched to the *New York Times.* He filed dispatches from the front as a "special," an embedded correspondent, except that specials also had to do chores for the army, ranging from burying the dead to interviewing prisoners.[22]

He wrote passionately against the Southern position. He reported on a Virginia tavern that was turned into a prison and hospital, imagining how the patients and prisoners, Confederate soldiers, might have visited that tavern in the past, growing their grudges against the federal government until they got into the trouble they were in today. "In its bar-room the local great men have met over their pipes and whisky . . . nursing their local pride until exaggerated notions of State Rights have finally wrought their ruin. . . . Virginia bears a heavy responsibility for this rebellion, which her efforts might have stayed, and heavily she is paying for her mistake—her crime."[23]

Church was a passionate Unionist, but he often criticized Union tactics. He complained that General McClellan's inability to keep a schedule cost the Union the Battle of Williamsburg. He wrote that McClellan's troops woke "to find the enemy gone in the morning."[24]

He quit journalism to be a captain of volunteers and provisional brigades for the Army of the Potomac in October 1862. He lasted eight months, a period in which he also fell in love and got married, then complained of boredom and went back to journalism. In June 1863 he became editor of the *Army and Navy Journal.* This wasn't an official military journal, but Church made it an influential publication that ran military accounts from generals on both sides. He ran a series by McClellan, and he published General Lee's account of Gettysburg.[25]

Church argued on the *Journal*'s pages against the country's patchwork of militias and armies. Church thought it was ineffective and anti-Unionist. He argued for a draft to teach Americans their responsibilities to the whole country. "We have heard a great deal about the rights of citizens," he wrote in September 1863. He wanted "to hear something about the duties of citizens. We have heard much of what the State owes to the citizen. Is it not now time to hear what the citizen owes to the State?"[26]

After the war, he promoted strong military control over the South. To Church, Confederates were traitors, at best. "Holding those views we do with the regard to the pernicious fallacy of State sovereignty and the dangerous prate of State Rights, we find secession a terrible crime, legally considered, at the outset." He wanted Jefferson Davis jailed for life.[27]

Church couldn't believe that the Civil War hadn't demolished once and for all the quaint notion of militias. The anti-federalists who were anti-standing army and pro-local militia had created what he called "infinitely false and fatal delusions" in the American psyche. The standing army, he said, was "to be our fate and fortune."[28]

Like the rest of the professional military community, he viewed the militia with not a little contempt. Military pros at the *Journal* viewed the militia with "suspicious distaste and looked on it as a non-professional organization of ill-trained, nondescript civilians," Donald Nevius Bigelow wrote in his account of the publication. The *Journal's* tactical editor Emory Upton wrote that the "difference between the Regulars and the State organization is that the one is a body of trained and disciplined Volunteers under the command of educated officers and the other is not."

Church wanted a professional army, but pervasive postwar anti-military sentiment made him settle for something less: that American soldiers be well trained and well equipped. During the Civil War, eighteen hundred men trained with the most accurate available weapon, a Sharps breech-loading rifle. These "sharpshooters" proved their worth, but the tradition-bound military resisted.[29]

If the army wasn't going to prepare American men for modern warfare, somebody had to. Church wrote a series of editorials on marksmanship. In the summer of 1871 he got Capt. George Wingate of the New York National Guard to write a how-to series that would later be compiled into a book.[30]

George Wingate, embraced as the other co-founder of the NRA, would be more to the liking of today's NRA leadership. He promoted the idea of the citizen soldier and defended the National Guard's shooting of civilian demonstrators. "The militiaman is often condemned. . . . The first stone thrown should be promptly met with a shot. If promptly fired, many broken heads would be saved."[31]

Charged with such a monumental task as teaching shooting, Wingate turned to England for help. A dozen years earlier Great Britain started a club called the National Rifle Association. It had been inspired by the success of German marksmen against the menacing French.[32] In other words, the National Rifle Association, far from springing from a unique American character, was copied from the British, who were copying from Germans. Throughout American history, Germany has been the original source of American gun culture. In colonial times it was German immigrants who became American gunsmiths in Pennsylvania. The Revolutionary War's famous Kentucky Rifle was really made in Pennsylvania by German immigrants known as Pennsylvania Dutch (from *Deutsch,* the German word for German).[33] Later it was the Germans who organized many gun clubs and militias.

The National Rifle Association of Great Britain had built a great shooting range near London called Wimbledon, where shooting could be scored according to hits on a target. The idea of turning shooting into a sport with measurable skill was nearly groundbreaking.

Wingate aimed his lessons at urban shooters who had no opportunity for live practice shooting. The technique, already used in London, was first to learn the workings of the gun and practice without firing, and only then go to a specialized range like Wimbledon—a concept then virtually unheard of in America. Wingate's book of *Army and Navy Journal* articles became wildly successful; it was the army's only official shooting manual.

"An association should be organized in this city to promote and encourage rifle shooting on a scientific basis. The National Guard is today too slow in getting about this reform," Church enthused in the *Army and Navy Journal.* "Let us have our rifle practice association, also a Wimbledon on American principles."[34]

Six years after the Civil War ended, current and former Union officers formed a club to encourage marksmanship among current and potential troops. They formed the National Rifle Association. General A. E. Burnside, a Union civil war hero, served as the NRA's first president. Burnside, the man who gave us the word "sideburn" from his distinctive facial hair, however, was really a figurehead. Within a year Church assumed the presidency.[35]

The first NRA meeting took place in the offices of the *Army and Navy Journal* in lower Manhattan on September 4, 1871. This meeting was at 39 Park Row in a building that no longer exists, across from City Hall.[36] The first official address of the club was a few blocks away in Wingate's office at 194 Broadway at John Street. There's no marker, but the curious can find it at a jewelry store next to the TGI Friday's. Until the turn of the century, the National Rifle Association would occupy at least nine different offices in lower Manhattan.[37] All were within a few blocks of City Hall. The only building that still survives is the Bennett Building, on Nassau Street between Ann and Fulton. The largest cast iron building ever made is now a pink mall of discount clothing stores. None of the sites is marked as a former NRA headquarters.

Church set out to find a location for New York's version of London's Wimbledon shooting range, which is now famous for tennis. He needed cheap land close enough to the city for easy access but far enough out so club members wouldn't shoot their neighbors. Hermann Poppenhusen, the German-American president of the Central and North Side Railroad of Long Island, was building a track to stretch the length of the island. He thought shooting would bring spectators out on his railroad, so he sold the NRA a seventy-acre farm abutting the tracks that he had just bought from a family named Creed. For years the fortunes of the NRA, shooting in America, and the Long Island Railroad were intertwined, with the popularity of one promoting the other.

The land sat near the border of Queens and was perfectly flat, like an English moor, so the NRA changed its name from the Creed Farm to Creedmoor. Then the NRA fixed Creedmoor up like England's Wimbledon range. The targets were concentric rectangles (instead of today's circles) on a piece of iron. The shooter would know a hit by its distinctive ping on the metal, then wait for a hidden signaler, protected and concealed in a pit, to raise a colored flag or paddle showing the results.

The NRA imported the 300-pound iron targets from England. The 570-foot-wide tract of land started near the railroad and ran 1,200 yards almost due north. That was ideal because shooters would never have to look into the sun. Because Wimbledon had been plagued by neighbors' complaints of stray bullets—a harbinger of things to come—Church designed a kind of berm backstop for the targets. The railroad helped build it and the NRA also got free labor from an army unit at Willet's Point, Long Island, because this site fit into military training.[38]

Shortly after Creedmoor opened, the Irish challenged America to a shooting contest. The match that would push Creedmoor into popular culture was held on September 26, 1874. The railroad ran special trains, which were packed with swells and Irish laborers alike. The shots at Creedmoor were heard around the world. A live news account was telegraphed back to New York and across the Atlantic. In New York crowds gathered around public news bulletin boards. Today the shooting styles would seem outrageously undisciplined and are as far from war preparation as the cheap handguns that flood the streets of urban America today. The American Henry Fulton would lie on his back, knees bent, left hand behind his head and gun barrel resting on his crotch and ankles. According to NRA histories, the match was close and came down to the very last shot by American John Bodine. Just before shooting Bodine took a bottle of ginger beer, which exploded in his hand. Bodine persevered even though his hand dripped blood. The crowd went quiet. Bodine waited for the right wind and light, then shot. The crowd cheered when they heard the distinctive ping of a bull's-eye. A white marker went up confirming the American win.[39] [40] [41]

Even Church, no fan of impractical shooting, would later boast that because of this match, "the name Creedmoor has become a synonym the world over . . . for the highest skill in marksmanship yet attained."[42]

Creedmoor was also a synonym for the NRA. While the offices of the association roamed around lower Manhattan, the base of its early operations was emphatically Creedmoor. The NRA held its first conventions at Creedmoor, starting in 1878. Remington, Sharps, Marline, and other gun companies used Creedmoor as a prestigious model name. Regular NRA matches reinforced Creedmoor's popularity.[43] There was even a "Railroad Match" sponsored by Poppenhusen.[44]

Shooting enthusiasts set up a "Creedmoor, Jr." range right in Manhattan.[45] It sat in the abandoned tunnel for New York's first subway, which was powered by fan and ran one block. The tunnel was under a building across the street from City Hall and the *Sun* building. Ironically, in 2005 Tom McDermott's own office would move to a building that sits, if not on the exact site, next to it.

MONEY AND LEGAL TROUBLES:
THE GOVERNMENT BAILOUTS THAT SAVED THE NRA

The good times couldn't last forever, though, and the NRA soon ran into financial problems. Because the NRA was founded to develop National Guardsman marksmanship, New York State taxes provided almost all of the NRA's initial funding. Those NRA shooting matches even included prizes supplied by New York State. But as shooting lost its novelty, the sport's popularity waned and the state began to wonder just what it had been subsidizing. Founder William Conant Church seethed in an *Army and Navy Journal* editorial in 1877 that the NRA was retreating from military skills.[46] He never had a formal falling out with the group, but his role in its history tapers off here.

That same year the army said Wingate's book was geared too much toward guardsmen rather than regular soldiers. It commissioned a new version, which borrowed liberally from Wingate's book. Wingate, who had originally co-founded the NRA to train soldiers, now found himself suing the army for using too much of his book. Wingate won the case in 1880.[47]

By then, though, the NRA's fortunes, in tune with the economy, were dwindling. Looking for budget cuts, Governor Alonzo Cornell cut the NRA off. He told Wingate: "The only need for a National Guard is to show itself in parades and ceremonies. I see no reason for them to learn to shoot if their only function will be to march a little through the streets. Rifle practice for these men is a waste of money and I shall not countenance in my presence anything as foolish as a discussion of the rifle shooting at Creedmoor."[48]

The NRA still had Creedmoor; what it lacked were state funds to run it. Without government money, the NRA was in serious trouble. The city office moved, again and again, to progressively smaller quarters. The NRA tried to put on another big international shooting match in 1885 but couldn't get another country to show up.

Complaints about Creedmoor were growing, too. Again, the Long Island Railroad greatly affected the NRA's fortunes, but this time negatively. The rail line was also in financial trouble, so it had cut service to Creedmoor. Now that it was no longer cheap and easy to get to Creedmoor, attendance dwindled even further.

Since at least 1881, the NRA had been negotiating with New York State to take Creedmoor off its hands. The NRA didn't want to spend money repairing Creedmoor because it was considering alternate sites, including Staten Island and Van Cortlandt Park, in the Bronx.[49] Without state funds, the NRA was having trouble drumming up the money for shooting prizes.[50] The NRA gave out $11,425 in eight-hundred-eighteen prizes in 1881.[51] A match prize of $50 then would be worth nearly $1,000 today.

New York State, however, was reluctant to take over Creedmoor, in part because of the legal liability. There had always been complaints about stray bullets. Groups of farmers were writing to the association demanding damages. They complained that they weren't safe farming on their own land. The National Guard feared it would have to close off a public road in Queens.[52]

The NRA and New York finally agreed in 1890 that Creedmoor would become state property. The key to the deal was a "Get Out of Lawsuits Free" card New York State gave to the NRA to protect it from potential lawsuits over stray bullets. However much the NRA protests today that shooting is a safe sport that is being victimized by frivolous lawsuits, its history shows it should be accustomed to the complaints. After all, sportsmen have been shooting innocent American bystanders— and getting sued for it—from the start. According to a September 4, 1889, *New York Times* article, "The National Rifle Association, on its part, is relieved of all responsibility for suits growing out of its occupancy of the ground. . . ."[53] Even in its formative years, the NRA understood that these lawsuits weren't baseless. The old indemnification deal may still be useful to the NRA today. Many old shooting ranges produced so much lead that they caused million-dollar clean-ups. Today New York City public schools built near the site came up with above average lead levels.[54]

The next governor cut the NRA off completely and the association soon withered. For all intents and purposes, the NRA was dead. The value of the state's taking Creedmoor and shielding the club from liability, however, continued to grow. In 1895 a Flushing man was shot in the woods near Creedmoor. The resulting public uproar led legislators to amend state law so that shooting victims could sue the state for up to $10,000 for similar mishaps at the state-owned range.[55] The state closed Creedmoor completely in 1907 because of the stray-bullet liability issue. The *New York Times* covered the grand jury investigation into the dangers of the range on June 30, 1907.[56] One farmer and his friends had collected 150 pounds of lead that had been shot onto their land over six years. Bullets had landed two miles southwest of the range, in the opposite direction from which they should have been shot. The testimony included: "About six weeks ago a Polish woman was stuck by a spent bullet. . . . A week ago, while Mrs. Emma Van Schenck, who lives a mile and a half away from the range, was drawing a pail of water in her yard beyond Little Neck Road, a bullet whizzed over her head and lopped off a branch from a locust tree. Phillip Hoeffner, whose farm is directly in range of the long-distance targets, a mile back of the park, has had two bullets imbedded in his market house this season and Charles Kinsch, who has a market garden nearby, told the members of the Grand Jury that a bullet passed under his horse a few weeks ago."

The district attorney said the case would decide if "the shooting at Creedmoor is a menace to life and limb and ought to be stopped." New York State closed Creedmoor and then, in a plan some current Queens NRA members claim was meant as a slight to their organization's fabled home, converted the Creedmoor Rifle Range into the Creedmoor Psychiatric Center.

The nascent NRA may never have recovered if it had had to pay for the mess that it made. But as the full repercussions of its former shooting range came to light, a group of people partially revived the NRA from dormancy in New Jersey, hosting big annual matches at Sea Girt, New Jersey, a site chosen for its proximity to New York.

To attract more shooters, Sea Girt offered the German sport of schuetzen matches. Schuetzen participants shoot at a model of an eagle, which represents a mythical eagle that flew off with a baby. For the rifle association, it was simply a way to capture the most enthusiastic supporters of shooting in America: Germans.[57] Germans ran many Schuetzenbunds (shooting clubs) around the country. The remnant of one, Amerikanische Schuetzen Gesellschaft, is on St. Mark's place, Main Street of the East Village, a formerly German neighborhood.

The NRA, which had been functioning merely as the New Jersey State Rifle Association since 1892, revived itself in 1900, then got a big boost when President Teddy Roosevelt signed a law in 1905 that created the National Board for the Promotion of Rifle Practice, which meant that the government gave the NRA its full blessing—and all the government subsidies it used to get from New York State (for its role training guardsmen), and more. The blurry line between the NRA and the government made it easier for the NRA to promote arguments about the right of every American to own a gun. This new National Board opened up military bases to NRA shooting. The military would also sell surplus rifles, ammunition, and other supplies to the NRA at cost. Americans had to join the NRA to buy.[58]

THE TWENTIETH-CENTURY NRA MARKETING AND GUN LAWS

"Shootin's really popular now, not like it was years ago when a feller with a few guns was looked upon as some kind of dangerous nut. . . .
"Yep, shooting's Big Business now, what with thousands of paying spectators, the television rights, and all. The NRA has become one of the most important organizations in the country. . . ."

—"Pistol Match, 1998, A.D.,"
A December 1948 *American Rifleman*
look at the future of shooting.

By the twentieth century, the founding mission of the NRA had been accomplished: The armed forces taught rifle shooting. In order for the NRA to survive, it necessarily shifted its target audience to civilians. The NRA continued the push for proper training of civilian marksmen and hunters—avenues that aid NRA recruitment. But for an organization founded on the principle that guns require training, it has spent the twentieth century fighting any attempt to require training or licensing of handgun users.

The first serious attempts at gun control was New York's 1911 Sullivan Law, which required handgun registration.[59] The NRA objected, but back then its main involvement with the government was obtaining funding, not changing laws. It promoted shooting as a sport—thanks to hundreds of thousands of dollars from the War Department—so this sport was encouraged under the pretext of military readiness.[60] NRA badges declared marksmen the country's second line of defense

The gangster violence of the 1920s and 1930s inspired the country to consider national gun laws. The NRA, which had been used to lobbying Congress to restore funds, even during the Depression, now fought against these laws with the same savage instinct for self-preservation.

On the table was what would become the National Firearms Act of 1934. The Justice Department's original idea was to require anyone who bought a handgun, machine gun, or sawed-off shotgun to apply, register, and go through a background check and fingerprinting. Exotic weapons and accessories, such as light machine guns and silencers, wouldn't be banned; rather, they would require an exorbitant tax of $200. Handguns would be taxed $1, and re-sellers would have to register changes in ownership, just as with cars.

The analogy to automobiles was apt, because the NRA felt that cars were much more dangerous consumer product than guns, an argument that Tom heard during the Great Neck gun shop controversy. The NRA had been using the car argument since at least the 1920s.[61] During 1934 Congressional hearings on gun control, NRA President Karl Frederick said, "Automobile owners are . . . as a class, a much more criminal body, from the standpoint of percentage, than pistol licensees." Democrat Congressman Robert Doughton of North Carolina was so stunned that he asked, "Do you make that statement seriously?" "Yes, sir," replied Frederick. Of course, as time passed and car companies were forced to include safety features, car owners paid mandatory insurance, and the license and registration of cars became an effective system, some of the steam went out of the NRA's position.

The NRA appeared willing to compromise and even helped write the bill. At the same time, it encouraged members to deluge Congress with complaints. Meanwhile, average Americans faced with a less tangible but more severe loss—the death of a son, daughter, husband, or wife through gun violence—did nothing.

Congress caved in and gutted the law. There's no telling how many senseless deaths and shootings could have been avoided with handgun registration. Sixty years later, Tom McDermott would get shot by a handgun acquired under dodgy circumstances. If Ferguson had had to get a license in California, chances are he would have been held up by his recent move to the state and hotel address. Now Tom was fighting for a gun law that offered just a fraction of the protection than one Congress had considered before he was born.

The Violence Policy Center's Josh Sugarman calls the 1934 act "the great lost opportunity in the history of gun control . . . [and] a reminder of how little has changed." The same tactics have been played out in battle after battle since: a mass shooting or assassination inspires a gun law, and the NRA waters it down or kills it.

From here the NRA became what Tom saw as a marketing machine. It marketed fear for the purpose of its own self-preservation. Americans started calling the enthusiasts "gun bugs."[62]

The next major push for gun control came in the wake of President John F. Kennedy's assassination. Lee Harvey Oswald bought the Mannlicher-Carcano Italian rifle he used by tearing out a coupon he found in the February 1963 issue of the NRA's *American Rifleman*. Oswald used a Smith & Wesson .38 Special, which he had also bought by mail order, to kill Patrolman J. D. Tippit.

Revolted Americans debated whether licensing and registration of guns would stop this kind of easy access, particularly to handguns. But rather than address the issue directly, powerful congressmen from states like Connecticut, the heart of New England's Gun Valley (home of Smith & Wesson and Colt), steered the debate to whether to ban competition from overseas, mostly Germany. C. R. Hellstrom, president of Smith & Wesson, wrote that "shabby hangers-on and junk peddlers" should be shaken "from the coattails of an old and honorable industry." The proposals were framed as necessary for national defense.

In 1968, after Dr. Martin Luther King, Jr.'s assassination, the NRA, seeing the tide for some type of effective gun control rise, submitted a bill to Congress that would have required an affidavit for interstate handgun sales. After Robert Kennedy's assassination two months later, Congress passed a tougher law.

The Gun Control Act of 1968 banned gun sales by mail-order and across state lines, and raised the minimum buying age to twenty-one (though minors could still receive guns as gifts). Perhaps most significantly, it banned the import of low quality "non-sporting" handguns, such as the Saturday Night Specials, but it didn't ban their manufacture, something that would prove relevant to Tom's quest to make a difference in the gun control movement. The act also instituted Form 4473, which for the first time asked gun buyers questions to see if they were legally banned from gun ownership. For most, though, the act just modernized previous gun laws that kept guns from criminals, kids, and lunatics.

MODERN NRA

The Gun Control Act of 1968 had more impact than its authors thought, but not in ways they foresaw. The restrictions on cheap, shoddy imported guns led to the production of cheap, shoddy American guns. And the NRA, which spent much of the 1960s buffeted by attacks—even its organizational history refers to 1967 to 1969 as its darkest days—became radicalized and vowed to block any further gun laws.

Meanwhile disparate law-and-order voices as Presidents Richard Nixon[63] and Gerald Ford[64] and Chicago Mayor Richard Daley[65] called for banning Saturday Night Specials in the 1970s. About all that happened was that guns did receive more official federal oversight in the form of the Bureau of Alcohol Tobacco and Firearms (BATF), a division of the Treasury Department, created officially in 1972. The agency had existed previously under a variety of names; guns had been lumped in with other taxed vices, alcohol and tobacco, as a result of the 1934 National Firearms Act. Their order in the name, though, generally reflected the order of priorities. The ATF focused mostly on catching moonshiners in the South, not gunrunners.

When guns received heightened attention in this era, the NRA pressed sympathetic congressmen to slash the agency's budget, prevent it from using computers, and then ridicule it for being inefficient. The NRA did have some valid criticism of ATF inefficiencies. Most agents worked in the rural South,[66] fueling both the South's contention that too many agents were going after harmless and petty rules violations and Northerners' assessment that there weren't enough gun cops around to cut off the flow of dangerous and illegal guns to the major urban centers, something Tom McDermott would also try to fight a generation later.[67]

The culmination of the NRA's modern metamorphosis came in 1977 when Harlon Carter, who was once convicted for killing a teenager with a gun,[68] led a more radical wing to take over the NRA, defeating those who wanted simply to promote shooting sports. The NRA, after many internal dramas, eventually made the young, public-relations-savvy Wayne LaPierre its public face, but it still advocated the philosophy that any gun law is a bad law.

The NRA marketed a fear of letting the government keep data on guns. It targeted Form 4473, a watered-down version of registration instituted by the Gun Control Act of 1968. According to the NRA, anti-American forces were poised to invade and seek out Form 4473 so they could take away our guns. The 1984 right-wing cult film *Red Dawn*[69] actually features this scenario as part of its plot. The Russians invade Colorado and use the 4473 to find gun owners but are ultimately thwarted by the likes of Patrick Swayze, Charlie Sheen, Jennifer Grey, and the local high school football team. Not recognizing the defense capabilities of America's varsity athletes, the NRA has staged a long-running campaign to keep all gun records from being archived, lest they fall into the hands of the imminent invading hordes.

In *Saturday Night Special*, Robert Sherrill pointed out one flaw in this reasoning. "What this [scenario] never has explained," he wrote, "is why The Invaders would bother making thousands of stopovers at minor bureaucratic file cabinets when in one quick trip to headquarters of the NRA they could get their hands on the membership list representing most of the hard-line gun owners in the country. Could it be that the NRA is our weakest security link?"

The attempted assassination of President Ronald Reagan in March 1981 produced the NRA's greatest challenge since the 1968 act. Reagan and his press secretary Jim Brady were shot by a .22 caliber Saturday Night Special that had a retail price of $47.50[70] and was manufactured by Roehm, a brand name notorious in the pre-1968 era. Roehm's makers had found a convenient loophole: They just imported the parts—not covered by the 1968 act—and assembled them here.

After the shooting, Reagan briefly toyed with eliminating the Bureau of Alcohol Tobacco, and Firearms. The idea was really nothing new: Because guns were more of a crime than tax issue, many wanted them licensed under the Justice Department. Reagan's idea was to let the Secret Service, which have a fearsome and clean reputation, handle guns.

The NRA, which had been pushing to get rid of the ATF, got cold feet. It didn't want the competent and respected Secret Service to handle guns. Neal Knox, who favored an even more radical approach at the NRA but who lost the power struggle, recalled the dilemma in a 2003 column in *Shotgun News*. He wrote:

> When Reagan Deputy Treasury Undersecretary Bob Powis (former Secret Service) came to my office to pitch the plan, he acknowledged the problems with BATF abuses (telling Federal Director Wayne LaPierre and me that on the Treasury law enforcement employment test the 90th percentile went to Secret Service, 80 percenters went to Customs and barely passing 70 percenters went to BATF).
>
> I told Bob I was willing to transfer the functions to either Secret Service or Justice, but not the agents—whose reputation as "cowboys" still holds, as indicated by a recent FBI official's leaked memo opposing the present transfer to DOJ.
>
> But Powis told me Secret Service needed the manpower to "monitor gun shows so we'd have intelligence about where the guns are, to better protect the President." I was stunned—and opposed the transfer.[71]

Gun control advocates worked seven years on the Brady Bill before it passed in 1993—just seventeen days before Tom McDermott was shot. Now dealers actually had to bother to check—somewhat—that the buyer wasn't one of those people who weren't supposed to be buying a gun. As big of a victory as it was, the Brady Bill didn't come in time to stop Colin Ferguson. Tom thought the NRA had weakened it so much it would be ineffective in stopping future Fergusons.

Events like the LIRR shooting didn't produce a change of heart in the NRA faithful. On the contrary, they emboldened the membership. Knox wrote an article in the December 1994 issue of *Shotgun News* asking whether highly publicized shootings were really a conspiracy by anti-gun forces to drum up support for gun laws. "Is it possible that some of these incidents could have been created for the purpose of disarming the people of the free world?" Knox asked. "There have been far too many coincidences to ignore."

Tom McDermott was amazed to read how the NRA complained that guns are "the most regulated business" in America, a claim that would be challenged by anyone trying to make a living in restaurants or healthcare. Guns aren't subject to the type of safety tests that other consumer products face, thanks to a bill introduced by Michigan Representative and one-time NRA board member John Dingell. "It doesn't seem to me to be a matter on which the consumer has to be protected," he said. "Nobody's ever showed me that there is any need to cover firearms."[72] In 1972 he helped ensure that when Congress created the Consumer Products Safety Commission, guns would be exempt from its jurisdiction. The commission is charged with protecting the American consumer from dangerous products by setting safety standards for—and occasionally banning—some fifteen thousand types of products. It regulates just about everything from TV antennas to pens—but not guns.

Gun control advocates frequently cited the lack of consumer safety laws for guns. "This teddy bear has more regulations to make sure it's a safe product," Carolyn McCarthy announced at one press conference, brandishing a fluffy toy as a prop. "This gun has absolutely none."[73]

Tom found the NRA would always try to promote itself as the go-to group on guns. In its bylaws, he found, the group saw its mission as not only protecting the country by promoting public safety, hunting, and shooting sports, but also training the police. Tom would try to get a laugh out of police groups by showing them the paper that said it was the NRA's job "to train members of law enforcement agencies, the armed forces, the militia, and the people of good repute in marksmanship and the safe handling and efficient use of small arms." A few years later the NRA took its role as the preeminent source of gun information so seriously that it successfully lobbied congressmen to cut funding to the Centers for Disease Control by $2.6 million, the amount the agency spent on a study that showed having a gun in the house triples the risk of homicide.[74] The NRA had first tried to dismantle the CDC's Center for Injury Prevention and Control, which also tries to thwart car wrecks, brain traumas, burns, and other common tragedies.[75]

Tom realized that for all the battles in gun politics, the Gun Control Act of 1968 has since served as a fifty-yard line that pro- and anti-gun forces would jostle over, with neither side making much forward progress. There haven't been any more touchdowns on either side since. Just a few field goals, if you will. Regardless of public sentiment, changing national gun laws has been a difficult task. Tom McDermott knew he wouldn't have it any easier.

MR. MCDERMOTT GOES TO WASHINGTON, 1994

Now that McDermott understood the role the NRA had always played in creating the country's gun laws—at times basically writing them—he girded himself to face them as the country considered a new national gun law: the proposed ban on assault weapons.

Tom had pushed New York to pass a more comprehensive assault weapons ban, but so far its state legislature hadn't done anything. The federal bill was weaker, in part because it was much more specific in its limitations, but it did include Tom's major goal, a law that would have thwarted or slowed down Ferguson: It banned clips of more than ten rounds.

"How the hell can our society, our Congress, allow a civilian to have a clip of fifteen rounds?" he asked. "I remember in the service there were six rounds. I remember the shooting on the train and it just never was going to stop. The fact of a fifteen-round semi-automatic is just overwhelming to me."

The Senate had approved a ban on military-style weapons before, but the House refused. Rep. Jack Brooks (D-Texas) kept holding the law up. The NRA-backed congressman had been in office since 1952 and was now chair of the Judiciary Committee.

Richard Aborn, president of Handgun Control Inc., an organization founded in 1974 and sister organization of the Brady Center to Prevent Handgun Violence, directed McDermott and McCarthy in their lobbying. Aborn would station McDermott in the hallway right before legislators got on the floor.[76]

Tom would have just minutes to tell his story and make his case. He was left queasy by the whim of legislative process, worried that he was using himself as a walking victim impact statement. People listened to him only because he had been shot—and because he knew how to speak to this crowd. He felt he was showing off—"Here I am, a white middle class guy"—to remind the public that black urban youths weren't America's only shooting victims. He was proud to speak up for shooting victims, but he also felt that it wasn't fair that the public paid attention only to the articulate victims of notorious crimes. Still, the only way he knew to help was to show up and make his case.

"Tom and Carolyn were like Federal Express," Aborn recalls. "I could call them on Monday and say I need you here on Tuesday and they'd be there by ten-thirty. I never got, 'Well, I've got a dentist appointment, a family commitment.'"

Aborn would send people to talk with their own representative. McCarthy and McDermott would meet their representative, Levy, at the victims' group. Throughout much of the spring, they knew they were fifteen votes shy of victory. Handgun Control knew the score because it would run a vote count every three hours, rating the likelihood of support on a one-to-five scale. The ones were with them, the twos leaning toward them, the threes were gettable, the fours were no way unless it's 70 degrees in December, and fives were just plain no way in hell, Aborn explained.

In one early vote Aborn sent McCarthy and McDermott through a tunnel under the House floor to tell Rep. Rick Lazio that they didn't need his vote because the measure was doomed. They knew they had Lazio on their side, even though he was a Republican from the next district over (and would later run unsuccessfully against Hillary Clinton for a New York Senate seat). He spoke on the House floor about how Tom and Carolyn had persuaded him: "I was contacted by the widow of one of the victims . . . I also spoke with one of the wounded victims. "Their message was how could anyone vote against this ban if they knew the carnage that they saw when the killer went down the aisle and executed person after person. Had this legislation been in effect at the time, fewer lives may have been lost."[77]

Tom also worked on congressional matters back home in New York. Katina Johnstone lived on Staten Island, a Republican enclave in New York City. She would bring Tom to speak at events designed to sway Susan Molinari, the only New York City congressperson intent on voting against the assault weapons bill. Johnstone valued Tom at these events because he looked as if he could have belonged to the NRA himself. "These guys that would be in the audiences, he could take care of them," Johnstone recalls. "I don't think anybody changes their mind at these things, but he could make them be quiet. The message they got was, *How dare you do this?* And they were dismissed. Tom would dismiss them. *You're finished.*"

New York Mayor Rudy Giuliani appeared at one event and as he was rushing out, Johnstone slipped him a printed article on Molinari's stance with the note, "Can you help?" Johnstone thought she had startled Giuliani by approaching him that way, but he came through.

Finally, House Republicans started to sway towards the Democratic side. The first was Henry Hyde of Illinois, famous for his anti-abortion stance. The second was Molinari.[78] Her office told a local paper that Johnstone and Giuliani had changed her mind.

On May 5, 1994, the House had a vote on the assault weapons ban.

"We had to reach into the fours," Aborn recalls, referring to the group who would support gun control only under extraordinary circumstances. "We literally did not know how the vote would turn out." The House rings a bell to signal there's fifteen minutes of voting. "When the bell went off I'm standing there telling people before they went on the floor, 'You gotta come, we need you.'"

Aborn was standing next to an assistant to Attorney General Janet Reno. The assistant called Reno to say the Clinton administration would lose.

"It was the longest fifteen minutes of my life," he says.

Then all that lobbying by Tom and other people hurt by guns paid off. The bill passed, but just barely: 216 to 214.

"I was too stunned to be happy," Aborn recalls. "I walked around the Capitol afterwards and sat on a bench. Only then did I think, 'Oh my God, we did it.'" Later, President Clinton called to congratulate him: "He was ecstatic. You could hear it coming out of the phone."

Here Tom was, just months after the shooting, making a difference in federal law. He thought the assault weapons ban itself was typical of most federal gun laws: so watered down as to be nearly useless. Indeed, gun makers found a way around the law, marketing new "AB" for After the Ban models. However, Tom was proud he had helped get the ten-round limit in. He wasn't able to stop Ferguson from killing more people, but he had effectively stopped some other killer from firing more bullets.

"It was not a huge victory at all, but it was a step in the right direction against massive, powerful interests on the other side," Tom said. "The mere fact that there was an achievement, albeit small, was phenomenal. It meant the stranglehold the NRA had exerted for years on Congress had been broken. It showed there was a way to defeat them."

These congressional proceedings, Tom knew, were just reruns of the ones the NRA had been orchestrating for decades that avoided meaningful change. Even after the bill passed, there was trouble. Their Congressman Levy had backed the bill but then voted against the compromise worked out between the Senate and House. McDermott and McCarthy missed the last plane and had to take the long train back to New York. McDermott wanted to fight back against the politicians who backed the NRA on both sides of the aisle.

"One of us should run for Congress," he told McCarthy.

Even though he was offended by the legislative process he'd seen, Tom had toyed with the idea himself. Leaders of Nassau County's Democratic Party called him and wondered if he would run for state senate. He went to one Saturday morning session in their office and figured he had passed their vetting process because the Democratic leader of the state senate wanted to meet him in lower Manhattan.

"We will support you," he said. Tom was relieved. But then he went on to say: "You raise three-hundred-and-fifty thousand dollars and we'll match that."

Tom almost burst out laughing.

"Well, I doubt that very much," he said. "I don't have the network or kind of friends to guarantee that kind of money." He felt sure they knew there was no possibility, but to be polite he begged off using everyone's favorite political excuse: He needed to check with his wife.

The next day he was amazed to see a newspaper story saying he was going to run. Tom's wife Rosemary was more than amazed. She was furious. She felt the Democratic party leaders were being manipulative. They were using the shooting as a publicity tool for their own goals. The McDermotts did it the other way around: they let themselves be used to further an issue for the public good.

"That was the start and the middle and the end of my political career," Tom says.

Tom quickly decided that McCarthy, a Republican, would be a much more attractive candidate. "There's no way they're going to elect a Democratic white male on Long Island," he said. Tom, Cuomo and many others encouraged McCarthy. It took two years, but in 1996 she would run.

CUOMO AND THE ELECTION OF 1994

The assault weapons ban gave McDermott hope that this time the legislative cycle would be different, that ordinary people would challenge the NRA. However, as the year wore on, it began to look more like the history he had read about: Every victory was eroded with compromise and defeat.

McDermott and McCarthy gradually shifted from campaigning with Cuomo for the New York assault weapons bill to working for Cuomo's re-election. Cuomo was facing George Pataki, the little-known, mild-mannered mayor of Peekskill. Suddenly, however, the death penalty became the big issue, partly because of Ferguson, and the race was close. Cuomo's Catholic anti-death penalty stance hurt him, but he didn't change his mind. McDermott changed his mind, though for reasons a little less beneficent than the pope's. Tom thought back to that calm moment on the train when he was resigned to die and reasoned that Ferguson did not deserve that serenity. Life in jail would be a more severe punishment, he thought. Plus, from an economic point of view, the death penalty was a waste. He'd rather give the extra millions each death penalty case costs taxpayers to crime victims. He saw for himself how many of the people from the LIRR shooting were struggling financially. One traumatized passenger lost his job and his marriage; one surviving family member was so pressed for cash she had to move in with relatives. McDermott was amazed at how the victims of the shooting, a nationally covered crime, had been left to flounder.

McCarthy and McDermott appeared on a TV ad together for Cuomo. McCarthy talked about Cuomo's work on the state assault weapons ban: "He's been fighting so hard to get this bill passed. I don't understand why the Republicans—and I'm a Republican, and this really hurts—they're fighting this." Then Tom said: "Frying them all is not the answer."[79]

On election night, 1994, McCarthy and McDermott went to Manhattan's Sheraton Hotel to hear the results. They were sure Cuomo would win. Would New Yorkers elect Pataki just because he was willing to kill killers? An aide took McDermott aside to tell him the news: private polls showed Cuomo losing. McCarthy and McDermott looked on amazed as Cuomo conceded the race. They had a slim chance of getting a bill passed with Cuomo in office. Without him, they had none. That night marked the end of their trips to Albany.

New York passed a new death penalty law within months of Pataki taking office. But it never executed anyone.

In 2000, New York finally passed an assault weapons ban. At the time, it may have seemed like a meaningless me-too gesture, considering the national ban. But when the federal bill expired in fall 2004, it became significant.

REPEAL THE ASSAULT WEAPONS BAN? 1995

Conservatives lost the battle over assault weapons, but they struck back hard in the 1994 elections. Republicans won both houses of Congress and Newt Gingrich swept in a new class of conservative Republicans. Dan Frisa, an NRA member and state legislator who had long wanted Levy's job, won the primary.[80] [81] The NRA reserved special treatment for those loyalists who had faltered. It turned on its longtime ally Jack Brooks for allowing the assault weapons ban vote to go to the floor. After forty years in Congress, he lost his re-election bid to a Republican, Steve Stockman, to whom the NRA donated $9,000.[82]

"They are not reliable," Brooks told the *New York Times,* referring to the rifle association. "If you are not 110 percent for them, then they are against you."[83]

One of the first items on the agenda of the new Republican Congress was the repeal of the assault weapons ban, as weak as it was. Then Senate Majority Leader Bob Dole (R-Kan.), had vowed that by summer he would put a bill on the desk of Bill Clinton, who in turn vowed to veto it.[84]

Tom would have liked to spend his time working on newer, stronger laws, but instead he was playing defense, protecting last year's meager gains. He went down to Washington and told congressmembers that if they repealed the ban on assault weapons they would have "disgraced, dishonored the lives of those six human beings who never got off that car."

Charles Schumer, then a congressman from Brooklyn, asked Tom to appear at a hearing on March 31, 1995. Testifying ahead of Tom was a tiny thirty-six-year-old woman in a red suit, Sharon-Jo Ramboz. She had brought props for the table: pictures of her young children. Ramboz said that in 1989, she was in her Rockville, Maryland, home with her kids when she heard a sound downstairs. Assuming it was an intruder, she calmly walked to the closet to get the family Colt AR–15 semi-automatic rifle. "I walked to the top of the stairs. Then I pulled back the bolt and, letting it go, chambered a round." The ominous sound scared off the intruder, she said.[85]

Ramboz pointed out that she was Jewish and said, "This is how Nazi Germany began, by taking away our right."

The NRA promoted guns as the equalizer of the vulnerable, so this tiny woman seemed like a convenient prop. A Republican on the panel, Fred Heineman of North Carolina, noted that Ramboz was "hardly a Rambo."

Tom leaned over and whispered to Ramboz, who would with her husband go on to speak out for sundry NRA causes, "Who the hell are you trying to kid?" She turned her head to him but said nothing.

McDermott wasn't alone in his disgust. A fellow panelist, Bryl Phillips-Taylor, testified how a gun-obsessed Virginia Eagle Scout had executed her seventeen-year-old son Scott with an AK–47. "It's made me physically sick," Phillips-Taylor told a *New York Times* reporter after Ramboz's testimony. "What was I supposed to do, arm my poor child? They're saying they want to arm themselves to protect themselves. So do you arm seventeen-year-olds to protect themselves? . . . When the hell is it going to stop?"

GUNS DETER CRIME?

> A lot of people who want to keep a gun at home for safety are the same ones who refuse to wear a seatbelt.
>
> —George Carlin

Many believe that guns prevent crime despite statistical evidence to the contrary. The confidence comes from statistics that, whether they know it or not, are probably from former University of Chicago researcher John Lott, who wrote the book *More Guns, Less Crime*. Slate.com columnist Timothy Noah calls it "the bible of the national movement to persuade state legislatures to pass so-called 'concealed carry' laws."[86]

The Justice Department's National Crime Victimization Survey reports 110,000 defensive gun uses (DGUs, in the parlance).[87] Even that number includes cops and anyone who answered that they had "used a gun, even if it was not fired, to protect yourself or someone else, or for the protection of property at home, work, or elsewhere." This wording could easily lure those who just carry or own guns for self-defense. Lott claims many people just brandish a gun, then don't bother with reporting their would-be attacker. So the Justice Department's numbers are wildly low and inaccurate, and the true crime-stopping value of guns is vastly underestimated.

There's no direct corollary between just brandishing and not reporting, but that's the general idea. The figure Lott always quotes is that " . . . 98 percent of the time that people use guns defensively, they merely have to brandish a weapon to break off an attack." Lott puts the real defensive gun use figure at 1 million a year. Except when he says it's 2 million.

Lott first attributed his data to a number of newspapers surveys (which Noah says don't exist). When other academics pressed Lott, he said he had done the survey himself. *Okay, where was it, then?* Lott told the press he was the victim of a computer crash when a bookshelf fell on his computer.[88]

Academic gun work appears to suffer some curse of destroyed data. The left has Michael Bellesiles, an Emory University history professor who argued in *Arming America: Origins of the National Gun Culture* that early Americans had fewer guns than people think. He used several arguments, including early guns' high price and probate records, which he said showed that guns were not passed down in household property. Others couldn't duplicate his work, and he said his research was destroyed in a flood at Emory. Emory investigated and found no evidence Bellesiles was deliberately cheating, but said he was sloppy.[89] A panel of academics at the 2001 Social Science History Association reviewing the controversy faulted Bellesiles's methods and concluded that in early America gun ownership was "neither rare nor universal." "Roughly 40% to 60% of wealth holders" had working guns, one report showed.[90]

But while Bellesiles's general thesis—that guns were more expensive and less pervasive than people think in early America—if not his probate research remains largely unchallenged, Lott's other treatises have been widely challenged. Other studies don't confirm his result that gun owners just brandish their weapons 98 percent of the time. Florida State University criminologist John Kleck conducted a number of other surveys and put the "just brandishing" figure at 76 percent. The National Crime Victimization Survey from 1992–2001 puts the figure as low as 66 percent.

Lott also says laws that allow people to conceal and carry guns bring crime down. John J. Donahue III, then a professor at Stanford who has since moved to Yale, counters that attempts to re-create Lott's work came up with different results.[91] Donahue himself, along with Yale law professor Ian Ayres, used Lott's own methods on crime data but continued the work forward from 1992, when Lott stopped, to 1999. They found that concealed carry laws probably don't reduce crime; if anything, they increase it.[92]

Lott failed to account for variables like national crime trends. Or the fact that the states that passed concealed carry laws tended to be rural, low-crime areas anyway. So, Donahue says, it's not fair to compare these areas to high-crime cities that were in the midst of a crack-fueled crime wave.

Lott's research has some inconsistencies. For example, he cites a University of Chicago's National Opinion Research Center report on gun policy as saying that "the less-educated and those who haven't been threatened with a gun are most supportive of gun control." The report, in fact, says the opposite: " . . . support for the general regulation of firearms increases with education."[93] Tom McDermott is not the only American galvanized by his experience with gun crime. Gun control is most popular in cities, where there's more crime.

Lott claims that it made no difference that he was a John M. Olin Fellow at the university's law school. Olin is the maker of the Black Talon bullet, which expands on impact, preventing ricochets, but enhancing injuries. Others didn't hesitate to praise the Olin foundation, which closed in 2005,[94] for its work promoting conservative causes. *The Christian Century* reported that Olin's non-profit arm was one of "four sisters," foundations that "have been willing to put their money into journals and think tanks in order to win the battle for hearts and minds."[95]

When academics attacked his work, Lott found solace in the postings of one Mary Rosh, who claimed to have taken a class from Lott. She claimed Lott had student devotees, was her best prof ever, and that he was no ideologue but a pure academic.

And then Julian Sanchez, a blogger who works at the Cato Institute, a libertarian think tank, figured out who Mary Rosh really was: John Lott himself. But the NRA still doesn't distance itself from Lott or his findings. Lott is no longer at the University of Chicago. He is now a resident scholar at the openly conservative American Enterprise Institute.[96]

The *New England Journal of Medicine* has done the most definitive studies on the topic. Arthur Kellermann, an emergency room doctor who heads Emory University's Center for Injury Control, wrote in a June 1986 article, "For every case of self-protection homicide involving a firearm kept in the home, there were 1.3 accidental deaths, 4.6 criminal homicides, and 37 suicides involving firearms." That research has been backed up by the Centers for Disease Control among other agencies.[97] [98] [99]

VIOLENCE KILLS REPEAL OF ASSAULT WEAPONS BAN

McDermott was right: No amount of congressional testimony could stop the bid to repeal the assault weapons ban in 1995. What stopped the push was the American people saw what happened when the NRA's militia argument was taken too far.

Gulf War veteran Timothy McVeigh hung around with the Michigan Militia and mulled over the prospect of starting one of his own. Instead he bombed the Murrah Federal Building on April 19, 1995, killing 168 people. It was the anniversary of the shootout at Waco and the eve of Hitler's birthday.

With the unwanted scrutiny McVeigh brought to the movement in 1995, not to mention the disappointment at the delay in the imminent apocalypse, many militias, including the Michigan Militia, disbanded. Its founder Norm Olson told Ron French of the *Detroit News* in 2001, "What this country needs is a good old-fashioned Waco, with fifty people dead on each side. That would put fear back in society. You need fear to create a militia."[100]

Even though McVeigh hadn't used a gun, after Oklahoma City, the attack deflated the assault weapons ban repeal. "I think it does conjure up a lot of things in people's minds," Dole said on *This Week with David Brinkley.* "I can't bring it up, don't have any intention of bringing it up soon. It may be later this year. It may be next year,"[101] he said of the repeal bill. Those who wanted the repeal knew they had to wait for the public to forget Oklahoma City, the way it had already forgotten about Patrick Purdy and his January 1989 shooting spree that inspired the law: Purdy took an AK–47 to a Stockton, California, schoolyard and shot thirty-five people, killing five.

Tom, as always, thought the media attention paid to spectacular mass killings—even the Long Island Railroad shooting—drew attention away from the larger menace of everyday gun crime. Still, he was grateful that public interest kept the law around.

Congress let the assault weapons ban expire in 2004.

MILITIAS

"We're soldiers but we're American soldiers. We've been kicking ass for 200 years. We're 10 and 1. We don't have to worry about whether or not we've practiced. All we have to do is be the great American fighting soldier that's inside each one of us."

—Bill Murray, *Stripes,* 1981[102]

The biggest battle the mythical American militia soldier fought in the twentieth century was for gun rights. The army never called up the "unorganized" militia. But the NRA has used the citizen soldier to fight for government subsidies and gun rights. By the 1930s Congress effectively put to rest the notion that Americans should be training at home for the country's military protection. The weapons most useful to the military—fully automatic guns—have been out of reach of the average citizen since the National Firearms Act of 1934. Still, more extreme groups take harbor in the vague language of the Second Amendment and the country's once incoherent military structure.

For much of the nineteenth century, the country went through convulsions toward a federal army. Until the twentieth century, according to Harvard University sociology professor Jason Kaufman, "responsibility for American national defense was loosely divided between federal, state and independent forces."[103] In 1903, Senator Dick cleaned up the messy militia system. The militia had some successes and supporters, but it had been disorganized and derided since it started in 1792. Here are some of the reviews the militia got from the press over the years:

> "Idle spectators . . . the militia made so much noise in the gasconating speeches . . . and everywhere but in the field"—*Enquirer,* 1812[104]
>
> "Promiscuous and undisciplined masses . . . languishing skeleton companies . . . drooping spirit"—*Columbian Centinel,* 1820[105]
>
> "Thin-skinned"—*Army and Navy Journal* (after the *Journal* refused to print notices of militia practices, which it called "flippant notices of frolics"), 1867[106]

The Dick Act of 1903 finally brought the unwieldy state and independent militia system into the National Guard of each state. And for the first time, it divided the non-professional soldiers into two classes: the organized militia (the National Guard) and the unorganized militia (anyone between the ages of eighteen and forty-five who could be called up, although at the time it would have only meant white men). "Unorganized" was the old term that states had used to circumvent the militia requirement, code for nonexistent. The unorganized militia has never been called into service. It's been largely ignored, except by extremists.

That same year, the NRA worked with Congress to set up a Civilian Marksmanship Program within the army, ostensibly to train potential soldiers. For seventy years the NRA practically ran the program, which included letting civilians use military bases and annual matches at Camp Perry in Ohio. Although the NRA was designed to serve the needs of soldiers throughout much of the twentieth century, the defense department supported the NRA through shooting matches and discount gun prices. During the Vietnam War, 3,000 soldiers kept house at Camp Perry and Marines at Quantico complained that they were threatened with court-martial if they didn't give up weekend leave to pull targets for NRA members.[107] Those who campaigned to end the subsidy during the Vietnam War thought that without government support the NRA would just die out. Only in 1996 did Congress move the civilian marksmanship program into private hands and off federal tax dollars.[108]

The NRA fought to keep its federal funding even though their sport became less and less relevant to the military. Some competitions involved muskets—something even the tradition-bound army had long since discarded. In 1990 the Government Accounting Office, Congress's investigative arm, reported what everyone already knew: The program was of "limited value" to modern military preparedness.[109]

The program was an excellent recruitment vehicle for the NRA because only NRA members could buy military surplus weapons until 1968, when other approved clubs were finally allowed to do so as well. The arrangement cost taxpayers $5 million a year until it was finally moved to a non-profit in 1996. Congress let the Corporation for the Promotion of Rifle Practice and Firearms Safety take $4.4 million in cash with it and then gave it $10 million in guns and ammo over the next two years. Even though the Civilian Marksmanship Program is officially off the dole, the group still relies on government support. The army sells it guns such as the M–1 for about $100, and the group resells the weapons for $450 to $750. The NRA and other program supporters claim that they're actually saving the army money because it would cost about $17 to destroy each gun.[110]

If this were any other business, Congress would simply change this program and auction off the guns to the highest qualified bidder. The taxpayers bought the guns, and they should get as much of their money back as the market will bear. Of course, the army would have to make sure buyers were legally qualified. And it turns out, that's more than this non-profit was doing. A 1999 GAO report found the group didn't bother to check out buyers as it promised.

Since the mid-1800s private groups have been trying to claim the imprimatur of the unorganized militia. These local groups were social. Instead of fighting foreign enemies, they fought ethnic battles under the aegis of being part of the American militia.

After the Civil War, Congress worried that the old militias in the south, fed by a glut of cheap military weapons, would terrorize blacks. After all, before the war, militias in states such as South Carolina and Virginia used to go on patrols to round up escaped slaves. Congress banned militias in the former rebel states in the Army Appropriation Act of 1867. The Radical Republicans decided to go a step further and create a black militia, the Union League.

White militias were eventually reallowed, and many sprung up about the same time as the Ku Klux Klan, which effectively took over the old militia's job of harassing blacks. According to a 1993 *Southern California Law Review* article, "These vigilante groups undoubtedly saw themselves as carrying on a militia tradition—citizen-soldiers defending their communities against tyranny, in this case 'Northern oppression.' They were led by 'the flower of Southern manhood,' including former generals of the Confederate Army."[111]

A century later, after the Ku Klux Klan dwindled, its members started seeping into a new militia movement alongside Christian Identity factions. (The movement had come full circle, as it was many of the old militia who had originally populated the Klan.) Louis Beam is emblematic of the new militia-Klan. Born in segregated Texas in 1946, Beam joined the Klan after Vietnam. He worked his way up with David Duke until he became Grand Dragon of Texas. He worked on the KKK's paramilitary arm, the Texas Emergency Reserve. Then in 1981, he switched over to the more militaristic Aryan Nations. Beam and thirteen others were tried for sedition in 1987 but acquitted. Afterward he stuck to fomenting revolution against the government through his newsletters. In 1994, he wrote in *Jubilee*, a Christian Identity newspaper, "Guns are not just for hunting, target shooting and sport, they are for control of the government. . . ."[112] The militia movement got slightly more popular in the 1990s, in reaction to the perceived federal tyranny of assaults at Ruby Ridge and Waco and the new federal gun laws. Hundreds of groups such as the Michigan Militia renewed interest in the 'volunteer soldier.'

The irony is that if they were recreating the American militia as lovingly and accurately as Civil War reanactors mimic the Blue and Grey, they would be squirming out of their duty as early Americans did.

The true heir to the American militia is the National Guard, men and women who give up their lives back home—sometimes permanently—to go fight in Afghanistan and Iraq, but who aren't above grumbling when the army asks too much. They probably didn't know it but the soldiers of Victoria, Texas's 288th Quartermaster Company[113] were just following a long tradition when they put the now-famous cardboard sign "One Weekend a Month My Ass" in their windshield that became the rallying cry of a war's worth of overtaxed soldiers.[114]

DAYTIME TALK EQUALS DISASTROUS DEBATE

Homer Simpson: But I have to have a gun! It's in the Constitution!

Lisa Simpson: Dad! The Second Amendment is just a remnant from revolutionary days. It has no meaning today!

Homer Simpson: You couldn't be more wrong, Lisa. If I didn't have this gun, the King of England could just walk in here any time he wants, and start shoving you around. Do you want that? Huh? Do you?

—*The Simpsons*, originally aired Nov. 2, 1997

As Tom McDermott has witnessed numerous times, in almost every public debate on guns, NRA members offer up one of three arguments: guns are effective self-protection and deterrents to crime; the Nazis instituted gun control, and look what happened; or guns were part of America's national heritage and birthright, necessary for national defense and to keep the government in line. Tom also learned that if you got back to the basic issue that too many guns were hurting people, NRA representatives would say the problem was that not enough people carried guns. The worst time he had with the NRA was on *Rolanda,* a typically sensational daytime talk show starring Rolanda Watts, a former TV news anchor. Richard Aborn, the president of Handgun Control, asked Tom to appear with him to discuss the potential repeal of the assault weapons ban.

Tom got a bad feeling about the show when he heard the staff "whooping" up the crowd. This wasn't going to be a public policy debate. This was a steel cage match.

Not only was the NRA debating him across the table, but it had turned out in the audience, too. An older man in the audience took on Tom.

"You should have jumped Ferguson when you saw him reloading," the man said.

This was a low blow. The NRA was blaming Tom for not being able to stop Ferguson's massacre. Tom knew it was ridiculous; he'd been standing ten feet away when Ferguson aimed his gun. But it was a sadistic suggestion since so many victims are plagued by regret, wondering if they could have done something different. People who thought shootings worked like that, Tom knew, had learned about them from the movies.

The old man went on: "If I were there I would have had a gun and I would have shot him."

Tom was affronted. He fired back that he'd never trust that man on the train with a gun. He'd likely shoot somebody else.

As soon as they broke for a commercial Tom started to get up to leave. Aborn convinced him it would make their side look cowardly. So Tom stayed. After the taping ended, he vowed never to go on a show like this again. Civil debate was fine. But it was a waste of his energy to spend time debating this nonsense. Now he had a sense of why previous-shooting-victims-turned-activists quit. There was no point in playing these games with the NRA, letting the organization frame the gun issue on its terms.

INSIDE THE MIND OF THE NRA

As Tom faced off against the NRA, he began to understand the organization and its members better. The NRA is absolutist, but many members aren't. Talk to any NRA member and chances are you'll find some ambivalence. Still, people join, just in case there is a threat to their way of life, just the way many animal lovers join PETA without endorsing all its way-out stands. *Sure, they're a little nuts, but they get things done.*

Even though most people don't believe the NRA, the fear it spreads is infectious. Richard Aborn says that the NRA's message has permeated even moderate gun owners, causing them to ask with some suspicion: *You really want to take away my guns, don't you?*

While liberal groups like to debate, "The NRA has people in a Zen like state," Aborn says, referring to members' almost hypnotic confidence in the organization. "To be an NRA member is to almost intuitively understand that if someone is talking about guns on a radio show, they've got to call in. . . . And when it comes to Election Day, they've got to pull that lever and there's only one issue that counts."

Tom had seen the full impact of the NRA's marketing of fear. The NRA makes people afraid their own guns might be taken, and then it teaches them to express that fear in more socially palatable forms. It frames any gun law in a broader context of the history of the Second Amendment, the history of the militia, dubious gun safety statistics from John Lott, the Nazi gun positions, or any number of absurdly irrelevant hot-button issues.

The average city council member or senator isn't going to know the entire history of militias, Supreme Court Second Amendment cases, or gun statistics, so the NRA successfully markets, even to its enemies, that NRA members are *the* gun experts; challenge them at your peril. During the assault weapons debate in 1994, NRA supporters would argue that anyone who wasn't a gun expert was not qualified to legislate gun excesses. At its most pedantic, the argument came down to how can you take these gun control nuts seriously when they don't even understand the difference between a machine gun and a semi-automatic pistol? Machine guns, which have already been banned, are fully automatic and require only a continuous trigger squeeze to keep firing. Semi-automatic weapons still require a trigger pull per shot, but they can easily be converted to fully automatic and can still fire 40 to 100 rounds per minute. It's unlikely that Mothers Against Drunk Driving ever faced a similar challenge if they failed to differentiate between a Rob Roy and an Old-Fashioned.

Most people, even most NRA members, didn't hold these beliefs that strongly. A 2004 University of Pennsylvania survey found that 48 percent of people in a NRA household backed the assault weapons ban, as did 71 percent of people in households without guns.[115] Similarly, most people largely favored moderate solutions and not absolutes. Just 16 percent of the population endorsed a total handgun ban, according to the University of Chicago's National Opinion Research Center, as opposed to 85 percent who wanted handguns registered or licensed. No credible or major gun control advocate has pushed for a total ban for decades, Tom notes, because it's just impractical. Even if it were, Tom himself wouldn't want it; he doesn't see the need to keep guns from people willing to show they are responsible.

He thought gun control activists who pushed for a total gun ban were just playing into the NRA's hands. It wasn't going to happen. And it let the NRA spread fear and pretend that was the real goal of gun control. And as with a great number of gun control activists, Tom's concern was dead humans, not dead animals, so he focused on handguns and largely ignored rifles or long guns.

For all of the NRA's chest-thumping of its political might, a closer look at its numbers shows this might be just a self-fulfilling prophecy. It has outsize political influence—in part because it flaunts that it has outsize political influence. The public believes and perpetuates the story. When you consider its financial and membership woes, the NRA may be the quintessential emperor with no clothes.

Jack Anderson reported in *Inside the NRA* that the group started the 1990s with $92 million on hand. As of December 2003, Dun & Bradstreet reported that the NRA had a net worth of negative $63 million, an improvement over the previous year's $77 million debt.[116] By 2003, the latest year for which tax returns are available, NRA Executive Vice President LaPierre made $644,875 with $164,000 in benefits.[117] Neal Knox complained to Stephanie Strom of the *New York Times:* "We shouldn't be going into the hole, which is what we're doing. . . . The deficit isn't there because we're taking in more or less money, it's there because we're spending more money than we have."[118]

When it comes to its membership, the picture's not much prettier. The NRA should know that the demographics of hunting are not in its favor. Two reports in 2001 found that for every hunter there are 2.6 anglers and 5 wildlife watchers.[119] In 1985 the average hunter spent twenty days in the field but by 2001 he spent only eighteen. Hunters are getting older, and young people aren't taking their place. A 1986 survey found 17 percent of hunters were between the ages of eighteen and twenty-four, but in 1995 only 8 percent were. The mean age for hunters went up from 37.7 to 43.8 over the same time.[120] The demographic trends are not the gun industry's friends.

That means the NRA has to market to a dwindling pool of hunters more aggressively. To get a state hunting license, you almost always need to pass a hunter education class. The classes, which take place in little shooting clubs around the country, are an odd mix of government-sponsored gun safety and gratuitous NRA propaganda.[121] In one recent class the teacher asked: Will you be one of the true sportsmen who protects the sport? Or just let others do the work? Throughout the class the instructor continually offers a discounted NRA membership price. This is the same pitch, however, that nearly everybody gets in the mail. Normally, an NRA membership costs $35. Okay, okay, stop, you win. For you the NRA will take just $25. Just this once, it'll slash the price to $25. According to Jack Anderson, one 1994 NRA membership committee report showed that only 43 percent of new members signed on for a second year.

That kind of churn rate in membership puts many of the NRA's efforts in vast relief: This is a desperate organization. Failing and flailing, it clings to what it has—a core of extreme loyalists and its façade of power. If it ever lost too much ground on a gun law battle, perhaps even the loyalists would see it for what it was.

Tom was tired of the inflammatory rhetoric on both sides of the gun issue and ready to move on from epic fights that yielded weak results. He thought if reasonable people worked together, they could fix the gun problem, allowing responsible people to have guns and keeping them away from criminals. Mental health screening, now popular with academics, the Bush administration, and some states as a way to deter everything from teen suicide to common depression to incompetent senior drivers, shows promise of one day keeping the Fergusons of the world from buying guns.

What Tom found as he encountered hunters or gun owners was that if they weren't there to represent the NRA, he could get a fair shake. One Saturday winter morning, Tom spoke to a group of men at a synagogue in Smithtown, Long Island. He disagreed with some of the men but noted that it was "a remarkable positive and civil discussion."

One man in the group identified himself as having a pistol permit. He said he needed it for work. Did Tom think he should have to give up his gun?

"Our course not," Tom said with a smile. "I have never maintained guns should be banned or illegal. There is no question, people have a need to possess a firearm for an occupation or profession: a doctor carrying drugs, or a jeweler or a courier."

He was impressed that the men who were most serious about their practical need for a gun were also the most earnest in taking responsibility for it. They all left feeling that there was a reasonable solution to gun laws, a way out of the mess America was in. As long as the NRA wasn't involved.

Five

THE COURTS: COLIN FERGUSON'S VICTIMS SEEK JUSTICE

THE FERGUSON TRIAL, 1995: WELCOME TO THE CIRCUS

Back in the more practical world, the first, most basic way the courts would seek justice for the people shot on the Long Island Railroad was Colin Ferguson's criminal trial. Typical criminal proceedings often leave crime victims feeling empty, unsatisfied. Imagine, then, how the victims of this extraordinary crime felt when the trial became one of the strangest American courtroom dramas ever.

Before the trial, Ferguson's famous lawyers, William Kunstler and Ron Kuby, were preparing an insanity defense. They wanted to argue that his violence was triggered by black rage after experiencing racial discrimination. The victims didn't like either part of that strategy. Ferguson didn't like it, either.[1] There are varying standards for sanity, but in New York, someone is considered sane if he or she understands the proceedings and can aid in his or her own defense. A psychiatrist found Ferguson fit for trial.

The shooting victims reunited to prepare for the trial. Prosecutor George Peck, who looked like a stereotypical hard-working prosecutor, with a graying, crinkly comb-over, gathered them in an auditorium at the Nassau County Police Department to tell them what to expect.

At the first meeting, the chief concern was the black rage defense. Tom was angry at Kunstler just for introducing the black rage excuse, which he saw as in the interest of Kunstler's politics, not his client's welfare. Peck told them that if Kunstler went through with the defense, their job as witnesses would be straightforward, because no one would be challenging their version of events.

Given Tom's experience as both a lawyer and a witness in many trials, a few of the other victims called Tom for advice after the meeting. "You look right at the jury, each and every answer you give," Tom would tell them. "Do not look at the lawyer."

The circus switched rings when Ferguson fired Kunstler and Kuby. Nassau County Court Judge Donald Belfi allowed Ferguson to defend himself.[2][3] Kuby correctly predicted the trial would become a spectacle "so horrible to imagine . . . it staggers the imagination."[4]

When the shooting victims learned that Ferguson would be defending himself, they redirected their concerns. They worried about their safety. Tom assured them Ferguson wouldn't be allowed to get physically close. "You're not going to choke up or break down," he told them, though he was privately worried some might grandstand. "It's something we have to do in a mature way. This is now the most important period of time. Convicting him is something only we can do, not the cops, not the rescue workers, as important as they will be. We have to do this now, very unafraid."

Meanwhile, the prosecutors interviewed each witness individually. Although about fifty people could place Ferguson on the train, Tom was one of only a few who saw Ferguson shooting. The investigator asked Tom about the woman whom other passengers had seen him sheltering under his trench coat. He said he just couldn't remember. "We left it out," Tom says. As a courtroom veteran, he thought it best: "In any witness you want a clear recollection of what transpired so you can testify about what you heard or saw, not what you imagined or what you don't have a recollection of."

Peck told all potential witnesses—that is, all the passengers—not to watch the trial on CourtTV. That way the defense couldn't argue that they were just parroting what they had heard.

As the trial got underway, Ferguson toggled between lucidity and lunacy. A lifetime of delusional arrogance seemed to prepare him for this starring role in the absurd courtroom drama. He was sane enough to mimic the motions and emotions of a lawyer, but his arguments were often nonsense.[5][6] Ferguson opened his defense by smugly insisting that the reason the state indicted him on ninety-three counts was that the year was 1993. "The evidence will show that Mr. Ferguson was a well-meaning passenger on the train," he said. "In short, this is another stereotype victimization because he, Ferguson, is black. This particular conspiracy is more wide-ranging."

Ferguson argued that he brought the gun on the train and fell asleep. Then, contrary to every witness's account, Ferguson claimed someone else grabbed his gun and did the shooting.[7]

Throughout the trial, Ferguson referred to himself in the objective third person: Mr. Ferguson. The people he shot would angrily turn it back to *you* and *me*. His interaction with Elizabeth Aviles was typical. Ferguson, wearing a brown tweed suit, asked if she really didn't see the suspect shoot anyone. "I saw you shooting everyone on the train, okay?" she responded.[8]

When it was McDermott's turn to testify, he reminded himself to keep his emotions in check, not to show bitterness or anger. If you lose control of your emotions, you can lose a case, Tom had always told himself. In this case, losing was all but impossible, but he still wanted to be professional. He was an ideal witness, calm and effective.

Newsday veteran reporter Maureen Fan was impressed: "Thomas McDermott chose his words carefully. He spoke slowly. And the attorney from Garden City kept his anger in check as Colin Ferguson loudly questioned him about how he tried to shield himself from the shot that pierced the back of his left shoulder.[9]

"I was able to get into the aisle and at that precise time there was no one standing . . . between you and I. And when I observed you raising your right arm with the pistol in your right hand, I made this movement to protect myself and that's when you shot me in the back."

Ferguson asked if Tom had told the police on the scene that he had been a prosecutor. No. If he had known Peck. No.

Ferguson asked what McDermott did to protect himself. "I turned my body away from you. I did not want to give you a full profile when you were raising your right arm with the gun. I was able to turn my body and give a side profile, at the same time lifting my left shoulder up towards my ear, towards my head, and bending my head down towards the right and to the floor to protect my head from being shot by you."

McDermott thought Ferguson seemed intent in court on inflicting pain on the same people he had shot.

Ferguson produced plenty of nonsensical drama. He alluded to a vast government conspiracy to frame him. Ferguson wanted to call a witness to the stand who claimed he had been on the train and that Ferguson was being framed. The judge wouldn't allow this would-be witness, who had just turned up at the courthouse.[10] The judge also denied Ferguson's demand to get President Clinton to testify. Clinton had met with the three rescuers, and Ferguson claimed Clinton could have special information from them. Ferguson kept asking for delays in presenting his defense, but finally Judge Belfi gave him five minutes to make his closing arguments, which he did in a disheveled and uneasy manner.

The jury deliberated one day before announcing it was ready with a verdict. Tom was driving on the Long Island Expressway when he heard the news around eight P.M. The jury delivered a guilty verdict on February 17, 1995, at 9:15 P.M. Cheers went up among the victims in the courthouse and across Long Island.

The *New York Times* noted how the victims, now united, used the occasion to call for stricter gun laws: "The half dozen people who gathered to speak after Ferguson was found guilty of killing 6 and wounding 19 had clearly coordinated their prepared statements and planned their strategy to make a strong stand against gun manufacturers and their political supporters."[11]

The *Times* quoted Tom's speech as starting: "We, the survivors of the LIRR 5:33 . . ." and noted that "until 10 minutes ago [Ferguson] could have purchased the gun." Only his felony conviction would now stop him.

Carolyn McCarthy said she did not want to hear Ferguson's name again but vowed that people hadn't heard the last from these shooting victims.

Robert Giugliano would say: "The manufacturers, the gun people look for the almighty dollar. Enough is enough."

Five weeks later, many victims went back to court to give victim impact statements for sentencing. They were finally allowed verbally to let loose on Ferguson.[12] Giugliano said in his victim impact statement: "I know I have an impossible request, Your Honor. But given five minutes alone with Colin Ferguson, this coward would know the meaning of suffering. . . . [To Ferguson]: Look at these eyes. You can't look at 'em, right? You can't. You remember these eyes. You're nothing but a piece of garbage. You're a [expletive] animal. Five minutes. That's all I need with you. Five minutes."[13] *Newsday* later reported that Giugliano would be recognized as "the 'five minutes alone' guy."

Kevin McCarthy testified, with his mother standing beside him with her hand on his shoulder, stifling his sobs. He said that Ferguson had sentenced him to a life of pain and suffering.

Parents and widows spoke.

Tom didn't give a victim impact statement, believing it was best left to those whose relatives had died.

Ferguson was sentenced to six consecutive life sentences.

Although the bizarre liberties Ferguson was allowed at the trial angered many, Tom, always the discerning consumer of legal performances, thought the judge and prosecutors did the right thing. This way there could be no successful appeal.

Tom has given Ferguson little thought since.

PLAINTIFF TOM MCDERMOTT, 1994

Tom was satisfied that Ferguson would be put away. Ferguson was an awful man and he would pay for his crimes, however inadequate his payment might be to his victims. But the trial still hadn't brought justice to the people who let Ferguson have the gun. Now Tom wanted to make sure they would be held accountable, too.

He got the chance when he met lawyer Stephen Glasser at a Unitarian church on Staten Island. Tom's speech awed Glasser.[14] The Ferguson shooting had made Glasser think about companies that effectively poured high-powered guns on the street, surely knowing that they would hurt and kill Americans, but not taking any responsibility for it. Glasser introduced himself to Tom, and they began to sketch out the vague idea of a suit. Glasser worked at Sullivan & Liapakis, then one of New York's biggest personal injury firms, and they agreed to take it on.

Tom also trusted the firm's judgment to go after not only the maker of the gun, Ruger, but also Olin Corporation, the producer of the expanding Black Talon bullet and Ram-Line Inc., which made the extra-large, fifteen-round magazine. They would argue that, like Saturday Night Special manufacturers, these companies surely knew they were arming criminals against ordinary Americans.

Tom knew only a little about this kind of law, just enough to know the odds were against them. Here he would be a plaintiff, though, not a lawyer. His job would be to corral his fellow shooting victims to join him in the suit.

Tom wouldn't be the first of the LIRR 5:33 victims to seek justice in the courts. At least five had sued the railroad for lack of security, but their suits was dismissed. Tom and Rosemary weren't blaming the railroad. Rosemary jokes that the only time she really got angry with the LIRR was when they wouldn't let her use her pass. She had wanted to say, *After what you did to my husband*, but thought better of it.

PRODUCT LIABILITY AND GUNS

Tom had been a lawyer for two decades, but he didn't have any experience in product liability, which is what this case was about.

He knew people had used this strategy before without much success. It was new to Tom, but people had been suing gun users, owners, and makers for centuries. The first recorded U.S. lawsuit about guns dates back to 1674, according to Windle Turley, author of a two-volume textbook *Firearms Litigation: Law, Science and Practice* (1988).[15] People sue gun owners for negligence and gun makers for product liability. (Lawyers, always fond of irregular plurals like attorneys general, call it products liability.)

Every manufacturer can expect some kind of product liability complaint. With guns, of course, the stakes are raised because a flaw that would mean a burnt hand from a toaster can mean death in a gun. The typical defective gun case involves a drop-fire: The gun fires when it's dropped, something that safety features like the trigger guard (the loop of metal around the trigger) are supposed to prevent.

The Smith & Wesson archives in the University of Massachusetts library in Amherst show the company's pre-printed affidavit form from the 1920s.[16] The form makes it seem incidents involving consumers were common enough: "I [fill in the blank], a citizen of [fill in the blank], being duly sworn, do hereby affirm that on the [fill in the blank] day of [fill in the blank] year . . . a Smith & Wesson Revolver, Caliber [fill in the blank] exploded in my hand." The form then requires that the user state the type of ammunition, powder, and firing conditions and have the form notarized. Gun makers used to be able to fend off consumers' claims like any other big company: by saying that they had no direct transaction—and thus no duty or contract—with customers because a middleman sold the customer the gun. (Conscientious Smith & Wesson, the forms indicate, handled the claims without having a gun put to its head by the courts.) The law demanded "privity," a direct relationship, a concept that harkens back to a day when ye olde local craftsman made buggies personally for his customers. Companies still used the defense, however, even in the era of mass marketing and advertising.

The case that largely did away with the notion of was *Henningson v. Bloomfield Motors., Inc,*[17] a 1960 ruling that law students learn about to this day. On May 7, 1955, Claus Henningson bought a Chrysler as a Mother's Day present for his wife Helen. A few days later, a defect caused the car to veer off the highway, totaling the car and nearly Mrs. Henningson. The car companies effectively tried to say, *Mrs. Henningson? Who's she? Never heard of her.* The court effectively said, *She's the woman you nearly killed. Now pay her.* And a revolution in liability had begun, allowing people to sue makers of consumer products that were defective.

The legal responsibilities of manufacturers continued to grow, with car companies again leading the way. Evidence showed that Ford Motor Company knew in its tests from the early 1970s that its rear-end gas tanks on the Pinto could explode on impact, but it calculated that the cost of a few lawsuits and lobbying against safety standards would be cheaper than a redesign. After public uproar following a *Mother Jones* exposé, Ford recalled the cars in 1978. About five-hundred people died from the defect, and the public was revolted.[18]

Gun makers had been comparing themselves to the car industry for decades, (Criminals use cars to get away. More Americans are hurt in car accidents than shot. . . .) Now that car makers were taking responsibility for public safety, however reluctantly, the meme "Why not guns, too?" shot through the legal community.

Enterprising lawyers attempted a number of legal theories to bring responsibility to the gun business. Many of these centered on the idea that if a danger was foreseeable, then the makers had a duty to protect the public from it. One idea was to define the gun business as a hazardous enterprise. This idea dates back to a British case *Rylands v Fletcher* (1865),[19] about a mill whose reservoir damaged a nearby mine. From then on, according to eminent legal scholar and textbook author William Prosser, the courts held that "the hazardous enterprise, even though it be socially valuable, *must pay its way*, and make good on damage inflicted."

In 1973, Jeffrey O'Connell, a law professor at the University of Virginia, made a controversial argument in his university's law journal: If car owners have to buy insurance, why not owners and makers of guns? "If the power of the gun lobby precludes regulatory legislation curbing the sale and use of firearms, that end might be achieved by charging gunmakers and sellers with the costs of killing and injuring people by gun. . . . Why shouldn't guns—like autos—be forced to pay their own way?"[20]

During this era, a number of decisions encouraged plaintiffs suing any manufacturer for product liability. In *Ford v. Evancho* (1976),[21] a Florida court established what was called a "crashworthiness" doctrine: Automakers didn't have to make cars that couldn't crash, but they had to realize that cars *would* crash and make them as safe as they could. Until then companies had argued that they made cars for driving, not crashing, and that accidents were drivers' fault. The court said: "The manufacturer should not be heard to say that it does not intend its product to be involved in any accident when it can easily foresee and when it knows that the probability over the life of its product is high, that it will be involved in some type of injury-producing accident." In *Moning v. Alfano* (1977),[22] the Michigan Supreme Court held another kind of weapon to this doctrine of responsibility. A slingshot manufacturer had marketed its product directly to kids, who, to no one's surprise but the company's, ended up injuring people; Moning had lost an eye. The court found that the company owed a legal obligation of due care to the bystander.

In 1980, Stuart Speiser wrote *Lawsuit,* a widely read book that offered arguments for suing gun makers on another theory: that they negligently distributed their guns, flooding the market, even though they knew the product was safe only in the right hands.

Other legal theories included the idea that guns created a false expectation that they would protect consumers. (This is one of the NRA's primary arguments for gun rights and one that Tom encountered repeatedly.) Some thought guns should be subject to risk-utility analysis: weigh benefits and costs to society against each other. In the early 1980s, more than sixty suits were filed against gun makers, using these various legal theories: negligent distribution, strict liability, or abnormally dangerous activity. The nonprofit Foundation for Handgun Education kept the momentum going by holding a convention on gun company lawsuits in 1982.[23]

Despite the impetus, most cases were dismissed right away. They didn't fit the traditional mold of a product liability case. That is, the gun did exactly what it was supposed to do: kill someone. That didn't bode well for Tom's case.

Sometimes plaintiffs took hope just from the wording of a ruling against them or from a ruling that would later be overturned. Windle Turley was one of several lawyers who represented a group of shooting victims and argued that marketing small caliber handguns to the general public was so dangerous the companies should be held strictly liable for the damage their guns caused. Kathy Newman was a Tulane medical student when a guy used a cheap Charter Arms handgun to kidnap, rape, and murder her. Newman's mother Judie Richman sued the gun maker. In *Richman v. Charter Arms* (1983)[24] the judge said: "The analogy here is manifest: if car manufacturers must reasonably expect purchasers of their products to speed periodically then surely handgun manufacturers must reasonably expect purchasers of their products to kill periodically."

The *Charter Arms* case was later overturned, but it still gave the shooting victims and their lawyers hope. Nobody was in this for a big, quick cash payout. This was a long, hard fight. Each shooting victim, widow, orphan, parent, and lawyer sued without much hope of getting money, but with a hope that his or her small victory would be give something to someone further down the line to mount another case on.

KELLEY V. RG INDUSTRIES

McDermott took real hope from one case. Olen J. Kelley, a grocery store clerk, had been held up five times before he was shot in the chest in 1982 with a Rohm Gesellschaft gun. Kelley sued, hoping to make sure fewer clerks got shot by cheap, easily concealable handguns. Maryland's highest court ruled in *Kelley v. RG Industries* (1985)[25] that "the manufacturer or marketer of a Saturday Night Special knows or ought to know that the chief use of the product is for criminal activity. Such criminal use, and the virtual absence of legitimate uses for the product, are clearly foreseeable by the manufacturers and sellers of Saturday Night Specials. . . . [I]t is entirely consistent with public policy to hold the manufacturers and marketers of Saturday Night Special handguns strictly liable to innocent persons who suffer gunshot injuries from the criminal use of their products."

This decision was a bombshell. If Maryland could hold certain gun makers liable, then other states would certainly follow. This case gave Tom hope for his case. The court didn't care if what it did was too radical, impractical, or unpopular; it simply recognized that Saturday Night Specials were crime guns. The court saw guns for what they were. "In language and reasoning that should have been seized upon by other courts," Tom said. "[The court] said enough was enough."

Tom read a story by Howard Siegel, the lawyer who had taken on the case when it seemed hopeless: "When Olen Kelley had first come to see me, I had warned him that neither one of us would ever see a nickel out of this case," Siegel wrote in *Litigation*. "Our defendant was a West German corporation with no directly attachable assets in the United States. We were not about to go chasing around West Germany trying to collect."[26]

Instead of going after money, Siegel was sharp enough to drop the case after the Pyrrhic victory. That way, the verdict would stand. The NRA lobbied the Maryland legislature to pass a bill negating the decision. It narrowly failed. As a compromise, Maryland set up a Handgun Roster Board to determine which guns could be sold in its state. The vast majority of handguns pass, so responsible gun consumers are largely unaffected, but one Johns Hopkins study showed the policy saved forty lives a year.[27]

MCDERMOTT V. RUGER, OLIN

Things were not as encouraging in New York, though. New York State courts said there was no liability because the gun worked just as it was designed to. Tom explained all he had learned to the other shooting victims and families. He said they needed to keep their expectations in check. "It's the eyelet of a needle, the hope, so slight," he told them. But he still thought it was worth a try.

"I thought we had to do something," he says. "Was there a glimmer of hope? Yes," McDermott says.

In the end, fifteen of the Long Island Railroad shooting victims signed on.

Sullivan & Liapakis worked out the framework of their complaint. They would argue that Ruger had to do more to keep this gun out of the hands of criminals. It would be easy enough to come up with a criminal profile, they argued. They even had a marketing expert to say that Ferguson, by only giving a hotel address, a freshly minted I.D., and no phone number, should have fit the profile of someone likely to misuse Ruger's guns. This was not racial profiling, but behavioral profiling. Airlines have adopted a similar approach that tells them that someone who buys a one-way ticket with cash needs a closer look.

The LIRR shooting victims also sued Olin Corporation, which made the Black Talon bullet. Olin was no fly-by-night company, like so many in the gun business. Its stock was publicly traded on the New York Stock Exchange. Olin and its subsidiary Winchester Ammunition had bragged in advertising that the Black Talon bullet can "cut its way through flesh."[28] The lawyers figured they could argue that this was the ammunition equivalent to the Saturday Night Special, a product that would appeal to criminals.

Jacob Locicero, the father of Amy Federici, joined in the suit and told a reporter from *The Independent:* "A Cadillac is not designed to kill. A Ruger loaded with hollow-point bullets has one function, to cause horrific injury to the human body. Its design gave my daughter no chance of survival."[29]

Olin had introduced the bullet, which would open into six petals on impact, in 1991. The next year, the NRA's *American Rifleman* magazine[30] gushed for five pages about the bullet and its "breakthrough technology." The bullet ended up in so many crimes and ungodly injuries, some wanted to ban it like Congress banned certain kinds of armor-piercing bullets, known as cop-killers, in 1986. ("Cop-killers" are designed to cut through what they hit, while Black Talons were designed to stop.)

Contrary to popular belief, hollow point bullets don't injure by exploding or bursting open and cutting tissue. What most people don't know is that the extent of a bullet injury depends on "the kinetic energy the impacting bullet transfers to the target," according to *Gunshot Wounds* by Vincent Di Maio.[31] The transferred energy creates a temporary cavity of pushed-back flesh, which causes far more damage than the actual bullet track. That's why bullets that fly in one side of a human and out the other—a "through and through," in the parlance of TV cops—do less damage. When the hollow point bullets open up, they function like a parachute that stops a racecar. The petals make sure the bullet stops sooner, transferring lots of energy right away. In November 1993, just weeks before the LIRR shooting, New York Senator Daniel Patrick Moynihan proposed a 10,000 percent tax on the Olin bullets.[32] Three weeks later, the company withdrew the product from the market.[33] However, that wasn't fast enough. Colin Ferguson had already bought them. And other hollow-point bullets remained on the shelves.

The shooting victims would not sue as a class; each would be an individual plaintiff. They met with their lawyer, Bob Sullivan, in his office in Mineola, right by the train station. Sullivan advised them not to expect any courtroom fireworks; their main battle would be getting their case to court. "If I ever get this case before a jury, there will be a billion-dollar verdict or I will give up practicing law," Bob told the little group. It was an easy enough boast to make: almost nobody suing gun companies for anything like this had ever made it past a judge's decision to dismiss.

THE LIRR LAWSUITS GET STUCK IN THE STATION, 1995–1996

Carolyn McCarthy had filed her own suit against the gun companies in the LIRR shooting. She didn't join McDermott's suit because she wanted to sue the railroad, recalls McDermott's lawyer Stephen Glasser, and Glasser thought that was pointless. So McDermott filed his suit in Brooklyn federal court and then McCarthy filed her own case in Manhattan federal court.[34]

Tom's case was creeping along at a glacial pace. McCarthy's was moving much faster. On March 4, 1996, Manhattan federal judge Harold Baer threw out McCarthy's case against Ruger, Ram-Line, and Olin. In his decision,[35] Judge Baer said, "This expansion dramatically increases the wounding power of the bullets. Unfortunately, it appears that the Black Talon ammunition functioned exactly as designed in this tragic occurrence." Baer said the law wouldn't let him decide otherwise.

A disappointed Carolyn McCarthy summed up what they were hoping to accomplish. "When someone is harmed by [firearms], I am hoping that the victims will stand up and keep trying," she told *Newsday* at the time. "Hopefully, someday a judge will listen, and we will be able to turn these things around. All we want is to get into discovery and find out what the manufacturers are doing."[36]

Tom thought the whole ruling was perfunctory, a waste of their best chance to force the gun companies into court. All the shooting victims figured the cases might not win, but at least they could get documents and evidence on the way the companies did business during the discovery process. Even if they didn't win themselves, they could help the next person fighting gun companies to win.

The judge in Tom's case decided to wait for the Second Circuit Court of Appeals to answer McCarthy's appeal before weighing in. That wouldn't happen for another year. The appeals court agreed with Baer, and then Tom's case was thrown out of court, too.

Tom estimates that Sullivan & Liapakis spent $250,000 working on the case. "It was not by any means an insignificant effort by the firm, but when the decision came down, it was really expected," he said.

Three months after she lost her lower court case, on Memorial Day, 1996, McCarthy announced she would run against for Dan Frisa for his U.S. House seat. Carolyn went ahead, switching parties to become a Democrat, despite polls that indicated she'd lose to Frisa. McCarthy found her role in the national gun debate, and in November 1996, she beat Frisa 57 percent to 41 percent. She's been the congresswoman from Garden City ever since.[37]

Six

FIRING BACK: TAKING ON THE GUN INDUSTRY

HAMILTON, 1997

After his own case, in which he was a plaintiff, was thrown out of court, Tom didn't try to find a new gun case; one found him. This time the suit didn't go after gun companies for having an inherently dangerous product to sell to consumers. Instead, it claimed the way they distributed the guns was negligent, that the gun companies mass-produced guns and didn't care where they went or what people did with them. It was a new way for Tom to tackle the problem of too many guns getting sold too easily and hurting too many people. There was another big difference in this case: This time Tom would be a lawyer instead of a plaintiff.

Tina Johnstone, who had worked with Tom on Staten Island, told him about a case she was a plaintiff in, *Hamilton v. Accutek et al.,* Johnstone had gone on to found a group, New Yorkers Against Gun Violence. A product liability attorney, Elisa Barnes, represented Johnstone and a group of people hurt by guns. The group would stand in for the victims of gun violence and sue the gun companies. Because there was no money to fund the case, the victims weren't just putting their names on the case—they were all volunteering their time and varied skills to work on it.[1]

Barnes had filed an ambitious case in *Hamilton v. Accutek.* The 1995 Brooklyn federal court case named an astounding forty-eight defendants, basically the whole gun industry, including distributors and associations. *Hamilton v. Accutek* was the biggest, most promising courtroom battle against the gun companies to date. For starters, the case had already survived the gun companies' motion to dismiss the case, the stage at which Tom's case had been thrown out.

Barnes argued that gun companies flooded the South—states with weak laws—knowing that gunrunners would shop there and haul masses of guns up I–95 (sometimes known as "the Iron Pipeline") to the streets of Washington, Baltimore, Philadelphia, New York, and Boston. The well-worn pattern defeated the tough northern gun laws. According to the latest ATF figures, only 15.5 percent of New York crime guns were originally bought in the state. The Carolinas supply one-quarter of New York's crime guns, and 70 percent come from down south.[2]

Barnes, forty-two, a well-educated, East Coast liberal, quickly became public enemy number one in gun circles. A *New York Times* profile by Lynda Richardson[3] noted that her husband, a real estate developer, "refers to her affectionately as Mrs. Trotsky." On pro-gun websites the little family joke turned into a sinister sneer: *even her husband thinks she's a commie.* "I could've come in there with a Bergdorf suit and what they would've seen is a patchouli-reeking, Birkenstock-wearing Upper West Side liberal," she says with some pride. Barnes's work background proved as big an asset as her personal profile was a liability. She had made her living successfully representing victims of defective products, including women harmed by diethylstilbestrol (DES), a drug given to their mothers during pregnancy. Doctors had prescribed DES to prevent miscarriages, but in 1971 the FDA banned DES after it was found to cause a rare form of cancer. As the years went by, women whose mothers had taken DES suffered reproductive troubles of their own. Due to the passage of time, the daughters had no way to tell which of the hundreds of companies that made DES manufactured the particular pills their moms took years earlier. Thirty-two companies made the drug.[4] Normally that would be a roadblock: The law demands that victims prove that a particular company made the product that hurt them. But Barnes successfully argued a theory called "enterprise liability": Companies would pay according to their market share.

As Barnes described to Paul M. Barrett of the *Wall Street Journal,* when she read about gun violence and all the crime guns police never find in the early 1990s, a light bulb went off: unrecovered crime guns were nearly as interchangeable as DES, so why shouldn't market share liability apply to handgun makers?[5] The key was that gun victims faced the same hurdle as the DES daughters had: They had a hard time figuring out which company had made the product that damaged them because cops often don't find the gun that was used.

Barnes asked for Judge Jack Weinstein. A childhood actor during the Depression, Weinstein worked on the Brooklyn docks to put himself through college. After serving as a navy lieutenant in World War II, he went to Columbia Law School, where he later became a professor. Athletic and casual, Weinstein was known to sit across a table from lawyers or hear testimony in the jury box. Weinstein had handled the biggest product liability suits of his generation: Agent Orange and asbestos. He was famous for corralling over six hundred cases from Vietnam vets and the makers of Agent Orange into settlement.[6] Because chemical injuries sometimes take years to appear, Weinstein even made sure the settlement would take care of future claimants. The deal had the hallmark of fairness—it annoyed both sides. Companies thought he was too generous in the face of ambiguous proof and victims complained they couldn't bring individual suits.[7] Always creative and practical, Weinstein had made sure the lawyers didn't take too much of the vets' money by grading each lawyer's performance and paying accordingly.[8] He was now on senior status, or semi-retired.

Normally lawyers don't get to pick their judge, but Barnes argued that Weinstein should hear *Hamilton* because he had handled two related cases: the DES suits and a case against Remington Arms[9] for a design defect. Weinstein hadn't shown any bias against gun companies: In the Remington case the jury partly blamed the company, but Weinstein agreed with Remington that the jury acted out of sympathy for the widow. He absolved Remington of blame. Nonetheless, the defendants fought (unsuccessfully) his presiding over this case.

Weinstein wasn't giving Barnes too many easy breaks. In a big class action suit, judges sometimes consolidate, forcing all the companies to team up and have only a few lawyers. Not this time. Barnes had to deal with each party filing its own motions. Some of the defendants paired up, but still, it was like fighting dozens of lawsuits at once.

Aside from Johnstone, whose husband was shot on a business trip to California, the other plaintiffs were mostly mothers of dead teenage sons. There was also one father. One surviving shooting victim, Stephen Fox, a teenager from Queens, was limping around because of a .25 bullet in his brain that a friend had accidentally put there.[10]

Barnes wasn't trying to make this a class action suit on behalf of all shooting victims—that would have been another legal hurdle. Instead the plaintiffs would represent the broad swath of everyday Americans whose lives had been wrecked by guns. Gradually, they assembled a group, though one that would grow and shrink as the case wended its way to the courtroom.

The gun companies were burying Barnes in paperwork, and she was trying to do it all alone. Since the gun industry doesn't have the deep pockets of tobacco, no big firms were signing up to help, taking a chance that one day they'd get paid. All she had was a secretary and a bunch of occasional volunteers, her plaintiffs.

Katina Johnstone tried to raise money so Barnes could hire some help. Tom tried to organize a telethon to raise money, but the idea never took off.

Barnes immediately liked Tom. "It always seemed to me that the lack of any meaningful regulation came as a profound shock to him as an American," Elisa says. "I'm not sure if he and I would've seen eye to eye on many progressive issues before this. I was taken with how offended he was, almost viscerally offended, as an American, that this could be. I come out of a whole different view and tradition: How could you possibly be offended after all the horrors that have been perpetrated on American cities?"

Tom tried to figure out how he could help Barnes on the case. He didn't think he'd fit as a lawyer because he had no experience with product liability suits. He was a fraud investigator. Nor would he be of much help as a plaintiff because Barnes wanted a group of typical murders that represented the well-worn crime patterns in New York. Colin Ferguson had bought his gun legally in California, an aberration.

Getting back into the gun battle would not be easy for Tom personally. It was a relatively light time at work, so he had the time to go to Barnes's office a few days or nights a week. The harder part was explaining to people why. One of Rosemary's friends asked her, "Why does he need to be in the limelight? When is he going to get over this and move on?" If anything, that comment spurred him on. That was what he always feared: that people would get weary of talking about the LIRR shooting and forget about it so they could get on with their lives. "People don't like to have a reminder of an incident like the 5:33 around, talking about it," Tom says. "It makes them uncomfortable. It makes them remember how close we all are to something like that happening."

Around the time he was debating whether to join Barnes's effort, he went off to see his son Ryan play college lacrosse and met Ryan's teammate's family. The boy's beautiful sister showed up to every game in a wheelchair and was her brother's biggest supporter. Tom figured she had been born disabled. No, he found out, an ex-boyfriend had shot and paralyzed her. One bullet and every day of her life would be different.

It was a turning point for Tom. He volunteered to help Elisa Barnes. He would be a lawyer on her team.

This time Tom wasn't just offering his wounds as an exhibit in the cause of gun control. He was no longer fighting about his own shooting. He was fighting about the torrent of firearms deaths that occurred each day in America. If the victims had died together, it would have been a national tragedy and led to massive outrage. Instead, they died discreetly, and few paid attention.

From now on, Tom would represent those average American shooting victims. He would use his skills as a lawyer practiced in sussing out crimes, especially financial misdeeds, to aid the cause of gun control.

Barnes sought unspecified damages. That's a deviation from the usual lawsuit pattern of asking for an exorbitant amount of money up front as part of a bargaining posture. Barnes anticipated a huge backlash from the NRA, so why give them a huge number that would let it accuse her of being greedy? Economically, making gun companies pay for just the medical costs of gunshot wounds predictably caused every year would put them out of business. Some have put the total liability figure at $4 billion annually. The point wasn't to get the money, but to force gun companies to behave responsibly so that the injury costs would go down.

The defense would be that gun companies were not responsible for what anyone did with their products. A criminal act normally breaks the chain of responsibility. The companies would argue that they couldn't know that their guns would be used to shoot, rob, rape, or murder people. It would be up to Barnes and McDermott to show why they should be held responsible anyway.

PARALLELS TO TOBACCO

For decades smokers or their widows had been suing tobacco companies. At first the suits were mocked, but by the mid-1990s both public and legal opinions started to sway. A pivotal moment was the April 1994 congressional testimony by seven tobacco CEOs. They held up their hands and swore that nicotine wasn't addictive—and that therefore their companies weren't liable for diseases people got from smoking. The public saw them as liars who just didn't care how many people died from their products. Forty states sued to recoup the public health costs of smoking.

Now that the tobacco suits were making headway, everyone thought guns were next. There were many parallels between the industries. Both were facing a boatload of potentially ruinous lawsuits accusing them of turning a blind eye to illegal distribution of their wares and causing a wave of deaths. Both make products that are vilified but considered a personal right by users. Their legal battles pitted the rural South against the urban North and personal responsibility against community responsibility. Both faced accusations of marketing to people who couldn't legally buy their products. For tobacco, that meant kids being wooed by Joe Camel. For gun companies, it meant allegations they marketed guns to criminals with promises of easily concealed pocket rockets or fingerprint-resistant guns.

The industries are so close in people's minds that when John Grisham's book *Runaway Jury,* which is about tobacco suits, was turned into a movie, the enemy industry was changed to guns. Dustin Hoffman played the Elisa Barnes character.[11] The sprawling legal team for gun companies in the movie went as far as surveilling and blackmailing jurors. There's no indication the gun companies' side could or would do such a thing.

The tobacco suits alleged conspiracy and fraud, saying that the companies had figured out the health effects of their products, ignored them, and even manipulated drug levels and willfully targeted minors. They focused on deliberate, provable action. The gun cases sued over negligence, which is fuzzier.

Even most gun control advocates didn't claim gun makers were overtly marketing to criminals. The most notorious exception was Navegar's promotion of the KOTE finish on its high-capacity Tec–9s as resistant to fingerprints. Timothy Bumann, an aggressive lawyer for gun companies, maintains that this is a simple misunderstanding: The skin's oil can corrode a gun's finish. "That was an unfortunate use of terms that has been thrown up in the face of industry ever since," he said. Even the KOTE finish is not magic, he points out, and if he were a criminal he would "know perfectly well my fingerprint would be wherever I leave it."[12]

In *Hamilton,* Barnes argued that handgun makers sold far more of their guns in the loosely regulated South than could be used there. Lucy Allen, an economist with NERA, an international economic consulting firm, studied the market and found that 13 percent of U.S. handguns were sold in Florida even though the industry's own market research put the Florida market at only half that size.[13] The gun industry argued it simply couldn't control what people did with guns once it sold them. A decade later, the U.S. pharmaceutical industry would take the opposite approach and threaten to cut off Canadian pharmacies who were ordering more than their market could bear and shipping drugs to the United States.

The crux of the *Hamilton* case was that gun companies knew that their products were going to criminals but didn't care and didn't take the care due to the public to stop it. (Barnes herself thinks that as much as the industry protests that it just hates that its products are used by criminals, thugs are an indispensable part of many gun companies' customer base.) The industry contends that fewer than 1 percent of the guns[14] it makes are involved in crimes; Barnes puts the figure closer to 20 percent.

There's no reliable way to calculate. Americans reported between 300,000 and 400,000 gun crimes every year from 1973 to 1989, according to the Justice Department.[15] The industry produced between 1 million and 2.5 million handguns in each of those years. The gun crime rate slowed in the late 1970s, shot up again in 1982, and then fell back.[16] Starting in the late 1980s—when domestic Saturday Night Special makers were ramping up production—the overall production climbed to a peak of about 2.8 million guns in 1993 and 1994. Gun crimes went up with the number of guns out there. During those years gun crimes took a larger toll than ever on Americans: They reported 560,000 to 580,000 gun crimes each of those two years.

Gun production and gun crimes may not exactly correlate but they seem to dance together. When production is high, so are gun crimes. During crime waves someone threatens or shoots someone with a gun once for every five handguns produced.

That's fast and easy math. Obviously, people don't use only new handguns in crimes. Studies of the "time to crime" for a gun have reached different numbers. A 1995 government study showed that the median time-to-crime was 4.5 years for pistols and 12.3 years for revolvers.[17] (Gun rights activists inevitably point out that the "time to crime" is a flawed concept because when cops arrest someone on any charge and find a gun, they might trace it even if the gun was not involved in their alleged crime. Critics also gripe because really old guns don't have serial numbers so they can't be traced and are left out of the equation.) The overarching flaw is that the data is not the whole universe of crime guns because cops don't get their hands on most guns used in crime. The annual ATF studies on gun traces include one gun for each six gun crimes.[18]

Gun advocates don't like the time-to-crime numbers perhaps because they refute the argument that *there are so many guns in America, even if you banned them tomorrow, there'd still be all kinds of gun crime.* There sure are a lot of guns in America, 200 million of them, including 65 million handguns.[19] But, the time-to-crime numbers suggest guns go quickly from legal commerce to criminals and that if that spigot were turned off, crime would drop.

According to the National Opinion Research Center at the University of Chicago, "from 1980 to 1997 the proportion of adults who personally owned a gun held steady at about 29%." The production numbers show only when a gun is "born," but they don't show when it "dies." No one keeps track of how many guns are rounded up in gun buyback programs (not very many), how many the owners give up as broken (lots of cheap guns), or how many are thrown in the water, buried in a hole, or dumped off somewhere (tons).

Barnes would try to prove that the gun companies had to be blind not to realize that guns were making it from the unregulated, rural South to the urban North. The Iron Pipeline theory, as it's known, was nothing new; according to one ATF agent, who spoke on condition of anonymity, the pattern has been obvious since the 1960s.[20] Cities in regulated, northern states each have their own source states, usually ones directly south. The East Coast gets guns from Virginia and Florida. Chicago gets guns from Indiana and Mississippi.

The agent, who helps trace New York crime guns, divides gun traffickers into two categories: professionals, who run guns to protect their drug trade; and amateurs, for whom gun running is just a crime of opportunity, a chance for quick money. "People from New York going down there, there's a family or military or drug connection," the agent said. "They know you can't get a gun up here, but they're down there and Billy Bob pulls out a gun and starts shooting at cans. They say, 'Wait, you can't do that.' And then Billy Bob explains how easy it is."

The ATF's main weapon to catch gunrunners is Form 3310, a multiple purchase form, the agent said. Gunrunners get around it by recruiting a "straw purchaser," someone who buys the gun for them. It can be homeless guys, beer-seeking teens, or girlfriends.

Barnes would argue that if the ATF, college kids, and drug gangs could figure out the system, then surely people who made their living making or distributing guns could not be oblivious. But could Barnes and McDermott prove it? The tobacco suits had an ace in the hole: research executive Jeffrey Wigand. Wigand, on whom the movie *The Insider* was based, not only testified about Brown & Williamson's extensive knowledge and use of nicotine, he also brought along a bushel of documents. Barnes found an executive whistleblower, too, but Robert Hass, a former executive at Smith & Wesson, provided no metaphorical smoking gun, no company study that found its products and distribution methods hurt people.

In 1996, Hass approached Barnes. Hass had boosted Smith & Wesson sales throughout the 1980s. In retirement, he said, he reflected on what he'd done and wanted to make up for it.

He provided Barnes with an affidavit[21] outlining how each time Smith & Wesson flirted with the idea of gun laws as a practical business tactic to avoid liability, the NRA and gun community would slam it. In 1975, Massachusetts considered banning handguns outright, and Smith & Wesson proposed a compromise of handgun registration. A boycott pushed Smith & Wesson to withdraw the proposal.

In 1980, Hass and a Winchester executive explored how the gun industry might break away from the National Shooting Sports Foundation, its NRA-backed lobbying arm, to have its own, more pragmatic and less ideological voice. The other gun companies shot their effort down.

"The company and the industry as a whole are fully aware of the extent of the criminal misuse of firearms," Hass wrote. "The company and the industry are also aware that the black market in firearms is not simply the result of stolen guns but is due to the seepage of guns into the illicit market from multiple thousands of unsupervised federal firearms licensees. In spite of their knowledge, however, the industry's position has consistently been to take no independent action to insure responsible distribution practices, to maintain that the present minimal federal regulation of federal firearms licensees is adequate and to call for greater criminal enforcement of those who commit crimes with guns as [the] solution to the firearm crime problem."

In the end, Hass told *Newsweek*'s Matt Bai he wasn't brave enough to appear in court, but his affidavit offered a rare peek into the business practices of a secretive lot of companies.[22]

Without Hass, Barnes had to find other evidence to show that the gun industry just didn't care about where its guns went.

Tom read an article in which Rex Davis, the former head of the ATF, complained that the NRA hobbled the firearms agency. Tom and Elisa went down to Washington to meet the distinguished-looking Davis for breakfast at a hotel. Davis told them a story of how the NRA had stopped his plan to use computers for gun crime traces in the early 1970s. Davis had come from the alcohol enforcement side, so he was naïve about gun politics. He was appalled at how long it took cops to trace guns. The gun trace records were kept on index cards. If cops found a murder weapon, they would have to call the manufacturer, who would use the serial number to find which distributor had bought it. Then the cop would call the distributor and on down the supply chain. He estimated the trace time could be cut from days or weeks to seventy-two hours. Who wouldn't want that? The NRA, that's who. They maintain that the government has no legitimate interest in keeping track of gun owners.

A senior Treasury official called Davis in on the carpet for provoking the ire of the gun lobby. To teach Davis a lesson, Treasury deducted the amount of the computer proposal from the ATF's budget.

In the end, Barnes decided not to use Davis because his knowledge of the agency was dated. Besides, Davis talked about the NRA defeating efforts to track down gun criminals, and Barnes was suing companies, not the NRA.

The marketing documents that Elisa and Tom did manage to pry from the industry during the discovery process showed how dismally ordinary and apolitical their businesses were. Again, no one document was a smoking gun, but in the aggregate the documents did show that the companies managed a detailed relationship with their wholesalers and dealers. The details were mind-bogglingly picayune: shelf space, what can and can't be sold at gun shows, ordering discount schedules. What was remarkable was only what wasn't there—namely, any mention of these products' role in thousands of American deaths. The gun business operated as if it were a mundane industry churning out widgets.

If you consider that the political right and the left hold similar feelings about their right to firearms and their right to abortions, then imagine how controversial it would be if there were a collection of for-profit abortion chains. And they were constantly trying to steal business away from each other with clever marketing and schemes to push the legal boundaries to the limit. "Abortions as late as eight and a half months!" "Screen for genetic defects, medical maladies or even gender, right in our facilities." While the left concedes its own queasiness about the specifics of abortion, the right's official line—though personally abhorrent to many gun owners—is to insist that no limits on guns will ever be tolerated. Anti-abortion and anti-gun activists may both consider their opponents merchants of death, but what these documents showed was how purely mercantile the gun business was.

ANATOMY OF THE GUN INDUSTRY

> Every gun that is made, every warship launched, every rocket fired, signifies in the final sense a theft from those who hunger and are not fed, those who are cold and are not clothed.
> —Dwight D. Eisenhower, from a speech to the
> American Society of Newspaper Editors, April 16, 1953

The point of going after gun companies in court instead of gun laws in Congress is that the NRA would always be able to defeat just about any meaningful gun law. The companies, however, were not so powerful. They were just like other businesses: pragmatic, not political.

Those who care about gun crime focus on handguns. According to a 1993 Bureau of Justice Statistics report, about 29 percent of all violent crime in the United States involves a gun and about 86 percent of those guns are handguns. About 70 percent of murder victims are shot with a handgun. To go after crime guns, you have to go after handguns.

And while the NRA might convince hunters or militia types that they should stand up for people who want a handgun in their drawer for self-defense, would they really be able to convince one gun company that it should protect the business of another? Or would companies be governed by the rules of capitalism and by their own self-interest to sell responsibly and accept some restrictions? In other words, would those companies who wanted to survive settle as did those in the tobacco cases?

Business is where the handgun industry truly differed from Big Tobacco. The gun industry is dinky. Handgun sales make up a small part of a relatively small gun industry, which sells three kinds of products: handguns, long guns, and ammunition. During the 1990s, handguns represented only between 24 percent and 34 percent of overall industry sales. At their peak in 1994, handguns accounted for $668 million in sales (or 35 percent) in a $1.9 billion industry.[23] If the fifty-five companies that produced handguns in significant quantities that year were all balled together in one enterprise, it would have barely clawed onto the Fortune 500. By 1997 the entire gun industry had $1.3 billion in sales, and handguns were $344 million of that. Even if the entire gun industry—including rifles, shotguns, and ammunition—merged into one company, that company wouldn't have half the revenue of 1997's lowliest member of the Fortune 500, Ventas, a healthcare REIT.[24]

The *Hamilton* case boldly sought to bring the entire gun industry to task for the destruction wrought by its products. Tom realized the image he and so many Americans had of the gun industry—big, powerful companies forming a monolithic front around NRA policy—didn't quite hold up. Guns are an hourglass business: There's a high end, a low end, and not a lot in between.

Most people will have heard of the high-end companies: Colt, Smith & Wesson, Winchester, and the like. These storied American brand names have survived more than 150 years. There are more companies, however, on the low end, companies that most people never hear about, the makers of Saturday Night Specials. From Colonial America right through the twenty-first century, the vast majority of gun makers have been tiny operations that teeter on collapse and typically last only a handful of years.[25]

Tom now needed to find out more about the industry itself. If some people in the industry favored pragmatism over politics, there was hope. The documents he saw gave him some optimism. If only the companies were as conventional about these suits as they were about their marketing strategies, some gun company would settle. After all, it would be better to change their sales and distribution practices than to have to pay for the medical costs of injuries their guns caused. If only the businessmen could be persuaded to make changes, Elisa and Tom wouldn't need to beat the NRA.

Gun advocates figured that whether any gun company was ever found guilty by a jury, the cost of defending the cases could put some companies out of business. If there wasn't one whopping verdict because the case involved product liability, higher insurance rates would follow. That's just like paying a big loss on an installment plan.

That would mean the issue of guns in America could be decided by the laws of economics, over which the NRA has no influence, rather than the laws passed by Congress, where the NRA enjoys tremendous sway. In response, the NRA typically continued its long history of asking the government to give the gun industry a helping hand: It wanted a federal law to exempt gun companies from this kind of lawsuit.

The insurance that backed the high-end and low-end companies turned out to be as distinct as the two halves of the industry. Any sensible manufacturer knows that odds are it can expect to be sued for product liability at some point, so it has insurance to manage the risk.

Giant companies can self-insure—that is, accumulate an emergency fund to pay off claims. Big, respectable companies can also buy product liability insurance from an insurance company, but it's expensive. And as the *Hamilton* case kicked off a wave of similar lawsuits, these insurance companies balked.[26] Wholesaler RSR got Weintstein to force its insurer to pay defense costs,[27] but gun maker Beretta lost its suit against its insurer, Chubb Corporation, and had to pay its own way.[28] [29]

A group of about twenty high-end gun makers got together and pooled their resources into an industry group called Sporting Activities Insurance Limited and bought insurance offshore in Bermuda. The group, managed by Bob Chiarello at his decades-old family business in Elizabeth, New Jersey, paid most of their legal bills.

Some low-end companies claimed they were self-insured, but unless a business is about the size of an Altria (née Phillip Morris), "self-insured" is just a euphemism for uninsured. Others had banded together to form their own insurance group. The group was about as ragtag as the companies it covered and, as Tom was about to find out, nearly as important in flooding American streets with cheap guns.

THE GOOD OLD DAYS OF HANDGUNS

> I was armed to the teeth with a pitiful little Smith & Wesson's seven-shooter. . . . It had only one fault—you could not hit anything with it. One of our "conductors " practiced awhile on a cow with it, and as long as she stood still and behaved herself she was safe; but as soon as she went to moving about, and he got to shooting at other things, she came to grief.
> —Mark Twain, *Roughing It*

The handgun industry as we know it started in the mid-1800s with the Civil War, mass production, and a few technological advances. Before then, guns were made in small shops, largely by or for the government, kicking off a partnership between gun companies and government that lasted centuries, even as the military significance of side arms diminished drastically.

Because the U.S. government couldn't acquire enough American guns during the Revolution, it started the Springfield Armory in 1794. Producing guns proved more difficult and expensive than Congress had hoped. Congress spent about $123 for each musket, the equivalent of about $1,300 today. So within four years, the government outsourced the job. That didn't turn out much better: The United States signed contracts with twenty-seven companies to make a total of 30,200 guns but got only 1,000 of them. Guns were in some ways the first American personal technology product, and businesses didn't understand how to account for research and development or the difficulties of skilled mass production.

As the weapons boom of the Civil War approached, massive government contracts made the business tenable. Two types of gun companies started to fill the need, models that survive to this day: high end, largely responsible companies and low-end renegades.

Smith & Wesson represented the staid and responsible model.[30] Daniel Wesson learned gunsmithing from his brother, and the older, fatherly Horace Smith learned it at the Springfield Armory. They sold their first company, the Volcanic Repeating Arms Company, to one of their investors, shirtmaker Oliver Winchester, who modified their repeating rifle design and put his name on the company.

Smith and Wesson's technological innovation was a self-contained cartridge; the bullet, gunpowder, and detonator were all in one weatherproof case. When Smith retired, he turned the company over to Wesson, whose family ran it for generations.

Samuel Colt's operation fit the other model: clever and entrepreneurial to the point of being a rogue, a model followed by Saturday Night Special entrepreneurs a century later. Colt perfected the cylinder revolver that could shoot six times; before that, guns could fire only one or two rounds.

The son of a slave trader, Colt was a natural mechanic, show-off, and opportunist.[31] At age eight he took apart and reassembled a gun. At age fourteen he posted a flyer: "Sam'l Colt Will Blow a Raft Sky-High on Ware Pond, July 4, 1829." The explosion drenched the townsfolk, who had turned out in fancy dress, in mud. Colt was a pioneer in gun design, mass production, and clever marketing, but he frequently had a whiff of scandal about him. He raised the money for his gun factory by touring as a "practical chemist": he'd give audiences laughing gas and have them do silly things.[32] Exactly fifteen years after his Ware Pond fiasco, he blew up a boat in the waters off Battery Park in lower Manhattan to show off his new mine technology. Congress even took the day off to see the spectacle. His biography, *The Flamboyant Mr. Colt and His Deadly Six-Shooter,* explains that some think he just attached the mine to the boat to ensure a hit. Colt was also embroiled in a bizarre love triangle with his brother. Colt married a woman who wound up living with his brother. The brother then murdered a man and shipped the body off to New Orleans in a trunk. When he was caught, he pleaded self-defense but was convicted. On the day of his hanging at the Tombs prison, he married his former sister-in-law. The cupola of the jail exploded and though a body was eventually found in his cell, people assumed Samuel Colt had blown up the jail so his brother could escape to Europe.[33]

Samuel Colt's first business, Patent Arms Company of Paterson, New Jersey, failed the same year as the love-triangle scandal. Colt then worked on telegraphs with his friend Samuel Morse but soon turned back to guns.

Colt's next company, Colt's Patent Fire Arms Manufacturing Company, made him one of the richest men in the country, a testament to both his technical ingenuity and capitalistic savagery. Colt's aggressive business style and sense of showmanship rarely failed him. Colt made his fortune selling guns to Russia, Japan, and perhaps most striking, because it was fighting a war against the United States at the time, the Confederacy.

He sent guns to Texas on the pretense of its arming against an Indian uprising when the Civil War was imminent. When the war started, the

United States declared an embargo on trade with the South. The official story is that Colt stopped shipping to the South then.[34] But some think he didn't stop. In 1863, Union authorities enforcing the embargo found Colt weapons on a steamer headed to the Confederacy. The barrels were innocuously marked "Lard."[35]

Meanwhile, he was charging the Union Army $25—roughly $500 in contemporary U.S. dollars—for his Colt Model 1860 when it cost him only half that to make them. Another gun maker, Eli Remington of Ilion, New York, testified to the Ordnance Commission of 1862 that he could make his 44 Remington, a gun that proved to be more accurate, for $12. He also offered to make any gun the commission wanted for $12, driving Colt's price down drastically. With the passage of time, Colt became an increasingly respectable company, but new outfits pop up all the time to fill the renegade role.

As soon as the Colt and Smith & Wesson patents expired, companies sprang up to make cheap copies of their designs.[36] They were called pocket pistols or bulldogs, but are now known as Suicide Specials, an early forerunner of today's Saturday Night Specials. It would have been suicide to fight with them, but they were suitable for the one-time application of suicide. They flooded the market in the late 1800s, much as Saturday Night Specials would later. Duncan McConnell, who popularized the nickname in a 1948 *American Rifleman* article,[37] viewed them as a fascinating detour on the road to better gun development: "These revolvers do show elements of ingenuity of design that are surpassed only by the poor quality of the materials used and the crudeness of workmanship."

The British gun historian W. W. Greener warned readers in his popular *The Gun and Its Development* against buying these cheap guns made poorly of poor material: "If its user survives 10 shots, the gun will not."

In a heavily researched 1958 book on the lowly subcategory, Donald B. Webster, Jr., described them this way. "Suicide Specials are unique in that they have almost no historical significance. They never won any battles, neither had they any part in winning of any frontier, with the exception of an occasional brawl." (Although a British bulldog was used to assassinate President Garfield.)[38] [39] The lowest known price was 60 cents in 1887 (about $11.60 in current dollars), but the Sears Roebuck catalog probably offered a more common bargain price. "Grandest Bargain Yet! $1.35 buys a $5.00 revolver!" The low-end models were so poorly made they were unsafe even when new, Webster says, and people probably knew that. "The point that many makers worked on seemed to be that a 10- to 15-dollar revolver should last 10 years, a 5-dollar model for a year or two, and a 1-dollar revolver should shoot at least once."[40] Translated into contemporary dollars, that would make the guns roughly $20 for the cheapest, $94 for the mid-range, and $185 to $280 for a good handgun.

The low-end gun makers back then sound remarkably similar to the ones around today.[41] Hood Fire Arms Co. was formed in 1870 and ended up making more than all the other companies combined, though the firm was considered a shoestring operation. Webster describes Hood as "a man of many colors with his thumb in many pies." Hood had an assortment of companies at his disposal. "The companies and factories which were directly controlled by Hood made a bewildering array of Suicide Specials of all possible types and qualities."

The longest-living Suicide Special maker was Iver Johnson, which is still around, though purists think the company really died when the Johnson family sold out in 1975.[42] The company did more than copy Smith & Wesson's proven designs; it also made innovations. It made the .22 revolver that killed President McKinley. The more typical Suicide Special maker flooded the market with cheap guns, giving out its guns as prizes with cigars, new wagons, or at carnivals. Some of them were regarded more as toys, coveted by boys to shoot off with blanks, especially on the Fourth of July. The easy availability of cheap guns, however, annoyed communities, which passed stricter laws. According to Webster, the guns were still in circulation until about the 1920s, but no one made them past 1890. "As law enforcement became more rigid and a few anti-gun laws came into effect, the need for personal artillery slackened. Actually the fad had died. . . . The manufacture of Suicide Specials was no longer profitable to the makers, in fact, most of the manufacturers had failed, or were in the process."

HIGH-END TWENTIETH CENTURY

After World War I, the American public turned against gun manufacturers as "merchants of death." As usual, military guns flooded the market after the war. Gangsters and their Tommy guns didn't improve the image of gun makers either. John T. Thompson had tried to develop a machine gun in time to fight the Germans in World War I, but he didn't get it ready in time and later sold it to civilians with the help of Colt. When a congressional committee considering gun laws in 1934 called Colt executive Frank Nichols to testify, he admitted the company executives had been "a bit careless in their method of merchandising"[43] the gun that became popular with gangsters. That mild admission could have cost them millions if they'd said it decades later in the *Hamilton* case.

Smith & Wesson, ever diligent and responsible, introduced the first Magnum revolver, the .357, so cops could compete with the increasing firepower of Tommy-gun-toting criminals. Magnums were tailor-made to each customer's specifications, with barrels from 3–3/4 to 8–3/4 inches.[44]

Smith & Wesson provided another unique feature for its guns, something that would be unthinkable today to the NRA. Owners proudly registered each gun with the company, and Smith & Wesson would give them a fancy certificate signed by a member of the Wesson family. There was no public outcry, nor did it lead inexorably to the confiscation of the guns. Instead, it just got too expensive to register each of the $60 guns, according to the NRA's *American Handguns & Their Makers* (1981).[45]

CORPORATE CONGLOMERATE ERA

From the 1950s through the 1970s, large conglomerates gobbled up gun companies as part of their diversification craze. The strategy would be unthinkable in risk-conscious corporate America today, akin to buying an insurer of airlines and an asbestos plant. Over time, the conglomerates realized the folly of their ways, but this era does reflect a time when the gun manufacturers were generally respectable enough to join a corporate family. The subsequent change in attitudes over just a few decades gave Tom McDermott hope. If big business could realize the liabilities of being in the gun business, perhaps today's gun industry leaders could do so as well and change their ways.

In 1955, Colt, under heavy debt and the victim of a kind of economic extortion known as "greenmailing," became the first gun company to try to save itself in a big corporation.[46] Buyer Leopold Silberstein described himself "a professor of sick companies" and *Time Magazine* dubbed Colt "a stretcher case."[47] The price was just $7.2 million. Silberstein had taken what he considered the sickest company in the sickest of industries, the Pennsylvania Coal & Coke Co., and turned it into the acquisitive Penn-Texas Corporation. That company bought out Colt and Pratt & Whitney, reorganized twice, and took on the solid brand name of Colt Industries.

Bangor Punta, another large conglomerate best known for its menagerie of textile, boating, and industrial companies, picked up Smith & Wesson in 1964. One of the last family owners, Cynthia Wesson, D. B.'s granddaughter, generously gave her share of the proceeds out to workers.[48] A few years later, Bangor Punta also bought a majority share in Taurus, a Brazilian gun maker that had just started to expand into the United States.[49] Lear Siegler Corp., a military contractor, bought Bangor Punta, and the conglomerate changed hands a couple times until a British multinational, Tompkins PLC, bought Smith & Wesson in 1987.[50]

E. I. Du Pont de Nemours started as a French family company in 1801 and moved to Delaware to become a major gunpowder maker in the 1800s[51] and chemical giant in the twentieth century. It bought Remington in 1980, and sold it off in 1993.[52]

What's striking about all these financial dealings is how peculiar it is for us today to think of gun companies like any other business, bartered around in financial transactions.

Gun companies that thrived were ones that diversified away from guns. The most successful gun companies of, say, 1900, are the ones that don't have much to do with guns anymore. They got out when the getting was good—or were forced out by prudence. Du Pont is into chemicals and healthcare, and Bausch & Lomb (which made lenses used in gun scopes) judiciously switched to other lenses. Abercrombie and Fitch (which made elephant guns and other aristocratic hunting and sporting equipment) went bankrupt and was bought by The Limited. Now a trendy teen clothier, Abercrombie and Fitch went public on its own in 1996. Krupp was a German family steel business that made guns for the Germans in World War I—including a howitzer named Big Bertha after Gustav Krupp's wife. Now its successor ThyssenKrupp is only a big steel producer.[53]

Aside from lawsuits over guns shooting people, there's plenty of other expensive liability in the gun business. DuPont had to spend over $130 million to tidy a munitions site on Canonball Road in Pompton Lakes, New Jersey, and after a jury found it should pay half a million dollars to a few neighbors who got sick from contamination, it settled with the rest of the community for another $38.5 million.[54] Smith & Wesson has set aside $3.9 million to repair environmental damage on a former Springfield site.[55]

Gun companies were once giants of American industry—back when canals and railroads dominated the stock market. But the American economy has grown so fast, it has overtaken these old-time businesses.

THE GUN BUSINESS THAT BARNES TOOK ON

> Thus the metric system did not really catch on in the States, unless you count the increasing popularity of the nine-millimeter bullet.
>
> —Dave Barry

The gun businesses that served as defendants in the *Hamilton* case bore little resemblance to the industry's earlier eras of innovation and corporate largesse. Barnes and McDermott's opponents had been weakened over the years. The high-end American gun makers, perhaps slackened by years of government help, lost business to wily low-end American gun makers and high-end European companies. European models even supplanted American guns on police forces and in the military. The problem was that American companies made revolvers, a design that originated around the time of the Civil War. Revolvers hold six bullets in a cylinder. Europeans make pistols, a term that once referred generically to all guns but now specifically means a non-revolver, a gun that holds ten to fifteen bullets in its handle. As demand grew for smaller, high-powered, high-capacity guns—the so-called pocket rockets—the big American gun companies were slow to adapt. The old joke among gun lovers is *I once shot a guy with a .22 . . . and the guy got really mad.* (As opposed to being really dead had he gotten shot with a 9 mm.)

In the 1980s, Colt suffered a painful, four-year strike and the loss of a dear government contract to make M–16s.[56] The company was still so important to Connecticut that the state helped bail it out in 1988 with an investment from the state pension fund.[57] In 1992 Colt filed for bankruptcy protection.[58]

In 1994 Colt found itself once again in the position of needing a turn-around artist. New York financier Donald Zilkha bought up 85 percent of Colt, hoping for a swash-buckling revival. In the mind of its CEO Steven Sliwa, what the company needed was a technological breakthrough, on the order of Colt's revolver. He wanted to make a "smart gun," a gun that is locked to all but authorized users by some device, such as biometric identification, a combination, or an electronic signal ring. Zilkha even confidently told the *Wall Street Journal's* Paul M. Barrett: "We're not gun nuts. We're businessmen with a business plan."[59]

By 1999, however, the company was in deep trouble, shoveling over $300,000 a month to its attorneys in legal fees to defend the company's distribution practices. *Newsweek* reported that Zilkha and his partner "secretly put up $1 million of their own money so that Colt could hastily build 1,100 modified assault rifles for the civilian market."[60] The rifles gave Colt a cash infusion so it could pay its factory workers. But it wasn't enough. Colt then announced it would stop making most consumer handguns, concentrating instead on law enforcement sales and the smart gun. Colt management touched off a minor boycott when one executive came out in favor of a federal gun permit.

Smith & Wesson's stock trades, but at a price of $3. Many brokers consider stocks priced under $5 risky. The company is under an SEC investigation for its accounting practices in 2002 and 2003.[61] In 2004, the *Arizona Republic* revealed that its chairman was a convicted armed robber. As a felon he was therefore not allowed to buy guns.[62] Smith & Wesson, like Colt, spent millions in federal funds trying to develop the still elusive smart gun.

The company that made Colin Ferguson's gun, Sturm Ruger & Co., is a small-sized company that's profitable and even pays a dividend. According to its SEC filings, it says its handgun sales are falling because of lower demand.[63] Winchester is part of the Olin Corporation, the maker of the Black Talon bullets that Ferguson used. It's a publicly traded chemical and metals manufacturer.[64]

Ellett Brothers, a giant wholesaler started in 1933, had shrunk so much that by 2001, Nasdaq delisted the stock.[65] RSR Group got to be the industry's giant wholesaler by doing distribution as well as Wal-Mart. But the company, which started in a Rochester garage, has shrunk considerably since its 1994 heyday when the Orlando *Business Journal* said it had revenues of $155 million and marked up the typical gun about 15 percent, making a 1 percent profit on every sale.[66] Hoover's estimates that in 2005 RSR will have $25 million in revenue.[67]

What's left, for all intents and purposes, is a ghost industry. Both Colt and Smith & Wesson have been reduced to trading on their past and their brand names. They make lots of commemorative guns. Colt has also tried to diversify by making bicycles. Smith & Wesson licensed its name extensively, slapping its brand on everything from plumbing supplies to handcuffs. In the Tompkins era, it considered opening a Smith & Wesson Heroes and Legends .44 Magnum Barbecue Restaurant in Las Vegas.[68] The old-line gun maker has a catalog full of stuff fetishizing its brand. In case you didn't hear that it isn't British anymore, it sells T-shirts proclaiming "American Made–American Owned."

LOW END

The low-end gun companies have their roots in American history, too. None of the companies around today goes back very far, but there have always been companies like them. The precursor for the low-end companies that Barnes and McDermott challenged in *Hamilton* came from post–World War II Germany.

According to Whit Collins, formerly an editor at *Guns & Ammo Magazine* and now a frequent expert trial witness, during World War II the Nazis worked furiously designing all kinds of guns, both high-end and low-end. They wanted to make guns progressively cheaper and easier to produce. Their answer: handguns made of zinc instead of steel. The process was much easier, but the metal could weaken and bend if the gun was fired much. After the war, German companies continued to make a prodigious amount of handguns, cheap and otherwise, flooding the United States, particularly with cheap handguns. The most notorious Saturday Night Special maker in the United States was Germany's Roehm.[69]

But there were some American Saturday Night Special makers, too. Robert Sherrill, author of the 1973 *Saturday Night Specials,* found one Nashville gun company president, Harry Friedman of Arms Corporation of America, who made about 35,000 .22 caliber revolvers that retailed for $16.95: "No, we don't test-fire our guns. Our pistols aren't for heavy-duty use. But the American people are entitled to this market. If you are a dollar-sixty-an-hour workingman and your wife is scared and you can't afford a $95 Colt, you may want ours for $16.95. Your wife will never use it.

How many women get raped, percentagewise? . . . I had a gentleman call me yesterday who said, 'I want one of those inexpensive guns to give to my wife to make some noise, to make her feel like she's got protection.' She doesn't know how to shoot it. She takes it out once and shoots it to see if she can do it, and that's the last time the gun is fired."[70]

In the 1960s Los Angeles was a hotbed of interconnected low-end, mail-order gun shops. Hy Hunter, who had started off in mail-order nudie pictures, was Mr. Saturday Night Special. He ran a confusing array of gun companies, including one he claimed had been set up by the CIA. Hunter was an expert at structuring deals to avoid taxes; for instance, he would import parts instead of whole guns.[71]

Then the Gun Control Act of 1968 came along and banned cheap, shoddy foreign handguns. Instead of putting Hy and his like out of business, the act created an opportunity: With foreign competition removed, suddenly there was a demand for cheap, shoddy American-made guns. The act put no restrictions on domestic guns but made sure that foreign handguns were "suitable for or readily adaptable to sporting purposes" by using a point system that rewarded guns that were bigger, heavier, and would not melt easily. The effect was to ban the import of Saturday Night Specials.

With so many notorious shootings in the news, public outcry rose against cheap handguns. At the same time, though, a new network of gun companies sprang up to churn them out. By coincidence, they set up around Hy Hunter's old backyard, Los Angeles. And like Hunter's enterprise, this interrelated group of companies had a complicated structure that helped its owners avoid taxes.

They are collectively known as the "Ring of Fire" companies. Dr. Garen Wintemute, an emergency room doctor at UC Davis who has studied handgun violence as a public health epidemic, gave them the name for a chain of volcanic islands, not the Johnny Cash song. He defined the ring as six companies, all generally unknown to the average American: Arcadia Machine and Tool (AMT), Bryco Arms, Davis Industries, Lorcin Engineering, Pheonix Arms, and Sundance Industries. Some also include Raven Arms, a company that burned down in 1991.[72]

These companies make guns from zinc alloy instead of steel, a penny-pinching, efficient design that Whit Collins, the former gun editor who uses his historical design expertise lobby for gun safety laws, traces back to the Nazis. The guns are usually small-caliber and have a small, easy-to-conceal profile. They are inexpensive—some would say disposable—at $50 to $200. Because the soft metal distorts with use, they're also harder to trace. According to ATF agents, gunrunners love these guns because they offer a much higher profit margin. They can quadruple the price of a cheap handgun but not even double the price on a high-end one.

At the center of the Ring of Fire was machinist George Jennings, who founded Raven Arms Inc. in 1970 outside Los Angeles. "The main strength the Jennings family brought to the table was to be able to originate guns like ones that had been made in Germany in the U.S.," Collins says. Because George was a skilled machinist, he knew how to make die cast molds for soft metals, which saved him the cost of a foundry. The barrier to entry in the low-end gun market is slight. Companies set up shop in industrial parks instead of trying to re-create the fortresses of Connecticut's gun valley. They cut corners, skipped safety features, and used low-quality materials and methods.

George's son, Bruce Jennings, started Jennings Firearms Inc. in 1978. George's son-in-law, Jim Davis, started Davis Industries Inc. in 1982. Jim's brother John set up Sedco, which the other members of the Jennings clan pressured out of business. One of George's nephews set up Sundance Industries in 1989.[73] And Jim Waldorf, a buddy of Bruce's in high school before they both dropped out, started Lorcin. Waldorf ultimately became the new king of Saturday Night Specials.

"They all could have been one big, happy family drinking beer," Larry Gudde, former plant foreman, told *Wall Street Journal* reporter Alix M. Freedman. "But they didn't choose to do that because they were afraid one would get a dollar more than the other."

The family members first divvied up the cheap, low-caliber gun industry by model but then started straying into each other's turf and into larger caliber guns like the .380 and 9 mm. Bruce was in danger of losing his firearms license because of a felony assault charge; he so badly beat his then-wife on Christmas Day 1994, he broke her jaw. "I lost my cool, and I hit her," he told Freedman. "My wife had taken all the bonds, the Rolexes, the diamonds and the gold." He ostensibly sold off the company to Gene Johnson, a former Jennings office manager, who changed the name to Calwestco. Bruce beat the felony charge and only served ninety days, but Sharon Walsh of the *Washington Post* investigated and found gun law experts who said he should have lost his license for just that. Released from jail, Bruce started a Nevada wholesaler called Jennings Firearms, which sold guns from Calwestco and from Bryco, a company he set up for his wife as part of their divorce settlement. Meanwhile, the original company, Raven, burned down, and George sold the equipment to a new company, risen from the ashes and winkingly named Phoenix, which was owned by his grandchildren.

The Treasury Department got wise to the sweet deal Bruce Jennings had set up for himself: He secretly controlled two manufacturers, which sold the guns at cut-rate prices to his distributor. Because a 10-percent excise tax is paid on the price of the gun going out of the factory, that meant an incredibly low tax bill. When Bruce admitted that he really controlled

both companies, the ATF could have taken away his license. Instead, it settled for the taxes.

By 1992, much to everyone's surprise the Ring of Fire had become a
major force in the American gun industry, producing 44 percent of its handguns that year. Taken together, they were bigger than any other company.
By 1993 the Ring of Fire made more than 900,000 guns, 46% of the handguns produced in America.[74] These guns were more than three times as
likely to end up traced by a cop than a gun made by one of the major manufacturers.

GUN COMPANY COMBAT

> Don't meddle with old unloaded firearms. They are the most deadly and un-
> erring things that have ever been created by man. Think what Waterloo would
> have been if one of the armies had been boys armed with old rusty muskets
> supposed not to be loaded, and the other army had been composed of their fe-
> male relations. The very thought of it makes me shudder.
> —Mark Twain, in speech known as "Advice to Youth," 1882

The documents piled up so high in Barnes's already cramped and cluttered
office in lower Manhattan that she had to rent a storage room down the
hall. Tom spent all his spare time in this room, with a bare concrete floor,
naked light bulb, and wall of banker's boxes, all crammed with documents.
Tom's responsibilities as counsel for the state's Thoroughbred Racing Capital Investment Fund had wildly varying hours. So whenever he could, often
several times a week, he would head downtown after his real job to pull another shift working on the *Hamilton* case.

The gun companies used the old bury-them-in-paper tactic. "That is really how the game is played, to overwhelm your opponent," Tom says. Of
course, first they frustrated Barnes and McDermott. "It was pulling teeth
to get them to produce anything," Tom says. "They adopted a stonewall
position, a unified stonewall that unless the court orders it, they don't give
it, and even then only begrudgingly." When the defendants did finally send
over documents, there were no highlights or Post-it notes to alert the victims' side to the juicy bits; instead they would send boxes of mostly useless
stuff. But Tom knew any one piece might reveal a secret of the gun industry. "You can't help but read every document that is numbered or you could
face a malpractice suit and that one document could be a smoking gun, but
if you miss it, shame, shame on you."

Tom didn't make an appearance in the case—meaning that he never
formally told the judge that he, a lawyer, was helping out, but he did attend
depositions in Barnes's tiny conference room. There he saw another part of
the defense strategy against Barnes: intimidation. "Within the first five min-

utes or so, I realized this was going to be the nastiest, most vile, knock-down brawl because of the obvious ability and opportunity that numerous defense attorneys had against one plaintiff attorney. Any one of those attorneys could have sufficed for the job. They were all very bright. They didn't have to jump on her," Tom recalls.

He'd never seen anything like it. These were discovery depositions, not death penalty courtroom dramas. The witness "just sat there motionless while objections and statements and histrionics were carried out. The court reporter was constantly saying 'hold it down' or 'keep quiet' or 'I'm not going to listen to five people at the same time."

Tom finally snapped. "Keep your mouth shut until it's your turn to question the witness," Tom remembers saying.

He was talking to Timothy Bumann, who he later learned was such a gun expert that he could take apart guns blindfolded. Tom says Bumann asked Tom who he was to talk to him like that.

"You heard what I said," Tom said. "And if you don't, we'll take this outside and we'll resolve this another way."

After that tensions seemed to ease, Tom says. "At least after that the deposition became a helluva lot more civilized."

It was one thing to try to bully lefty Barnes, but they somehow paused before law-and-order McDermott. "Tom looks like the genuine article," says Barnes. "And if they've lost him, then it's much more dangerous."

Bumann recalls nothing of the confrontation with McDermott but says that half the people who meet him think he is the biggest jerk and half think he's the most laid back guy in the world, depending on which side they're on. It's hard to imagine anyone thinking this hard-charging lawyer is laid back, even when he is representing his other major client, horse dealers. Bumann, a lawyer from Atlanta, got into these cases the way Barnes did: He was a product liability attorney. The difference was that his experience—and loyalty—lay with the manufacturers. He had represented foundries and the makers of high heel shoes and reclining chairs. He figured most injured people had themselves to blame. "If someone has a product and they have disabled a safety system, which is designed to prevent a particular kind of accident, while I have sympathy for them as a human being, I don't have a lot of sympathy for their case." What if there was no safety system? "The number one safety system on any product out there is the brain of the human being that is handling whatever it is," he says.

Barnes says gun company attorneys are usually aligned almost spiritually with their clients. "The attorneys are partisans for the most part and have worked almost exclusively for gun companies for their whole professional lives," Barnes asserts. "They find cases against gun companies scary and offensive. Tim Bumann . . . is the most partisan of the partisans."

THE MURDER INVESTIGATIONS: TYPICAL AMERICAN GUN CRIMES

Since the *Hamilton* case relied on a set of specific murders and assaults, Barnes and McDermott had to reopen and reprove all those cases and then show where the killer got the gun in order to present enough evidence at trial about what gun was involved.

Tom hoped he had found his niche here. People knew little about the business of gun traffic. If he could document how gun runners really worked, he could make a real contribution to the gun cause. There was plenty of statistical evidence to support the Iron Pipeline theory, but he and Barnes needed flesh on the bones. The death of Japanese college student Kei Sunada on August 7, 1994, was a fairly typical American gun murder. It got little attention here, but in Japan, where handguns are outlawed, it raised a furor. Sunada, twenty-two, was in the United States to go to college. He lived in Lefrak City, a giant Queens apartment complex. Sunada was an avid kickboxer who conditioned his legs by walking up the seventeen flights of stairs to his apartment. On August 7, neighbors heard shots fired in the stairwell and found Sunada face down in blood. He died four days later. Police caught two local teens.[75]

Reggie Cameron, the son of a schoolteacher, told police that Sunada kicked at them and that "Junior," formally Armond McCloud, Jr., shot him. Reggie didn't know that Junior had a gun. For his cooperation, he was sentenced to eight-and-a-half to twenty-five years, while Junior got twenty-five to life.

McDermott went to see both of them at the Clinton Correctional Facility, a massive stone, maximum-security prison upstate in Dannemora. They asked Junior where he got the gun.

"What? Why would I cooperate with something I don't know about?"

"What do you mean something you know nothing about?" McDermott asked. "Weren't you convicted of this murder?"

"Yeah, but that was all bullshit, man. My appeal is pending, I'm gonna be outta here in less than six months," Junior boasted.

Holy shit, talk about delusion, McDermott thought.

Reggie's mother had spoken to her son about McDermott and the case, so he was ready to help.

He told them the gun was a Lorcin .25—a cheap gun popular with criminals. According to the ATF, Lorcin was the gun of choice among criminals aged twenty-four and younger. That's remarkable considering Lorcin had been producing guns for only a decade while other companies had been putting them on the street since the Civil War. A Bureau of Justice Statistics study called "Guns Used in Crime" showed that in 1994 the Lorcin .25 pistol was the gun most frequently traced from criminals. Ring of Fire guns took seven of the top ten spots. Wintemute found that as a class, "junk guns" were 3.4 times as likely to end up used in a crime. The ATF's 2000 Gun Trace Report found that the median time a traced Lorcin .380 pistol had been out on the street was 4.5 years. Sometimes it was a matter of hours. If a Smith & Wesson revolver got into trouble, it took about a decade longer.[76] The shorter the time to crime, the more likely it is the gun has been trafficked.

Reggie didn't know where Junior had gotten the handgun, but he taught Tom about how commonplace handguns were in his city school. "You guys just don't understand. Every kid in high school carries a gun," Reggie told them. "You gotta do it for your own protection."

Tom didn't think Reggie was being cocky. He was just stating the facts.

Reggie said he didn't carry a gun every day, but he had to have one "just in case anything happened."

The closest thing Tom could relate this to was a white suburban kid's desire to have a car to drive to high school.

Reggie's Letrak City apartment building was just miles from the McDermotts' Garden City home. But when Tom went home to Rosemary that night, he told her, "We live in a different world."

The murder of Kei Sunada was obviously tragic for the young man and his family. But Tom now saw that the little Lorcin had hurt Reggie and his family, too. Without that gun that one night, Reggie would probably be leading a normal, productive life. If there were some group for all victims of gun violence to join, the Camerons should sign up, too. The makers of this Lorcin may have known that some of their guns would end up in the hands of someone trying to steal someone else's cash. But in this case the handgun stole human beings from families.

All those lives brutalized by one handgun that had cost less than $100.

Seven

FOLLOW THE MONEY:
THE LORCIN BANKRUPTCY

ONE LOW-END GUN COMPANY GOES BANKRUPT

Tom was about to find out much more about Lorcin. The biggest and seemingly most successful Ring of Fire company, Lorcin, filed for bankruptcy protection in October 1996[1]. In 1993 alone the company had produced 341,243 guns, which each sold for about $85.[2] To Barnes and McDermott, it was a suspicious move for such a successful gun company to go under. They figured it was just another ploy to drag out the proceedings and make Barnes go broke.

In the war between gun control advocates and gun companies, bankruptcy was shaping up as a major weapon.[3] One Ring of Fire owner, Bruce Jennings, later told *BusinessWeek*[4] that the gun companies "can file for bankruptcy, dissolve, go away until the litigation passes by, then re-form and build guns to the new standard. . . ." Three other Ring of Fire companies—Davis Industries, Sundance, and Bryco—would eventually file for bankruptcy.

So it really wasn't that remarkable that Lorcin, facing an onslaught of eighteen lawsuits, decided to file for bankruptcy. Most of the lawsuits it faced were not so big or politically charged as *Hamilton*. Customers were simply claiming that their Lorcin guns malfunctioned and caused a wrongful death or personal injury.

There are two common kinds of bankruptcy. In Chapter 7 bankruptcy you turn off the lights, lock the door, and the court sells your stuff. On the other hand, Chapter 11 is "bankruptcy protection;" it means the court literally protects the company from claims while it reorganizes. All lawsuits are automatically halted and handed over to the bankruptcy court.

Lorcin faced so many personal injury lawsuits that the court hired a lawyer to estimate each court claim's worth. That estimate determines how much say the claimant has in the proceedings. Claimants don't have to settle in bankruptcy court, but typically they do because even if they manage to get permission to proceed in an outside court and then win, the bankruptcy court can decide to pay only pennies on the dollar. So, for many companies filing for bankruptcy is more of a financial planning strategy than a cry for help.

The people suing a bankrupt company get doubly screwed: They typically settle for little money and no jury trial. A jury doesn't decide liability or damages; the decision is left to a harried bankruptcy judge whose mission is to settle claims efficiently and reorganize the company so it can stay open.

Barnes couldn't afford to hold up the entire *Hamilton* case for Lorcin's bankruptcy; she planned to ask the bankruptcy court to lift the stay so that Lorcin would still be included in the *Hamilton* case.[5]

In August 1997, just as Barnes was preparing to head to the Lorcin bankruptcy court, she got a phone call. Her nine-year-old son was at a sleepaway camp upstate. He had been swimming with his friend and bunkmate, and the other boy drowned. Her son wasn't in danger, but she wanted to see him. "I just didn't feel comfortable not being there," she said. So she asked Tom to fill in for her. Little did anyone realize that this random tragedy would alter Tom's course in pursuing justice yet again.

WHY IS THIS MAN LAUGHING? A PORTRAIT OF JAMES WALDORF

Jim Waldorf, the man Tom would face in bankruptcy court, was not your typical gun manufacturer. He was a clever, charismatic, outgoing, and skilled businessman, always working an angle.[6] He was a modern day Sam Colt.

A successful entrepreneur even before he entered the gun business, Waldorf recalled his career in his self-published 1992 autobiography, *Landing on Your Feet*. Waldorf[7] worked as a regional sales manager for a machinery company, but after he got laid off in 1982, he became disillusioned with corporate America. To support his wife and two daughters, he went to work on his own.

His first shaky opportunity was brokering the sale of a silo. He knew someone who wanted to unload the large piece of farm equipment. He scrambled to find a buyer, collecting phone books from friends to make cold calls. "They always asked why I needed them. I would mumble my plans of putting a silo deal together," he wrote. "I later learned from other friends that after I left they would talk behind my back about how desperate I had become."

He put together the unlikely silo sale, earning a huge commission worth three months' salary. From there, he got into the business of selling used machinery by running a newsletter with ads. Instead of eBay it was like HeavyEquipmentBay. It took off. He didn't charge to advertise but took a 6 percent to 10 percent commission on sales. In his bankruptcy deposition, he explained his reason for that decision. "Well, you know, when you offer Jewish people something for free, they always take advantage of it."[8]

"You felt like taking a shower after you talked to these guys," said Alan Stomel, a Los Angeles bankruptcy lawyer who worked on the case.[9] Stomel has been practicing bankruptcy law since 1986 and says bankruptcies are a success when both sides work together, but this one failed because it was "extraordinarily nasty." A bearded father of three and a gun owner, says "I'm not anti-gun at all. I'm anti–cheap gun and I'm anti-criminal."

Waldorf sold the newsletter business to get into manufacturing, despite an earlier failure in making army-style flashlights. "Why did I want to tread away from what had apparently been my calling?" Waldorf asked rhetorically in explaining his decision. "Well, I knew of an opportunity that could be very profitable in the manufacturing of a certain type of firearms," referring to the Saturday Night Special segment of the market. "The only thing in the way was a company that had monopolized that particular market segment for over 20 years. Now you must be saying, wow, this is really sounding dangerous, right? Wrong. This reason this was such an opportunity was because of the company's dominance for over 20 years without competition."

Waldorf wasn't really talking about one company; he was referring to the network of gun companies known as the Ring of Fire. Waldorf had gone to high school and been friends with Bruce Jennings, Saturday Night Special scion. Both Waldorf and Bruce had dropped out of high school. Bruce went to work in the family business and started Jennings Firearms in 1978.[10]

In the deposition, Waldorf explained how the business worked: "The gun industry is interesting in that there are no degrees in gunology. You don't go to school to learn how to build guns. You know manufacturing principles and you apply them from work experience." He didn't make guns to prove any political point; it was pure practicality. He found handguns an attractive business proposition "as measured by its return on investment and risk/reward ratio."

In 1988 Waldorf and machinist Errol Brown each put up $110,000 to start Lorcin Engineering (named for Waldorf's two daughters, Lori and Cindy). They started with only 100 square feet of space.

Waldorf saw an opportunity no one else in the low-end gun business did. "Well, the niche was affordable firearms. Basically, there were just very few companies that were building affordable firearms. I felt that they had an Achilles heel. They had some problems and I felt that their market share was pretty easy to take away from them. . . . Their Achilles' heel is that they didn't pay any attention to their market. They became complacent."

To attract this business, Waldorf explained in the deposition that he hatched a theory that product liability insurance would enable him to outdo his Ring of Fire rivals. "We provided product liability insurance," he explained. "They never had product liability insurance. Wholesalers like to be indemnified with the product liability. We pursued the pawn industry. The pawn shops throughout the country that sell handguns. We took a very aggressive position in marketing them."

Pawn shops were becoming a big, uniform business. Waldorf courted them and struck a deal with Cash America International, a publicly traded pawn shop chain.

The insurance was crucial. The only way to get into a big chain store was through a wholesaler. And the only way to get picked up by a wholesaler was to show a certificate of insurance. Waldorf needed that piece of paper. Without it, the other Ring of Fire companies were condemned to work out backdoor distribution channels.

The distribution is so key that Waldorf said in his deposition that before he offered insurance, he tried to open his own distributor, modeled after the Bryco plan, but the IRS didn't care for that idea.

Waldorf did very well for himself. He found a way to make the guns exceedingly cheap. He could make them for about $30 each and sell them to wholesalers for about $65.[11] That means Lorcin had a pre-tax profit margin of more than 115 percent. By comparison, Ruger had a pre-tax profit margin of 28.8 percent and the metal fabricated products industry was scraping by with 12.6 percent. Waldorf called those margins "sad."

Over its lifetime Waldorf's company put more than 1 million handguns on the street. By 1993, Waldorf had surpassed his high school buddy and his family, becoming the number one handgun maker in the United States. Waldorf credited his success to his insurance company, which allowed him to mass distribute the guns.[12] Waldorf also made forays into the African market, where he exported loads of his guns.[13]

Well-informed gun owners stay away from Lorcin guns. *Gun Tests,* the *Consumer Reports* of the gun world, has rated Lorcin guns "unacceptable" and "not durable or reliable."[14] Their researchers found the guns were rickety and often misfired or failed to load. The gun aficionado site Packing.org runs a bulletin board, which sometimes acts as a virtual support group for disenchanted Lorcin customers. Some list their complaints:[15]

> It is a jammatic, and not fun to shoot.
> The darn thing jammed, leaving what I could see were 2 bullets in the chamber. I felt like a dork. . . . I totally agree that ANY Lorcin is pure junk,

and a dangerous weapon. I have read about several Lawsuits against the owner of this company, who was named as Jim Waldorf. . . . This man shouldn't be able to manufacture any firearm in my opinion.

I joked to the seller that I better get someone with the first shot because I don't know if I would get a second (ha, ha) if forced to use that gun.

The more experienced gun owners then chime in with their words of wisdom:

It can't be fixed. It's junk . . . it's the definition of junk. Chalk it up to a lesson learned.

It does make a half way decent fishing sinker.

. . . this weapon is low end (at best), poorly made, unreliable, and inherently unsafe. If you come across one in your travels handle it with EXTREME care. Actually, run away, run far away! It is literally an accident waiting to happen.

Waldorf defended his company, saying that he was only selling "affordable" guns and that poor people had a right to buy guns to protect themselves. He was acknowledging the call for a tax that would raise the price of guns as a method to keep them out of the hands of low income people, who criminologists say commit more crimes. Waldorf calls these efforts "more discriminatory than slavery." There's the issue, of course, of whether guns actually do their duty of protection or if they do more harm than good.

When Waldorf divorced his wife, he listed among his assets two homes in swank areas outside Reno worth $1.8 million; a Mercedes, a Porsche, and a Jeep Cherokee worth a combined $156,000; and "the lowest-mileage DeLorean in the world." He did not estimate its value, saying the rare car, with only sixty miles on it, was for his grandson's college tuition. In the three years leading up to filing for bankruptcy, Waldorf and his partner Brown paid themselves $925,000, $668,750, and then $700,000 each, according to court documents.

While the media made much of gun companies going bankrupt in light of cases like *Hamilton,* the case filing cited decreased annual sales,[16] from $14.7 million down to $4 million. With those sales the company couldn't ward off their other big problem: product liability suits. The suits increased five-fold from 1993 to 1994. Their biggest headache was the case over Alice Mae Johnson in Texas.

Waldorf claimed he filed for bankruptcy only because one Texas court was unfair to him, allowing the plaintiff to shift theories and experts without giving him time to come up with a new defense. Here's how Waldorf described the case:

Johnson's accident happened on Christmas Eve 1992. He murdered his wife. We have established through discovery that he was drunk, working on his

stereo, watching television and playing with his dog and he put his gun together backwards. Supposedly, the pit bull came in, jumped in his lap, supposedly his arm went up, the gun went off and killed his wife. They had to
sue her life insurance carrier to collect and they didn't pay for two years because they were sure it was a homicide. This was going to go to trial in eight
days and . . . they had amended their complaint six times to reflect the different theory of what was wrong with the gun. There is a Texas law that says
you have to name your expert witness 30 days prior to trial, but the plaintiff amended the complaint seven days prior to trial. . . . So here we have a
new theory of what was defective in the product and our hands were tied
from naming an expert plastics witness. If we had gone to trial, we would
have lost.

Here's what the court records show:[17] The wife was in the other room
and the police quickly exonerated Johnson. The change in strategy was
from simple negligence, over a manufacturing defect in a critical safety
mechanism, to gross negligence. A gun expert told Lorcin's lawyer he was
prepared to testify that the gun part should never have been made of plastic. (Because the NRA made sure guns are exempt from Consumer Product Safety Commission regulation, there would be no government
investigation into whether any other guns Lorcin produced of this model
should be recalled.)

Waldorf, however, was sure all the complaints against his company
were without merit. He referred to anyone who sued him as a blackmailer.
He called all the suits "ransom notes" from greedy customers and attorneys. "The gun always just goes off," he would say mockingly. "No one
ever fires a gun."

CALIFORNIA SOUTHERN DISTRICT

Lorcin filed in about the most overburdened bankruptcy court in the
country, the federal court in the central district of California, Los Angeles. In the year that Lorcin filed for bankruptcy protection, one of that
district's judges, Lynne Riddle, told an anti-fraud group that of the 1 million bankruptcy proceedings open nationwide at any one time, this district, one of ninety-two in the country, saw 10 percent of the action. She
had nine thousand cases assigned to her in one year. "Admittedly, not all
of those nine thousand cases are highly active, but just one case can have
hundreds of lawsuits associated with it," she said. "I have a colleague
who had five thousand lawsuits in just one case . . . so the workload is
staggering."[18]

The Justice Department has estimated that 10 percent of the bankruptcy cases are fraudulent. So approximately ten thousand California cen-

tral district cases fell into that category. Yet the district prosecuted only a handful of those cases. Resources to ferret out bankruptcy fraud were scarce.

By the time McDermott got to court, the creditors were already suspicious that Waldorf was using the overburdened bankruptcy court system to take everything he could from the company and leave the plaintiffs with nothing. Without insurance, it was doubtful the company would have enough money for the people suing Lorcin.

Bankruptcy proceedings divide creditors into two categories, secured and unsecured. Secured creditors—who hold a contract or collateral-like real property—get priority over unsecured claims like personal injury lawsuits. The debtor files a list of the twenty biggest unsecured debts and then a bankruptcy official picks which of those to invite onto a committee that represents the group. Stomel represented the committee.

Meanwhile, both Waldorf and Brown asked the judge to approve salaries of $7,500 per week each, which would amount to $780,000 per year for the pair. Stomel hired a compensation expert who said that they should get only $2,000 a week. The sides initially agreed on $3,500 a week but kept arguing from there.[19]

Early in the case, just as the injured parties were getting organized, something peculiar happened with Lorcin's product liability insurance. Howard Holladay, an insurance salesman from Boston, filed a claim in the bankruptcy proceeding for $132,756 on behalf of Control Systems Inc. CSI claimed to be Lorcin's insurance company's third party administrator, a company that typically handles the paperwork and claims for an offshore carrier.[20]

Nobody knew much about Howard Holladay, a lanky, grizzled old man. Public records,[21] [22] showed that he was born in 1928 in Orangeburg, South Carolina. He attended the University of Georgia and became president of its Sigma Chi fraternity and the interfraternity council. An early resume makes him sound extremely social: he was a member of a series of clubs: Sphinx, Gridiron Secret Society, Blue Key (which honors service to UGA), Omicron Delta Kappa, and a business fraternity. He graduated with a bachelor's degree in business administration in 1953. Holladay, who also lists a stint with the army, married Jonnet Kerns, a Stanford grad, in 1961, and they had two sons. Holladay worked for National Life of Vermont and Equity Services. He was well-off and lived in an expensive townhouse in Boston. Howard Holladay was a member of some national insurance associations and at the time appeared to be fairly respected. There was no public record of any wrongdoing on Holladay's part.

Holladay tells good stories in a Southern accent. Like how he was related to Wild West hero Doc Holiday, spelling idiosyncrasies aside. He'll say he's Doc's great-great-nephew. He's not sure exactly how they were related. "My mother used to keep up with all that stuff," he'll say. He clearly has been asked about the relation repeatedly and delivers a treat of a story.[23] "He was born in Griffin, Georgia," Holladay will start out.

> After the Late Unpleasantness he became a dentist and he developed consumption. In modern lingo that means tuberculosis. Back then the only cure was to go west. So he went west and I don't know why the hell he stopped in Dallas, though. He tried to reestablish his dental practice and he didn't get very far with it because people didn't like to be coughed on. So giving that up, the one thing he was good at, that he knew very well, that he learned in the Confederacy was how to shoot a gun. So, he took up playing poker. And when you play poker with some big burlies and you reach in to pull the pot and somebody raps your hand with a six gun, you're not too eager to leave your hand out on the table. But Doc Holiday was a good card player and he learned pretty quick that he had to have himself pretty well armed if he was ever going to pick up any of his pots. So he had a derringer strapped on his leg and two six-guns on each side and a knife, I think, he kept, so nobody fooled with him pretty much. He actually wiped out twenty-six people. All in self-defense over a period of years. He died in a Colorado sanitarium.

When pressed to draw out the lineage and the source of his family lore, he'll say, "My family never mentioned it. I didn't know anything about Doc Holiday 'til I went into the army and subsequently into university and the legend began to unfold and somewhere I picked up a book on his life."

Still, it's a good story.

It's unclear whether Holladay realizes the discrepancies from one end to the other of this tale. Probably no one challenges the yarn. In the bankruptcy court, however, there was no generosity about his claim against Lorcin. The claim struck everyone as odd. CSI claimed that Lorcin had agreed to pay a special surcharge on top of its insurance premium to reimburse its insurer for paying claims.

Even if you know almost nothing about insurance, this doesn't sound kosher. If a business has to pay back an insurance company every time a claim is paid, that defeats the purpose of having insurance. Imagine if Geico tried to tack on a special supplement to a driver's bill every time there was a car wreck. It wouldn't fly. (Because of the accident, you would be considered more risky and Geico would raise rates for future risk, but that's a different story.) The insurance company doesn't know who in particular is going to make a claim, but it's the company's job to figure out the odds of a claim over a large group and spread the cost of risk around.

Adding to the intrigue, Lorcin's insurance company was named Leeds & London Merchants Insurance Co. That's right, not Lloyds of London, the insurance marketplace that dates back to 1688 and is backed by billions of dollars and a prestigious coterie of private investors known as "names." Leeds & London was incorporated in Costa Rica and the name seemed designed to conjure up the insurance icon.

That's precisely the kind of behavior people don't want to see in an insurance company, which ideally has bags of money, a long history, and teams of actuaries toiling away in a marble fortress. Instead, Leeds was like the company that makes cheap electronics gear and then sells it under a name that sounds like high-end maker Sony. The average consumer considers buying an off-brand CD player too risky. So the decision to insure a gun business with a company with that branding strategy reflects poorly on the foresight of company owners. The risk would obviously be much higher. The insurance policy would jeopardize the entire business.

If Lorcin had adequate product liability from a solid insurance outfit— say, Lloyds of London—it never would have needed to file for bankruptcy. The insurance company simply would have paid any jury verdict.

This peculiar setup of Leeds & London, Holladay, and Control Systems Inc. set off Stomel's alarms. Insurance is the linchpin of any bankruptcy with lots of personal injury claims. Bankrupt companies are inherently troubled, so the insurance is expected to have to pay off many claims. Bankruptcy courts typically demand that a debtor company keep insurance going so if there's a new accident, the insurance company will handle it and the resources that should go to the people it currently owes won't be eaten up. If there was something funny about Lorcin's insurance company, Stomel knew it could negatively affect the entire plan for the company to settle its personal injury claims.[24]

Stomel didn't understand the exact structure of Lorcin's complicated insurance apparatus. Usually, though, insurance companies file a small claim for premiums and then are on the line for other claims against the company. Stomel figured that Howard Holladay, the man representing the insurance company, just filed a big claim for CSI to have a considerable say in the bankruptcy. When Stomel and the other creditors raised a fuss, Holladay backed down and reduced the claim to $12,000.

But the incident raised Stomel's antennae.

He grew so suspicious he took the drastic step of pressing for a Chapter 11 bankruptcy trustee, someone to take over and manage Lorcin during the bankruptcy reorganization. It may sound strange for a court-appointed agent to run a Saturday Night Special maker, but the alternate universe of bankruptcy court has produced federally operated brothels, too. When Nevada's infamous Mustang Ranch was in bankruptcy protection in 1990, Jeri Coppa, a Chapter 11 trustee, told the *San Francisco Chronicle* that she would keep it open "like any other business, a bar or a store. The point is to pay off the government taxes and other secured creditors."[25] Lorcin argued that turning over the company to new management would jeopardize, of all things, their insurance. To keep Stomel and a Chapter 11 trustee at bay, Lorcin reluctantly produced more documents on its insurer. Stomel had also hired an insurance expert, Wayne Kreger of Kreger & Stein, to act as "special insurance counsel." He would check out this strange insurance company.

Kreger discovered there were at least three entities involved: There was Control Systems Inc. of Boston, where Holladay worked adjusting claims. There was Leeds & London Merchant Insurance Company S.A., in Costa Rica, which was the actual insurance carrier. And then there was Assurance Buyers Cooperative Inc. (ABC) of California.

ABC was a newfangled, obscure non-profit entity called a Risk Retention Purchasing Group. Even people in the insurance industry were still sorting out how these new insurance animals functioned. In the 1970s, many high-risk small businesses were hard pressed to afford product liability insurance. Congress passed the Products Liability Risk Retention Act of 1981 to allow hard-to-insure industries to pool their resources and form their own insurance company just for members.[26] But because of the hodge-podge of state laws, some of which banned pooled insurance or selling across state lines, hardly any groups started. Congress subsequently strengthened the act and told states to back off. The new law said states couldn't ban these new groups so long as they met the qualifications of one state's insurance regulator. Once they did, no other state could say no to their selling insurance to group members located in their jurisdiction. All the group had to do was notify the insurance regulator of each state it operated in; it no longer had to follow each state's rules. The move was risky because it meant that one state could set very low financial standards to attract the business, thereby authorizing companies to spread havoc to other states. These laws also created a whole new entity, a Risk Retention purchasing group. Instead of acting as insurance companies themselves, these purchasing groups were limited to buying insurance from licensed carriers for their members.

Leeds was ABC's "captive carrier." ABC used Leeds just to handle its insurance needs. It wasn't an independent company that wrote policies for other people; ABC was its only customer. ABC and Leeds were linked, but CSI was supposed to be separate, like a hired claims adjustor.

Kreger found that Assurance Buyers Cooperative Inc. had incorporated in California in 1986, but the company didn't pay its franchise fees, so the state dissolved the cooperative in 1988. When Kreger raised the issue, Holladay turned over a new registration: The company "A-Buyers Co-operative" was registered in Massachusetts on March 19, 1990 as a not-for-profit.[27] The lawyers for Holladay continually referred to the groups interchangeably, as if the difference were some typographical error.

Kreger noticed a problem. "A-Buyers Co-op" had been incorporated in Massachusetts, all right, but it was merely registered as a non-profit, not as a purchasing group. When Kreger raised an issue about the legitimacy of ABC, Leeds, or CSI, Lorcin's lawyer, Robert Pitts, would argue that Leeds had paid out $627,000 in claims for Lorcin. Stomel pointed out that Leeds still came out ahead in the deal. Lorcin had paid in far more than $627,000 in premiums and special supplements. This wasn't so much an insurance company as a structured payment plan, he claimed.

Tom McDermott's head was spinning. He had never dealt with these kinds of obscure insurance entities—risk purchasing group, third party administrator, captive carrier. How was he to judge whether they were doing what they were supposed to do? He put his doubts aside until his next visit to the courthouse a few weeks later. After the hearing, Tom sat with Kreger, the insurance counselor, on a bench outside the modern courthouse. They discussed how they could investigate the insurance company even though the judge seemed uninterested in the insurance issue.

Kreger sent Tom to talk to Jacqueline Schroering and Harry Gregory III. These two lawyers, based in Louisville, Kentucky, had already started to scrutinize Lorcin's insurance. They represented the family of Timmy Jones, an army vet who was killed when his Lorcin pistol dropped from his holster. Their product liability suit claimed that if Lorcin hadn't used such a cheap safety, the gun wouldn't have gone off and Jones would still be alive.[28]

When Tom got back to New York, he called up the Kentucky lawyers and heard their theory. Schroering didn't understand why a legitimate insurance company wouldn't just pay up after such an awful accident. Gregory told Tom he thought it looked like there was something phony going on. Still, they needed proof.

Tom told Elisa Barnes about the strange insurance saga out in California. As they sat in her lower Manhattan office, he picked up a phone book and found the local Costa Rican consulate. He figured someone there should be able to tell him if Leeds & London was a legitimate insurance company or not. It turned out the consulate was right in the neighborhood. "You know what? I'm just going to walk down there and find out," McDermott announced.

The consulate was surprised by his inquiry. Since 1924 Costa Rica had only one insurance company, the Instituto Nacional de Seguros (National Insurance Institute), a state monopoly. (Costa Rica would agree in 2004 to open the market by 2011.) The government didn't allow any other insurance company to do business in Costa Rica. Leeds was incorporated in Costa Rica, but not as an insurance entity.[29]

The consulate helped McDermott find the original public incorporation papers. At first it looked as if Leeds was perhaps a legitimate independent business. The papers showed two Costa Ricans as its officers. Tom had no idea who they were. But as he looked more carefully, he saw what appeared to be proof indicating that something was wrong with this insurance company. The papers showed that the company had incorporated with only 20,000 colones—or the grand sum of $86. Obviously, there was no way it could ever pay out all the Lorcin claims.[30] He found that Leeds & London was formed in Costa Rica on October 6, 1994. But Lorcin claimed in the bankruptcy that it had been using Leeds as its insurer since 1989. Tom thought of three possibilities to explain the discrepancy. The first possibility was that Lorcin had no insurance before 1994. But Waldorf had presented his early policies from Leeds in court. It would be beyond brazenness; it would require a massive conspiracy between Waldorf and Holladay. Tom dismissed the idea as unlikely. Alternatively, Leeds might have been based outside of Costa Rica before 1994, which could be perfectly legal. Tom's final thought was that Leeds existed before 1994, but only as a paperwork entity, with no real incorporation as a legitimate insurance company. If that were the case, it could have violated an enormous number of insurance rules.

Tom didn't have much to go on to determine Leeds & London's origins. He remembered that Waldorf claimed in his bankruptcy deposition that Howard Holladay sold him insurance from another company—just briefly—before Holladay switched to selling Leeds insurance. Waldorf was very vague about the details: "You know something, there may have been one other carrier. . . . I think in the beginning there was one other carrier. What comes to mind over longevity, of course, is Leeds & London. I believe that Leeds & London did acquire the initial carrier. [Its] name I don't recall. It was a very short period of time."

This other carrier didn't explain away the gap in Leeds & London's registration. But it did make Tom begin to suspect that this insurance business—already complicated by three guises of Leeds, ABC, and CSI—could be an even more sprawling empire with more players. And if one had already disappeared, it made him worry about the rest.

McDermott excitedly told Barnes the news. The consulate found him a lawyer, Rodrigo Soto, to chase down Leeds in San José. Soto found the lawyer who had incorporated Leeds, Alberto Raven.

Raven laid out the details to Soto, who wrote up a report for Tom. The report said that in June 1994, Howard Holladay had called Raven from Boston saying he wanted to set up a company in Costa Rica. He was planning to come down to Costa Rica in a few weeks and he wanted the paperwork set up by then. That's how the two strangers got on the incorporation papers: Raven needed people to sign the documents right away, so he got two of his office workers to be the stand-ins. Raven said this was standard operating procedure in Costa Rica.

Soto found out that originally Holladay had wanted Raven to file papers for Leeds Y Loundres Seguros Merchantiles Sociedad Anomia (Leeds

& London Merchants Insurance Company). The Costa Rican registry rejected the filing right away because, as Tom had learned from the consulate, Costa Rica doesn't allow any insurance companies but its own to do business there. The government doesn't even let people use the word Seguros (Insurance) in their company name.

Raven told Holladay he'd have to change the name. They came up with Leeds Y Loundres Proteccion Merchantiles (Leeds & London Merchants Protection Company). The Costa Rican government approved the amended name for Holladay.

Raven also revealed that his dealings with Holladay were even more complicated. Holladay had him transfer ownership of Leeds to yet another company, Universal Management, in yet another Caribbean corporate haven, the Bahamas. This company was still on the move.

HAMILTON TOSSED FROM LORCIN

Just as he was getting interested in Lorcin's insurance setup, however, the claims estimator in the Lorcin bankruptcy said the *Hamilton* case was worth nothing in the proceedings. The judge agreed that it was too much of a novel case theory to bother setting aside money in Lorcin's financial plan. That meant, effectively, that the *Hamilton* case and Tom were thrown out of the Lorcin bankruptcy.

The Jones case would also be excluded from the proceeding; the claims estimator said Lorcin's liability for Timmy Jones's death had not been established. Harry Gregory and Jacqueline Schroering represented Jimmy Jones over the death of his son Timmy. On November 1, 1995, Timmy, thirty-five, a father of two young teenagers, went shooting with a friend. Timmy bent down to clean off his boot by the friends' garage and the Lorcin pistol fell out. The drop was no more than two feet, his mother, Myra Jones, says. At first Timmy didn't even realize he'd been shot. "He told his friend, 'I think I've shot myself,'" Myrna said. They only found the bullet hole by lifting up his shirt. Timmy was still talking when the ambulance picked him up, but that assurance of health was deceptive. Doctors said the bullet had cut off a major nerve. His parents raced to the hospital but by the time they got there, Timmy was breathing with assistance, seemingly unconscious. The nurse told Myrna to talk in her son's ear, that he could still hear, but as she tried to talk someone pulled her away so Timmy could go to surgery. "I didn't say everything I wanted to say," she recalls. The surgery wasn't successful and he died. Timmy's brother's wife knew Schroering and introduced them, Myrna says. The wife, a blind diabetic, postponed a kidney transplant to attend Timmy's funeral, then died six weeks later herself.[31] His father sued Lorcin, and Schroering found a ballistics expert to testify that Lorcin used a cheap zinc rotary safety switch on a primitive pistol design when it could have used a steel switch for $2 to $3 more per gun. The claims estimator and the judge, however, had valued the case at nothing, saying Jones might not be able to prove that the safety was on.

CSI's lawyer, Kurt Gerstner, who worked at Campbell Campbell Edwards & Conroy, a prestigious firm in Boston, tried to use the decision to push the Kentucky duo to settle.[32] "Perhaps you felt that the Claims Estimator would make an award far in excess of the settlement offer I made on behalf of Lorcin Engineering," Gerstner wrote. "Your office has steadfastly presented unreasonable settlement demands which were clearly nowhere near the true value of the case. . . . The fact that the Claims Estimator and the Bankruptcy Court judge now have both reached the conclusion that there is no liability against Lorcin supports my view that the settlement value of the case is a lot closer to $0 than it is to the numbers you have been suggesting."

He went on to make his clients sound nearly altruistic: "They were always willing to negotiate reasonably." The estimator's finding "would justify my clients withdrawing their prior offer [but] they will not do so."

Jones's second lawyer Gregory wrote back, effectively saying thanks, but no thanks; we'll take our chances in court. The claims estimator just got it wrong, he said they could prove that Jones had the safety engaged and Lorcin was at fault. The decision by the estimator and the judge were "clear error," Gregory wrote.

When Schroering pressed Gerstner on Leeds' financial stability, Gerstner would just say, "You're spinning your wheels. You'll just waste your time."

Tom had gotten a similar response. "Something about their explanations for the operation of this insurance company didn't ring true to me," Tom says.

Tom and the Kentucky lawyers compared notes. They all felt confused by Gerstner's role. And they all felt that even if they never got paid for it, what they really needed to figure out was, What was Holladay really up to?

CHANGE IN DIRECTION; THE END OF HAMILTON

In the months after he uncovered all the strange details about Holladay's insurance business, Tom sat in Elisa Barnes's office, working on little details of the *Hamilton* case, but he kept thinking about the Holladay insurance operation. Tom wanted to keep on investigating Holladay and the insurance companies, but it was really no longer relevant to Hamilton. Distracted at his desk, he thought that the Holladay enterprise could really be an enormous fraud, one that wasn't getting enough attention. "I needed to do something," he said. "This could be a major, major scam."

Gradually, he stopped spending time on the Hamilton case.

Johnstone, meanwhile, had come through with funding from liberal philanthropist George Soros for Barnes, so more help would be on the way. Tom was completely out of the picture by the time *Hamilton* went to trial, after four years of preparation, on January 6, 1999, in Brooklyn federal court.

"This is a simple case about accepting responsibility,"[33] Barnes said in her opening statement. She said the gun industry had "taken a head-in-the-sand approach to the problem of gun violence." She said she would prove that it had saturated the market in lightly regulated Southern states, knowing the guns would end up on the streets of New York.

On the other side, attorney Anne Kimball said Barnes just wanted to "blame someone else for pulling the trigger, to shift the blame away from the cold-blooded killers in this case."

Over the next five weeks the families of the shooting victims would make a grim parade. In each case the mothers would get on the stand to talk about their lost boys. Dignified Freddie Hamilton had to reveal that her dead son had been diagnosed with manic-depression—or the defense would. Afterward, she told Jennifer Gonnerman of the *Village Voice* how mortifying it was. "At one point I thought, 'If he was at this trial, he would die all over again.' If he saw me sharing all his personal business, he'd say, 'What's wrong with you?'"[34]

Later in the trial, as Gonnerman reported, the only surviving shooting victim, Stephen Fox, testified how he struggled to relearn walking, talking, and dressing. Fox was hopeful even though he still carried the bullet in his brain. He said he was studying for his GED and wanted to be a carpenter. After Fox was ushered out, Barnes called a rehabilitation expert who said that Fox had lost thirty-seven IQ points to the bullet. As he was giving his grim assessment, Fox and his mother reappeared in the courtroom and testimony was halted until they left. A gun distributor's lawyer, E. Gordon Haesloop, suggested that Fox's prospects wouldn't have been promising, even without that bullet in his brain.

Judge Jack Weinstein told the jurors to ignore the raw emotion of the case and concentrate on whether the gun makers used "reasonable care" or not in marketing and distributing guns. They debated in turmoil for five days, sending notes of distress to Weinstein. One said that ten jurors had "decided to work together to reach a verdict," but that the eleventh "refused because he or she feels the verdict "will open the floodgate of lawsuits across the country."[35]

On February 11, 1999, the Brooklyn jury reached a verdict so complicated it took forty-five minutes to read: Fifteen of twenty-five gun companies were negligent in their marketing. They tied nine companies to two murder victims, but didn't award damages. The only award, $4 million, was to the sole shooting surviving victim, Stephen Fox, and his mother. Three companies—American Arms, Beretta USA, and Taurus International—made the type of gun that injured Fox. The jury apportioned blame by market share. Together the three only comprised about 13 percent of the market so they had to pay $560,000. Just as in the tobacco cases, this long history of public skepticism and resentment, of court losses and industry arrogance was overturned by angry jurors. "I thank God, we absolutely won," Hamilton told reporters. Barnes said it had all been worth it. At times, she said, she felt like she was fighting the federal government itself when she fought the gun industry.

By the time the verdict came in, local governments around the country had decided to sue the gun industry. The verdict encouraged more to join in. Meanwhile, the NRA had already started working on state legislatures. They were lobbying in states to pass laws that would ban cities from suing the gun industry for the cost of gun violence. Despite the ostensible conservative trust in local control, the NRA had already made progress passing these laws in numerous states and the U.S. House of Representatives.

The biggest court victory against the gun industry, the *Hamilton* case, proved short-lived. On appeal the federal circuit court directed the state law claim to New York's highest court, which ruled on April 26, 2001,[36] that gun makers had no duty to the general public because they had no relationship with them. In other words, the ruling smacked the public back to its 1950s standing. Just because gun makers could foresee criminal use of their guns didn't mean they had to do anything about it. "Foreseeability, alone, does not define duty—it merely determines the scope of the duty once it is determined to exist . . . the connection between defendants, the criminal wrongdoers and plaintiffs is remote, running through several links in a chain consisting of at least the manufacturer, the federally licensed distributor or wholesaler, and the first retailer."

There was one sentence that gave Barnes hope: "Without a showing that specific groups of dealers play a disproportionate role in supplying the illegal gun market, the sweep of plaintiffs' duty theory is far wider than the danger it seeks to avert."

Most people would read this decision as a door closing completely in the face of gun victims. Elisa Barnes, however, saw it differently. She figured she could readily demonstrate that there was a specific group of dealers who played a disproportionate role in supplying criminals with guns. The federal gun cops had said as much themselves. According to a 2000 ATF study, just 1.2 percent of current dealers (1,020 dealers) accounted for 57 percent of crime gun traces.[37] They were an easily definable group. She would keep looking for a new case to bring back to Judge Weinstein.

The initial *Hamilton* victory spurred on dozens of suits by local governments, the NAACP and the Department of Housing and Urban Development (whose concern was over handguns in housing projects). Mayor Richard M. Daley of Chicago sued the gun industry for $433 million for creating a public nuisance in his city.[38] Chicago bans handguns and it had sent undercover cops to the suburbs, where gun shops sold to the cops even when they professed to be gang members, buying for criminals or taking the guns to Chicago. The suit was dismissed in 2000, reinstated in 2002 and ultimately dismissed in 2004.[39] Five of seven Illinois Supreme Court Justices signed a separate opinion urging tougher gun laws.[40] Daley also led an epic court battle to get gun data out of the ATF for the case.[41]

The Clinton administration struck a deal with Smith & Wesson patterned on the massive settlements that ended the states' suits against tobacco companies. The gun settlement was more effective in changing behavior than in getting a booty of cash. Smith & Wesson would spend 2 percent of its annual revenues to develop a smart gun within three years and to impose a host of new requirements in its contract with dealers. Gun shops would have to carry $1 million of liability insurance coverage per year, sell only to those who passed a certified safety course or exam, and bar individuals from buying more than one gun every two weeks.[42] "Certainly if the market for guns wasn't declining, I probably wouldn't have needed to sign the deal," then CEO Ed Shultz said.[43] "But how can I justify paying legal bills instead of research and development for other products?" The incident highlighted how the industry and the NRA can have different interests. Shultz thought he was being a pragmatic businessman; the NRA labeled him a sellout and led a boycott against the company. "The demons for them are industry folks who may settle lawsuits," Shultz said. "The NRA thinks if we need to sacrifice a few manufacturers, so what?"

Eight

THE CHASE: UNRAVELING AN INSURANCE SCAM

THE END OF THE LORCIN CHAPTER I I BANKRUPTCY

Tom let Hamilton advance without him so he could concentrate on the case where he thought he could do the most good: the insurance mess in the Lorcin bankruptcy. He didn't have an official role there, but the case involved the kind of financial shenanigans he was good at figuring out. He would have to work on his own time and dime.

Holladay and Waldorf were releasing only a reluctant trickle of information on their insurance deal, but it was becoming apparent that the policy was a lot less valuable than Waldorf implied when he had big yellow signs at the SHOT Show, the industry's big trade show, bragging of a $1 million product liability policy ($3 million in later years). Customers figured it meant the policy would pay up to $1 million for each liability claim. But there was some confusion. The $1 million limit was for all claimants for the year. Holladay claimed ABC had five hundred members.[1] The group had four Ring of Fire companies—Lorcin, Davis, Sundance, and Arcadia Machine and Tools. Stomel wondered what would happen to the insurance company if all these other companies had claims like Lorcin's.

Originally Lorcin's policy type was "claims made": It would cover "claims made" against a policy in a given year. But Lorcin went along when Leeds changed the policy to an "occurrence" policy, in which claims are assigned to the policy year in which the accident occurred. Claims-made policies aren't necessarily better than occurrence policies, but a switch from one to the other can create a gap. This switch suddenly dumped $34 million worth of claims from sixteen personal injury lawsuits all in the 1994 policy year. Sixteen lawsuits now had to compete against each other for the $1 million available. Lorcin itself would have exposure for any damages above the $1 million, but oddly, Lorcin didn't object.[2] [3]

Finally, in early 1997, Lorcin came up with a reorganization plan and promised to pay off all the claims the estimator had said were legitimate.[4] Most of the people Lorcin owed agreed to take a down payment up front and wait for the rest. There was one holdout: Riley Beckett, the lawyer for Frank McDowell. A pawn shop worker, McDowell was shot in the leg when he tried to fix a Lorcin gun. The claims estimator said McDowell would probably win $242,000 in court. Refusing to pay all of it, Lorcin offered to buy an extra policy from its current insurance company, Leeds & London, just to cover the McDowell case in the event he won at a later trial.[5] This policy didn't make economic sense: Why would Leeds write a retroactive policy for an injury that had already taken place? Sure, there was a chance Lorcin could win at trial and pay nothing, but the expert had already judged it a good case. Insurance is supposed to cover unlikely mishaps, not almost inevitable judgments. This was more like Leeds co-signing a loan to Lorcin.

Creditors saw this as another example of Lorcin working with Leeds when their interests should be opposed. Lorcin's lawyer, Robert Pitts, said that fighting lawsuits just put Leeds on Lorcin's side. "The insurance company was clearly separate from Lorcin, though some people didn't want to believe that, but it was," he said in an interview. "They also paid the claims they were supposed to, which some people didn't want to believe."[6]

Predictably, this peculiar retroactive policy brought Lorcin's insurance back into the spotlight. The injured parties suing Lorcin had persistently tried to find out about its insurers. Stomel wrote to Craig Barbarosh, an attorney Holladay hired from a prestigious firm then known as Madison & Sutro, asking to clarify Holladay's role, name ABC's other 499 members, and provide financial statements and registration documents.[7] Barbarosh wrote back that "my client advises me that Control does not possess financial statements or other documents relating to the solvency of Leeds & London."[8] So far neither Holladay nor Waldorf had produced any helpful documents on Leeds. Waldorf first asserted that he had no idea whether his insurer was solvent. Eventually Waldorf filed a sworn statement saying, "I undertook my own investigation . . . [C]ontrary to the allegations and innuendos raised by Mr. McDermott," he found the company was just fine.

Judge Meredith Jury, the official presiding over this and probably countless other bankruptcy cases, held a hearing on the proposed plan.[9] Stomel and Beckett argued that the retroactive insurance policy didn't make any economic sense. What company in its right mind would write such a policy to a bankrupt company?

Although this circumstance had no obvious precedent, in Judge Jury's analysis, the most analogous situation was an appellate bond. When a defendant loses a verdict, it has to put the judgment money aside, in the form of a bond, during the appeal. To get such a bond, the company normally has to post the money or pay a very high fee. But Judge Jury emphasized that plaintiffs deserved the security of an appellate bond only if they'd already won a case in court, which Beckett hadn't. Lorcin wasn't providing many details on this retroactive policy, but it was clear it hadn't put up as much as the estimator said the claim was worth.

Beckett pointed out to the judge that "there's some kind of amazing things on this," meaning the copy of the policy. He went on to describe how the only evidence that the policy even existed was an unsigned letter from Leeds & London authorizing a $250,000 retroactive policy from Costa Rica. Normally, evidence rules are a little more stringent. Beckett wondered "how that document could with no fax marks, or anything—end up being part of this brief served on me on the last day." McDowell's only chance of getting any money now depended on this unusual policy. Beckett and Stomel protested that this policy was worthless because they had never resolved whether the insurance company was for real.

The judge seemed like she was getting weary of the insurance discussion. "I have never made any type of analysis of that insurance company," she said. "I've heard arguments about it, but I have never uttered a word of whether I thought it was a legitimate insurance company or not." And it appeared that she had no intention of investigating it.

Lorcin's attorney Robert Pitts evoked the comparison with the appellate bond, and Judge Jury kept getting tangled in it. "I mean, there's nothing nefarious here," Pitts said. "There was never a promise that we would provide an appeal bond." Beckett kept pointing out that he wasn't asking for an appellate bond. He would accept an insurance policy—as long as it was a real policy from a bona fide company.

"What they have at this case, Your Honor, is a Costa Rican retroactive insurance company that is not authorized to sell insurance in the United States," Beckett said. "They are dealing through a claims administrator who is out of Boston. And it's my understanding that with quick research . . . that there's a question of whether Howard Holladay and the CSI, which is his business, is authorized as required by the federal Risk [Retention Act]."

Judge Jury picked up language Pitts had used and called the whole insurance issue a "red herring." Then she circled back to the bond issue. "I mean, you're basically saying unless there's a bond, I shouldn't confirm the plan. And I'm not going to find that. I don't think your client is in the situation where they have a right to a bond. . . . I do think that this company . . . if it had to find $240,000 because you had a final judgment in that amount, would have it." Presumably, she was relying on Leeds' past record of paying out Lorcin's claims. The judge approved Lorcin's plan to emerge from Chapter 11 bankruptcy protection.

At one of the final hearings Tom attended, he saw Waldorf for the last time. Waldorf mocked Elisa Barnes, saying she was just out for a huge payout but would get nothing from Waldorf. "You think this is the end, but it isn't. This is just the beginning," McDermott spat in the direction of the lanky Waldorf as he stepped into a stretch Mercedes limousine. "I'll see you again."

PICKING UP THE COLD TRAIL

Survivors of gun violence find their own ways to contribute. Some work to heal their fellow crime victims. Katina Johnstone would get the public involved with the Million Mom March and the Silent March,[10] the parade of empty shoes that travels the country.[11] [12]

Tom had finally found his niche in the gun debate—gun industry insurance. It was an stunningly obscure and arcane niche, yes. Certainly it was one that he never would have conceived of as he paced his backyard five years before, wondering what he could do to keep guns off the street. But he knew this insurance issue might just be the handgun industry's Achilles heel that he'd been seeking. Let others go after gun laws, go on talk shows, take abuse at town halls, put their wounds on display. Leave the rallies and legislation to those who could do those jobs best. Investigating the financial underpinnings of the gun industry's insurance—it would be like going after Al Capone for tax evasion.

Howard Holladay's enterprise seemed to be protected from public scrutiny by, if nothing else, the wall of boredom that surrounds the topic of insurance.

If low-end gun companies were ever going to have to "pay their own way" for the damage their products did to the public, someone would have to hold not only the low gun companies but the flimsy insurance behind some of them accountable. The states were supposed to regulate insurance, but this kind of sprawling, international case was beyond their grasp. (These were all years before the general policy debate over whether to scrap the states' lax, hodgepodge insurance regulation system for federal oversight.)

Tom tried to get the FBI involved. The Los Angeles office, however, said the case was too small. He asked the other lawyers suing Lorcin to work with him. He didn't get an enthusiastic response. "My district attorney days are done," said one.

Because no one else would tackle the issue, Tom made Howard Holladay's insurance operation his own case. If he could prove fraud, he could even reopen the Lorcin bankruptcy, perhaps even go after the personal assets of Holladay and any gun company owner who was in on the scheme. He would be like a prosecutor, but he would have to work without the power to bargain with witnesses, the staff, or the badge. And without the money. In fact, he would spend hundreds of thousands of dollars of his own time and money. When later asked how much he had actually spent, he would usually try to dodge the issues. "Now you're talking like Mrs. McDermott," he would joke, hinting at Rosemary's rare instances of skepticism.

He was following other lawyers who had tried, over a lifetime, to eke out some gains against the mass marketing of handguns, each standing on the shoulders of the other. Elisa Barnes got years of harassment—and a few words of judicial encouragement—for all her troubles. Windle Turley didn't get the big court win he had been working on since the 1970s, but he did write a textbook on gun lawsuits. Michigan lawyer Robert Garvey was one of a few lawyers who successfully sued K-mart and other large retailers over the way some of their clerks carelessly sold guns, forcing them to revise policies.[13] [14] [15] [16] Countless others fought in obscurity and defeat. All gun control activist lawyers faced the same irony: Their enemies see their work as the perversion of American history, a nuisance that would not exist except for a few pesky individuals. Their supporters love them, but figure if they didn't file the cases, someone else would. Their work is revealed only incrementally, in slow but inexorable social progress.

Tom would now join this team, which so far had an abysmal win-loss record. There was no clear roadmap for the investigation. There were very few public records. Besides avoiding taxes, the big benefit of incorporating overseas is secrecy. Rather than being able to follow Holladay's footsteps as the insurance empire evolved, Tom would have to track his quarry from a parallel path, gathering any witnesses, documents, and information he could find about any part of the enterprise's timeline.

If only he could show that the business was based on a fraud, he could "pierce the corporate veil," meaning he could go after the personal assets of whoever was behind the company.

ASSURANCE BUYERS CO-OP

To figure if Holladay had done anything wrong, Tom had to learn insurance law. During the bankruptcy, Stomel raised questions about whether ABC abided by either the federal risk retention laws or the various state regulations. But, no one's investigation caught fire. Again, blame the soporific power of the word *insurance*.

Tom turned to the *Risk Retention Reporter*'s, managing editor, Karen Cutts.[17] She knew right away something was wrong. ABC included bungee-jumping companies, ultralight aircraft makers, and all kinds of injury-prone enterprises that would have been hard-pressed to find affordable insurance. These insurance groups are authorized to buy insurance only for their members, who must be involved in the same business. States originally banned pooled insurance because all members have different risks.

She had an easy way to think of the two possible entities: The highly regulated Risk Retention Groups (RRGs) sold insurance, and the lightly regulated Purchasing Groups bought it.

A Missouri insurance salesman named Arthur Blumeyer had already manipulated the confusing patchwork of risk retention laws.[18] He was convicted of fraud for setting up a string of fancy sounding companies like Bel-Aire. He concealed his interest by having the companies based offshore and by putting two nominees on their paperwork. He also put a legislator on his payroll, who retaliated against an investigator at the Missouri Department of Insurance by stripping the investigator's salary from the budget.

"A lot of guys [have the] same M.O.," Cutts said. "They sound a lot alike."

At the other end of the spectrum, there was the SAIL program that Bob Chiarello ran.[19] [20]

SAIL operated in the unlikely setting of an enormous house in industrial Elizabeth, New Jersey, near Newark Airport. Inside are all the trappings of an insurance business: desks, workers, dreary-looking binders. Chiarello, a friendly white-haired middle-aged man, sits in an office with a fireplace and toy train, and airplane antiques.

This is no fly-by-night operation: Chiarello started selling insurance to gun businesses in 1979 at the company his dad started in 1934. His company handles all but a handful of the big responsible gun companies. SAIL's program for dealers, distributors, and the like has a giant American insurer behind it. The program for manufacturers is based in Bermuda, one of the rare islands with real insurance regulation.

Chiarello's program is profitable every year because he knows how to assess and avoid undue risk. His fourteen-page application covers the company's accident history, premises, practices, subcontractors, everything imaginable.[21] Then it can send inspectors to check the details. And SAIL members can and do turn down customers.

SAIL isn't a Risk Retention Group. It's an industry captive. The policies are individual; they don't all share the same pool.

Chiarello often saw Holladay at the annual SHOT Show and was familiar with his business. Some industry friends had asked Chiarello about Holladay's unusual retroactive surcharges to cover claims.

"It's not something insurance companies do," he emphatically says. "It's either in the contract or it's not. Insurance is all about a contract. It just doesn't make sense."

Holladay would tell Chiarello that he had sent SAIL the companies that ABC couldn't insure. "I thought, 'Jeez, if you can't insure them, I sure don't want them,'" Chiarello says. Holladay even offered to sell him his business.

Chiarello insists that insurance is designed to manage risk, not make products safer. But if a company wants SAIL's insurance, it has to meet its standards, which are designed to make the company less risky. It's like a homeowner's policy offering a discount for having a fire extinguisher and smoke alarm: The insurance company makes the rule for financial motives, but the end effect is that its policyholders are safer for it.

Now that Tom understood the structure, he still needed to understand who was behind all these parts. Were ABC, CSI, and Leeds really all separate entities, as Holladay claimed? Or were they simply different corporate identities for Howard Holladay?

Holladay claimed to be a third-party administrator, something like a claims adjuster, in Boston. Tom had linked Holladay to Leeds & London in Costa Rica. His investigator Soto found out that it was really Holladay behind the company. However, Tom needed hard evidence to back up this claim. Now that avenue hit a roadblock. Holladay's old lawyer, Raven, kept stalling on documents.

Tom needed to find out who started Assurance Buyers Co-op. Public records showed that a lawyer named Daniel Simon from Los Angeles had incorporated the company in 1986.[22] Tom called Simon to ask who the real force behind the company was. Simon said attorney-client privilege prevented him from discussing the matter. "He would hardball me," Tom recalls. Frustrated, Tom pulled what would become his trademark move: He showed up at Simon's office, three thousand miles away from Tom's home, unannounced. He still got nowhere.

THE OTHER LAWSUITS

Tom's next step was to track down any other people who had tried to sue Holladay or any of his companies. He had no idea if there would be five, fifty, or fifty thousand. After all, many of the companies Holladay insured seemed to go out of business. If someone walked into a lawyer's office, injured by a defunct company, the lawyer might turn to the insurance company. Even if they found the insurer they would have found little encouragement they could collect a verdict. Most lawyers would have found these cases pretty hopeless and advised clients not to file.

Probably no one knew all the details of Holladay's enterprise except Holladay himself. But together all these injured people might establish a pattern of how Holladay operated. And then maybe they could pool their information and go after him.

Jacqueline Schroering had a suit in Kentucky federal court alleging bad faith in an insurance policy. Tom knew that self-appointed prosecutors only got so far; he needed an actual client. Not someone to pay the bills—Tom would be footing those himself. He just needed to represent someone so that he could build a concrete case. He went to Kentucky to discuss strategy with Schroering and Harry Gregory. He left Kentucky with a new client: Jimmy Jones.

Schroering and Gregory were doing their own investigation, but if Tom found something relevant he'd pass it along. He would go out and look for some of the cold cases filed against Holladay, bring them back to life.

GETTING THE FARRELL CASE

Stomel sent Tom a list of potential suits against Leeds from a legal database.[23] Many companies named merely had names similar to Leeds. He decided to look up the one cold case: *Farrell v. Leeds & London* (1992). The only way for him to find out what the case was about was to head to the courthouse where it was filed to read the complaint. Tom waited until there was a break at work, then headed down to Philadelphia.

The clerks at Philadelphia's ancient Court of Common Pleas were stunned by his request for such an old case. This gritty courthouse serves up common man's justice quickly. Bigger, more complicated get to go to federal court, which sets high standards for admission. So six-year-old cases are considered ancient history.

Clerks sent Tom off in the freight elevator to the dark, castlelike archives tower, where a stooped clerk practically shouted, incredulously, "You want me to find *what?*" He scuffled off and came back an hour later with the entire case file: a single page. All the paper showed was that the judge had dismissed the case because the lawyer could not find the company on which to serve papers. But it did have the plaintiff's lawyer's name: Roger Harrington.

Tom called up Harrington and explained that he was tracking down Leeds. Harrington explained the Farrell case. Leeds had insured the maker of a paintball gun that shot out the eye of Harrington's client, James Farrell. The company that made the paintball gun was called National Survival Games. It went out of business because of so many personal injury suits. Harrington learned that NSG had insurance with Leeds & London. The policy named Kurt Gerstner as the insurance company's attorney. When

Gerstner said he didn't have to and wouldn't appear in Philadelphia for Leeds, Harrington dropped the case. As Harrington finished his tale, he agreed to send Tom the whole case file.

Tom was amazed by all the new information. He could now approach people hurt by the defunct paintball company's guns. But for his lawsuit, the story was useless without the documents. Weeks went by and nothing arrived. McDermott called. Harrington promised to send them. Nothing arrived. Finally Tom pulled a variation on his trademark investigation move. He had a friend call down and set up an appointment to make sure Harrington would be in the office. Then he showed up at Harrington's elegant Center City office unannounced. Tom figured that Harrington somehow felt he should have done more, even though he had gone further than any other lawyer suing National Survival Games. "Harrington had hit a real major black hole," Tom said later. "I really don't know if there's anything else he could have done."

Harrington was expecting a new client, but in walked Tom: "You've not been returning my calls and you're really hurting my case," McDermott told him. It was a bluff. Tom was just starting his investigation and he barely had a case.

Harrington had pulled the files; they were sitting in a box in a closet down the hall. He handed over the entire case file, including copies of his notes.

With the benefit of Harrington's work, Tom pieced together this narrative:

James Farrell was playing paintball in a friend's backyard in northwestern Pennsylvania. The teenager hosting the game didn't notice that Farrell had taken off his glasses to rest and accidentally shot him in the eye.[24]

The game was designed to be safe and perhaps even an expert in risk assessment wouldn't have predicted the toll it would eventually take. Paintballs are just gelcaps filled with colored water. But their velocity when fired, which can reach 200 miles an hour, rips through eyes with brutal force. Eye injures were common in paintball. By 2000, there would be 1,200 severe paintball eye injuries annually, mostly among boys and young men.[25] Roughly half would lose an eye.

Farrell's doctors wanted to remove the eye right away, but Farrell tried everything to save it. After a year of painful surgeries, he let the doctors take it out.

Farrell sued the homeowner and the paintball maker.[26] The homeowners argued that it was all Farrell's fault for taking off his goggles, but on the eve of trial, the homeowners' insurance company settled for $300,000. That left the suit against National Survival Games, the gun maker. The owner of the company, Bob Gurnsey, also turned out to be one of the pioneers of the sport.

According to paintball lore (and the *Boston Globe*), back in the late 1970s some guys drinking gin in New Hampshire's woods came up with a game to settle who had the best survival skills, cutthroat urbanites or outdoorsmen.[27] [28] Early on, Hayes Noel and Charles Gaines used loggers' tree-marking tools. Gurnsey was one of the twelve players in the first-ever game in Henniker, New Hampshire. As more people heard of their game, Gurnsey used $10,000 to start National Survival Games to make more sophisticated equipment. He told the *Globe* that he was down to his last $400 before the sport took off. Eventually it grew to be a $100 million industry. Gurnsey hadn't patented his designs because he wanted to let people copy the idea and spread the sport. Since he hadn't been greedy, he saw only a small sliver of the industry profit but did well enough for himself: He drove a black Porsche with the license plate SPLAT and employed thirty people.

When Harrington went after the paintball company, he found that he was the last in a long line and that the company was on the brink of collapse. The business had turned out badly for Gurnsey, not only because so many people wound up hurt, but because he bought insurance from Howard Holladay.

By the time Harrington reached National Survival Games, Gurnsey had hired a former cop, Ron Lemay,[29] to handle and settle all the complaints. Lemay told Harrington that National Survival Games's insurance companies had collapsed—twice—but that Gursney was trying to pay off the injury claims himself.

Lemay mailed Harrington the insurance policies,[30] which named Leeds & London as NSG's carrier.[31] The policy said that Leeds was based in the Turks and Caicos, a chain of islands that used to be part of the Bahamas, and that claims against the policy should go to the Boston law firm of Campbell and Campbell. Harrington figured if Leeds could afford that expensive a law firm, there must be some money for his client. So in 1992 Harrington sued Leeds and served the complaint on Campbell and Campbell.

What happed next was more than a little unusual.

Kurt Gerstner, the same lawyer who had brushed off concerns about Leeds to Tom and the Kentucky lawyers, wrote Harrington on November 29, 1993,[32] saying he wasn't coming. Pennsylvania courts could make him travel only 100 miles, he said. Besides, he claimed the policy was incorrect and that he was the lawyer for Control Systems Inc., the third-party administrator, not for Leeds.

Harrington was stunned.

With Campbell and Campbell denying it had anything to do with the case, Harrington had few options. Because the parties were in separate states, he would qualify to move the case to federal court, where Gerstner would have to show up. Or he could hire a lawyer to bring the case in

Massachusetts. Both options would take lots of time and money and even then would probably not produce anything. Harrington and his clients, who already had a settlement from the homeowner, let the matter drop.

GURNSEY & LEMAY

Tom tracked down National Survival Games founder Bob Gurnsey in Arkansas.

Gurnsey said he got suspicious of Holladay after the first company he sold insurance from, Colony Insurers, collapsed. Holladay blamed an insurance company in Louisiana for ripping them off. Gurnsey said he'd hired a private investigator, Ron Lemay, to track down Holladay's business. The two had even taken a trip down to Louisiana to try to untangle the mess of a company, but they had wound up only more confused. Gurnsey's company had collapsed the same time as his marriage, in the early 1990s. When Gurnsey moved away, he told Lemay to haul their mountains of legal records to the town dump.

A few years earlier, McDermott and Gurnsey would have been on the same team, pursuing Holladay. Gurnsey sympathized with Tom but wanted nothing to do with that old mess.

The next time he was able to get out of the office for a few days, Tom McDermott called Gurnsey's old investigator, Ron Lemay. He got no response to his messages, but he drove up to New Hampshire anyway. He didn't know whether Lemay would be there or if he'd willing to help. Tom hoped Lemay would be one of those investigators who hangs onto evidence even in—or perhaps especially in—cases that don't pan out, in the hopes that the evidence can be used someday.

Lemay's office was in Georges Mills, New Hampshire, in a small building with a travel agent and post office, right across from Lake Sunapee. Tom found nobody there. A little desperate after his six-hour drive, Tom tried the town dump. He kicked around for a while but came up empty— not that he was expecting to find a giant pile of boxes labeled "Leeds & London documents."

When Tom went back to the office, a mailman told him Ron was forty miles away at the Dartmouth Medical Center in Hanover, possibly dying after a heart attack.

Tom drove to Hanover, but when he saw Lemay unconscious, and hooked up to tubes and monitors, he couldn't bear to question him. He left. But he couldn't bring himself to go home defeated just yet. He headed back to the hospital.

This time McDermott found Lemay—a white-haired man of about sixty—awake. He boldly approached, explaining what must have seemed like a surreal request. Imagine being woozy from hospital sedation when a stranger asks for documents from a job you worked on five years earlier.

He asked Lemay if he'd really destroyed all the documents as he was supposed to do.

"No, I saved them," Lemay said.

"Where are they?" McDermott asked.

"In a file," Lemay answered cryptically. Then he fell back asleep.

McDermott waited out Lemay in the cafeteria. When he returned, he found a woman in Lemay's room, Jean Rooney, Lemay's common-law wife.[33] Before Tom had a chance to ask any more questions, Rooney scolded Tom for harassing Lemay on his sickbed. Tom apologized, said he agreed. He'd gotten carried away. He left. On the way out of the hospital, he sent flowers up to the room.

The flowers worked. When Tom called a few weeks later, Jean was no longer angry with him. Lemay had been so sedated that he didn't even remember Tom, but he invited him up to go over the documents. In a way, he was waiting for Tom—or someone like him—to show up one day.

He and Lemay hit it off right away: They were both natural investigators, working-class kids who'd dreamed of becoming prosecutors. Lemay was working as a New Hampshire state trooper when his patrol car rolled over. He broke his back and that started a string of further injuries and surgeries. He retired and started a travel agency, which is where he met Jean. One surgery went terribly wrong and put Lemay in a wheelchair. He then decided to return to his dream of being a lawyer, no small feat because he was already forty-five and didn't have a bachelor's degree. One school in Oregon enrolled him. He returned three years later, walking and a law school graduate. But he never did pass the bar. So he became a "legal consultant."

When Gurnsey, who lived in the next town over, needed someone to handle his insurance mess, he called Lemay. By the end, Lemay had practically taken over National Survival Games for Gurnsey. He had amassed about ten full-sized file cabinets with legal documents, customers going after National Survival Games, which in turn went after Holladay. "Ron was incredibly angry," Jean recalls. He thought right at the outset that there was something fishy. "It wasn't just some poor insurance company that went belly up.' His instincts were really good and he was very angry." Jean said Lemay was determined to get to the bottom of this. Lemay arranged for Tom to work in an empty office across the hall. Jean owned the travel agency downstairs named Holiday Travel. The name became ironic as Tom and Ron were now chasing down the travels of Howard Holladay.

Ron would sit and tell the story of each case and document.

"It was a gold mine," Tom recalls.

HOLLADAY, COLONY, AND
NATIONAL SURVIVAL GAMES (1989–1992)

With Ron Lemay's help, Tom was able to recreate some of the early history.

In January 1986, Howard Holladay came up to the National Survival Games' New Hampshire office to talk with Bob Gurnsey about insurance. They struck a deal.[34] Holladay would sell insurance not only to Gurnsey but also to owners of small fields around the country where people wanted to host paintball. Insuring all those unknowns in all those backyard battlefields seems like a risky business. Perhaps that's why CSI copyrighted a document called "Injury Statistics at Home, at Work, and at Play." Most of the numbers are from the National Safety Council on yearly injuries per 1,000 participants. The paper shows that Lacrosse produces 223.79 severe injuries per 1,000 participants while bicycle riding produces 11.3, boating 0.92, and bowling 0.5. Amid these verified stats is the one CSI inserted for paintball games. Coming in at 0.31 injuries per 1,000 participants, it's the safest game in town. The National Safety Council, however, has repeatedly quarreled with another sport that uses this particular statistic to show how safe it is. That sport is hunting.

The International Hunter Education Association Manual, which is handed out in many states in classes people have to take to get a hunting license, uses similar injuries per 1,000 participant stats. With 15 million hunters and 880 injuries, hunting looks great. At least one teacher points out that people are 10 times as likely to get hurt playing tennis as they are hunting and that when hunters do get hurt it's usually because they sat on an arrow or fell out of a tree stand—an unusual message in a course designed to make people conscious of safety risks.

The National Safety Council has been trying—obviously without much success—to get them to knock off using its data this way. For starters, John Ulczycki, NSC spokesman, points out, it's not mathematically fair: People who ride bikes might do it every day but hunters only go a few times a year. So, bikers have a much greater exposure to injury. The NSC also has a quarrel with the severity of injuries. "We would never say that a sport where 75 people die every year is safer than another sport," says Ulczycki. Only boating has more deaths. "And I wouldn't equate a sprained ankle with a gunshot wound. Some people would, but I wouldn't."

Perhaps Colony Insurers, which covered paintball, was oblivious to their potential to harm like Steve Martin in *The Jerk*: He got rich making eyeglass pads but didn't foresee people going cross-eyed. At any rate, the insurer one day went belly-up. Things seemed fine until one day a strange letter arrived at Gurnsey's office from "Michael Gold, liquidator." The unsigned letter was addressed to all clients and creditors of Colony and said the company was broke, but fighting in court to get its money. The letter said Colony was suing Louisiana Underwriters Insurance Company and a Texas bank for fraud for taking the premiums. The letter said Colony owed its clients $150,000 in premium refunds, $200,000 in unpaid claims, $500,000 in accounts payable, and had $1.5 million in claims under litigation.

With Colony gone, Gurnsey's company would have to pick up the tab for injured customers. Holladay said he had found a new insurance company: Leeds & London. It wouldn't pay Colony's bills, but it would make things right from now on.

Gurnsey was wary, so he demanded proof that Leeds was solid.

Holladay supplied a letter written by a CPA[35] addressed to the board of Leeds & London in the Turks and Caicos saying the firm had $6 million in Treasury notes in a bank in New York to pay out any U.S. claims. That was enough to satisfy Gurnsey, a mistake that would ultimately cost him his business.

Years later, when the claims were piling up, Holladay suggested that Gurnsey place the company in bankruptcy. He did, but he hired LEMAY to sort out the claims and be fair to the injured. Tom was impressed that Gurnsey had used his own money to help them. "He was trying to do the right thing," Tom said. "He took care of himself, like any businessman would, but then he tried to take care of anyone else, too."

O'LEARY

Early Control Systems Inc. documents referred to another worker at CSI Systems besides Howard Holladay: Arthur "Jeff" O'Leary, but he was nowhere to be found in the later documents. McDermott wondered whether Jeff O'Leary might have quit CSI because he had developed some misgivings about Holladay. He tried to find him in Boston, but all he found was his ex-wife, who, based on his initial phone call, was in no mood to help anyone who had anything to do with her ex-husband. She kept saying she didn't know, they weren't in touch. Finally, on the third call, she said that Tom might find O'Leary in northern Florida, area code 904.

Tom set to work. He tracked O'Leary the way any computer illiterate would: He looked up every J. O'Leary in northern Florida until he found the right one. Tom flew down with a set of documents and met O'Leary, a dignified sixtyish man, in a hotel lobby restaurant, next to a ballroom noisy with an evangelical revival. O'Leary said he'd worked with Holladay setting up ABC to handle liquor liability risks for the hospitality industry with the help of a California lawyer named Daniel Simon.

So Tom realized Simon was a useful guy to have tried to question. What's more, O'Leary told Tom that when Simon didn't get paid, he sued Holladay. Simon had asked O'Leary to testify but then settled the case.

ABC had started off working with big insurance names, but when ABC strayed into other industries besides hospitality, those insurance companies backed out. When they left, O'Leary left, too. He said Holladay found a new insurance company through a friend in Louisiana named Barry Trevitech.

MATTHEW SCHELLENBERGER, 1986

Aside from O'Leary, Tom had another lead through Lemay's documents. He looked for suits against Holladay's previous insurance company, Colony Insurers, and found one. A Cleveland lawyer, Peter Weinberger sued Colony on behalf of the family of Matthew Schellenberger, a boy who was severely injured in a waterpark Holladay had underinsured.[36] Weinberger was completely open to talking to Tom. He certainly had nothing to hide. Many lawyers faded away when they met Holladay's stonewalling, but Weinberger had been clever. Holladay's insurance was so bad Weinberger sued the broker who sold the policy to the waterpark. He got more than $1 million for his clients. And he had a trove of documents on Holladay that he happily passed to Tom.

Putting the documents together with O'Leary's help, Tom pieced more of the history together.

Waterparks were a nascent industry in 1986. A joint between two plastic pieces stuck out onto the track of a high speed water slide at Ohio's Wildwood Lake. When a healthy Matthew Schellenberger, fifteen, went down the slide on June 7, 1986, his head hit this obstacle and snapped back. His brain was permanently injured.[37]

Matthew's father, Russ, said he was stunned when he learned that the owner of the park had designed the slide himself and not had anyone test its safety. The Schellenbergers first sued the waterpark for their son's care. The accident had practically scalped him and if not for the effort of a heroic lifeguard, Russ said, Matthew would have died in the pool. Although medical care could treat Matthew's urgent brain trauma, it wasn't yet advanced enough to help with the mood swings and depression that followed. He was probably one of the first human beings to survive with such a devastating brain wound. Eventually, he committed suicide.

The Schellenbergers realized it wouldn't be easy to get money for Matthew's injuries. The waterpark was transferring its assets, and the insurance company, Colony Insurers, acted as if it would fight the claim tooth and nail.

Weinberger and Colony met for a settlement conference, and that's when the company surprised them. The representative said Colony had no money.

"They would litigate extensively and make it look like they would have the wherewithal to defend the claim, but when push came to shove, when it was time to make [a] decision of whether or not to settle," Weinberger explained,[38] [39] "they would come in with the financials and say, 'You have a meritorious case, but if you hit us with a $1 million or $2 million verdict, it's going to throw the company into liquidation. We can only pay you a couple cents on the dollar.'" The bizarre financial papers showed Colony owned thousands of acres of land in South America. When push came to shove, Weinberger was warned the company was "a shell upon a shell" that would yield nothing.

As soon as Schellenberger, who has an accounting background, saw the documents, he thought that they "gave an odor of fraud or RICO violations that almost jumped off the page. I said 'Yo, there's a problem here.'"

Their best chance of seeing money was to accept the settlement, but Weinberger and the Schellenbergers decided to refuse the paltry offer and fight on. "What had happened to Matthew was so compelling. His father was [a] fighter [and] he was not going to just take what they gave him," Weinberger said. "When we got just a hint of how this insurance program was put together, it just stunk."

The insurance was so bad that Weinberger decided to sue the insurance agents who had sold it to the waterpark, essentially for malpractice. (This novel strategy wouldn't have worked for the later gun victims because Holladay had sold the policy directly to companies, with no broker in between.) The waterpark bought the policy through a major broker, Lockton Insurance Agency, which had an "errors and omissions" policy. The waterpark agreed to pay about $200,000 and assigned the Schellenbergers its right to sue over the policy. The insurance broker's insurance company paid about $1 million.

What kept nagging at Schellenberger was that the man who installed the slide didn't think about the ultimate consequence of having an unsafe slide that kids played on. Instead he just thought about getting cheap insurance. "The only reason anyone did anything was that people were willing to hand them a sheet of paper that said they had insurance for an unbelievably low price."

If it weren't for the bargain-rate insurance, Schellenberger thinks the waterpark would have been forced to get real insurance. And real insurance would have come with real safety conditions and inspections. "In my profession I know what insurance companies do and they would've had someone out there inspecting those things," he said. Were it not for the lousy insurance, Matthew Schellenberger might be alive.

LORCIN GOES UNDER, 1998

In early 1997 Lorcin emerged from bankruptcy protection, but not from trouble. Out of protection, it could again be sued in real courts. Over the next year and a half, that's just what happened: twenty-two cities and government agencies sued Lorcin for providing criminals in their cities with cheap, easy access to guns.[40] Some, like Elisa Barnes, claimed negligent distribution. Others would argue that Lorcin's cheap handguns created a public nuisance. Lorcin's sales had dropped significantly, from its high of 341,000 guns in 1993 to just 92,000 in 1997. But the company remained good at making the ATF's crime gun list. The Lorcin .380 clocked in at the number one position for guns traced to young criminals.[41] Meanwhile, California, tired of being home to the Ring of Fire, was getting ready to pass a law (with the help of former gun editor Whit Collins) that put handguns made there through tests like the ones foreign handguns had to pass to get imported to the United States.[42]

On August 7, 1998, Lorcin converted to Chapter 7 bankruptcy. The company was closing up shop.

For public consumption, Waldorf cited a deteriorating personal relationship with Errol Brown, his partner, as the reason for shuttering Lorcin. He also blamed the onslaught of municipal suits. Around the same time he was closing Lorcin, he filed papers to open another gun company, Standard Arms, in Reno, Nevada.

Gun supporters bemoaned the demise of gun companies, which they framed as a result of the pressure from politically motivated suits. The libertarian *Reason Magazine* blamed "municipalities looking to squeeze money out of the gun industry."[43] It's reasonable to connect the companies' collapse with the suits, but a cursory financial analysis shows the Ring of Fire companies weren't spending much on the political suits. The more responsible gun companies were pitching in for the common defense with a fund that the National Shooting Sports Foundation (NSSF) set up called the Hunting and Shooting Sports Heritage Fund. Even retailers who sold plenty more than guns, such as Bass Pro Shops or Field and Stream, kicked in. But, Lorcin or the other bankrupt Ring of Fire companies never joined. The low-end companies were, however, under serious pressure from basic product liability suits. That pressure was only severe because they didn't have adequate insurance for the quality and quantity of handguns they were selling.

What got little attention was what had happened to people who had settled with Lorcin: They got screwed again. The second part of their payments never materialized.

Meanwhile, the bankruptcy of Davis Industries[44] was playing out like a rerun of Lorcin, with all the same characters: Stomel, Holladay, and Judge Jury.

Stomel pushed Holladay even harder for answers in the Davis bankruptcy. After years of proclaiming that Leeds was absolutely safe, Holladay said the company was going out of business.[45]

Holladay then presented a letter he said he had received from a law firm called Ryan and Co. in the Bahamas. The letter said that Leeds had decided voluntarily to liquidate. Holladay said that he talked to "Mr. Kenneth E. V. Reid, the accountant with Ryan who is handling the liquidation . . . Ryan has shut down Leeds & London's insurance and other business operations." He went on to say that Leeds's lawyers have "been informed by Ryan that Leeds & London no longer has the funds to continue to pay their fees." So they quit. "Leeds & London has ceased to pay claims on existing insurance policies and has ceased to pay CSI for claims and administrative services. According to Mr. Reed, claims will be paid, if at all, in a percentage that is unknown, only at the conclusion of the liquidation. Leeds & London has therefore for all intents and purposes shut down and is out of business. As a result of the liquidation, I believe that Leeds & London will be unable to pay or defend the claims of Madonna L. Fultz, Robert Curtis, Celia and Rodolfo Campa and Malcolm and Mary Ann Stritzinger," people suing Davis for injuries.

After years of warning Judge Jury that this insurance company was unstable, Stomel was vindicated. Because bankrupt companies have to have insurance to operate, Davis was forced to buy it at market prices. Davis had to pay $250,000 for a $1 million policy.[46] They had bought a similar Leeds policy for $40,000.[47]

After the rash of gun company bankruptcies, particularly Lorcin, Sen. Carl Levin of Michigan introduced a bill to keep gun companies from going bankrupt in order to dodge lawsuits.[48] Waldorf was smart enough to realize that tort reform would become the rallying cry of his industry. "Tort reform is the determinant of whether we stay in the gun business or not," he said. "If we get tort reform, that will stick these lawyers' dicks in the dirt."

Meanwhile, without tort reform or Holladay's insurance, Waldorf's new company, Standard Arms, wasn't doing too well. He had to distribute the guns himself, and sales were nothing like the good old days.

SIMON V. HOLLADAY (1986)

After talking with O'Leary, Tom went to find the suit Holladay's own lawyer had filed against him.[49]

It started out as a simple billing dispute. According to the court papers, when Holladay formed Assurance Buyers Co-operative, he agreed to pay Daniel Simon $50,000 but paid only $20,000. Simon sued for the balance of his fee. He sued both but he didn't sue the flimsy company he had helped create—he knew that would get him nowhere. Simon sued Howard Holladay personally and Control Systems Inc. for the $30,000, plus he asked for $250,000 in punitive damages for "fraudulent and malicious conduct."

Holladay had tried to defend himself by arguing that he was only an agent of the principals who were on the board of Assurance Buyers Co-op.[50] He had been singing the same tune in the Lorcin bankruptcy. Now Tom was starting to see this as Holladay's modus operandi.

Simon replied in court papers that Control Systems and Holladay were really the same thing: "Plaintiff is informed and believes and thereon alleges that Defendant HOLLADAY was at all times herein mentioned, the owner of all the stock of Defendant CONTROL . . . there existed such a unity of interest in ownership between Defendant HOLLADAY and Defendant CONTROL, that any individuality and separateness between Defendant HOLLADAY, on the one hand, and Defendant CONTROL, on the other hand, have ceased, and Defendant CONTROL is the alter ego of Defendant HOLLADAY."

Simon argued that it "would promote fraud and sanction injustice" because Holladay has operated Control Systems Inc. "in an effort to avoid his obligations to Plaintiff and . . . substitute an insolvent corporation as the obligor of his own debts."

Simon also asked the judge to declare that Holladay and Control Systems were the same entity. The judge never issued such an order; instead, Holladay settled the case. So there wasn't a legal finding. If Tom had been able to find these court papers before the settlement of the Lorcin bankruptcy, he felt that the judge couldn't ignore the pattern.

ASSURANCE BUYERS CO-OP, 1985–1986: THE EARLY YEARS

In the late 1980s O'Leary did marketing for Holladay's insurance consulting business. He told Tom they thought Risk Retention Purchasing Groups would revolutionize the industry, and starting in 1985, when California passed a law to accommodate the groups, they worked on their own group so that they could get in on the ground floor.

They knew the hospitality industry—hotels and bars—needed insurance coverage. Hotels and bars were having a hard time getting insurance because of "dram shop" laws that would allow someone hit by a drunk driver to sue the bar where the driver had gotten sloshed.

Holladay already had a good connection with the hospitality industry through his college fraternity buddy, Sonny Seiler,[51] an influential Savannah attorney. Seiler has a few claims to fame. First, he is the caretaker of the University of Georgia dog dynasty. He has owned a series of beloved white bulldog mascots, each of which has been named UGA (the current mascot is UGA VI). And each must be charming enough to inspire the Georgia stadium to yell "Damn good dog!" Second, Seiler was the defense attorney in the case dramatized in *Midnight in the Garden of Good and Evil,* a murder in the eccentric high society of Savannah. Seiler was also the past president of the Georgia Bar Association and the president of the University of Georgia Alumni Association.

He and Holladay went to Daniel Simon, a California lawyer, to set up Assurance Buyers Co-op.

Once the group established ABC as a purchasing group, they had to buy some insurance. No U.S.–based company was interested. They went shopping offshore for both insurance, the main policy, and re-insurance, the back-up policy.

ABC worked out a deal with American British Insurance (ABI) of Bermuda., a prestigious firm. ABC would collect $5 million in premiums and American British Insurance would issue one master policy to Assurance Buyers Co-Op.[52] American British insisted on some safeguards: Damages were capped at $5 million, and ABC had to get some re-insurance.[53]

They started to negotiate the deal with Hannover RE for reinsurance. The group brought Simon to Germany because he had some connections there.

At first ABC seemed to get off the ground. Holladay and O'Leary would hold informational seminars around the country to recruit customers. They would sign these companies up as "members" of the co-op for a $25 fee. ABC incentivized clients to lower their risks. It offered a 5 percent discount for attending a class on "alcohol awareness." It raised rates if there was live entertainment or dancing.[54]

The big problems started after ABC overstepped its bounds with the insurance giants. After a seminar in St. Louis, an insurance agent asked Holladay and O'Leary out for a business drink. He explained that he worked for Lockton Insurance Agency, a big broker in town. Lockton had sold insurance to waterparks, but the insurance carrier had just said it wasn't going to renew the policy. The guy was panicked: It was nearly summer, waterpark season.

ABC accepted the waterparks as members without approval from American British or Hannover RE, the companies that would have to pay out claims on these policies if ABC undercharged for the risk.

That one step radically changed the business plan.

By the time American British realized what was going on, Assurance Buyers Co-op and the Lockton Insurance Agency had already issued liability policies to waterparks around America. ABI was not happy. It had $1.4 million in premiums in the Assurance Buyers account, but only $600,000 was from the hospitality industry it had agreed to insure. Another $400,000 was from the waterparks, and another $400,000 was from various businesses in other fields that Holladay had signed up. All these changes to the agreement were unacceptable to American British, and it pulled out of the deal.[55] The implications for ABC and its clients were enormous: It meant there was no real insurance in their insurance policy. The only thing they had was all the money that had been collected in premiums so far.

In August, Lockton got another letter from another ticked-off overseas insurer, Hannover RE.[56] Its officials had gotten wind that Lockton was selling a Risk Purchasing Group policy in America to waterparks that claimed Hannover RE was the re-insurer. The letter abruptly stated: "Please be advised that neither Hannover Re nor [its Illinois subsidiary] is participating in this program. Preliminary discussions with the principals of the Assurance Buyers Co-op Inc. and Hannover Re were terminated, and any quotes which we may have given have been withdrawn."

When the big insurance carriers backed out, Holladay scrambled for another offshore carrier. O'Leary said that one of Holladay's insurance cronies from Louisiana, Barry Trevitech, helped Holladay find a company through a friend called Island Group, Ltd. O'Leary knew nothing about this Island Group. Compared with the previous insurers, which had international reputations, it was like going from Marshall Field's to a street vendor plunked outside the store. O'Leary thought it was all too risky. He walked away.

BARRY TREVITECH, LOUISIANA

Tom brought Ron Lemay, who had interviewed Trevitech before, along with him to Louisiana. The first time he didn't get much information, but this time Trevitech was gaunt with cancer and he spoke freely. Tom guessed it was either because he knew he wouldn't be around long enough to get into trouble or because he wanted to make amends. He was so weak that he sometimes needed to rest from the exertion of their conversations.

Trevitech said he and Holladay went to a little insurance company for ABC after the big insurance companies had backed out. A Florida businessman named Bob Entin ran an insurance company called Island Group in the Turks and Caicos. After a while, though, Entin wanted out. That's when Trevitech and Holladay hatched the idea of starting their own Turks and Caicos insurance company, Colony Insurers. To seem more legit, they would need the backing of an onshore company, and Trevitech found one right in the neighborhood. The company turned out to be a big fraud that walked away with all of Colony's money. They collapsed Colony, and Holladay took control of a new company in the Turks called Leeds & London.

Meanwhile, Tom tracked down Sonny Seiler[57] and asked him how he got mixed up in all this. Seiler said he had just worked on a project with his college friend, but got out early on.[58] He even faxed Tom his letter of resignation[59]—he had quit before things got strange.

After talking with Trevitech, Tom tracked down Entin, who confirmed his role. Then, with the help of court documents and Lemay's research, he was able to piece together the rest of the story.

ISLAND, COLONY, AND LOUISIANA UNDERWRITERS (1986–1988)

When American British Insurance and Hannover RE backed out, Trevitech said he helped Holladay find Bob Entin, a Miami businessman who ran an insurance company in the Turks and Caicos called Island Group, Ltd.

Entin had some conditions for Holladay to use his Turks company.[60] Lockton would do inspections and get a fee. Damages were capped at $5 million. He didn't want the insurance sold in his home state of Florida to steer clear of violating state laws.

After Entin pulled out, Trevitech said he and Holladay figured they could just set up their own company without Entin. After all, the Turks and Caicos was one of many small governments around the world that offer competitively lax corporate registrations to attract entrepreneurs: the Cook Islands in the South Pacific, Malta in the Mediterranean, Dubai, Hong Kong, Mauritius in the Indian Ocean, the Isle of Man (between England and Ireland), Gibraltar, and (to a lesser extent) even Delaware.

The Turks had two advantages. Turks law makes it a crime for government employees to divulge who is behind secret companies. And it's only a daily, seventy-five-minute flight from Miami.

Businessmen show up and either start up their company or they pick up a premade company off their lawyer's shelf. These so-called shelf or shell corporations don't exist in the real world. They just spend years waiting for someone to breathe life into them. The early incorporation date can lend an air of desperately desired legitimacy. Lawyers' doors are decorated with hundreds of tiny little signs indicating all the corporations that claim to be based there.

Holladay put "Since 1981" on Leeds & London's letterhead.

Trevitech said that he and Holladay started Colony Insurers in 1986 with the $1 million left over in premiums they collected from ABC members while they were using Island Group as their carrier. They also had lots of leftover clients who thought they were insured. The $1 million was all Trevitech and Holladay possessed; they had no real insurance company.

Trevitech said Holladay worked out a deal with the son of the manager of the hotel at which he stayed on Grand Turk Island: Every week or two, the kid would gather up all the mail for Colony in a box and mail it to Holladay's office in Boston. Then Holladay and his assistant would answer all the letters, put them back in a box, and mail it off to the hotel manager's son in the Turks and Caicos. Holladay would pay the kid to mail it from there so that each piece would have a Turks and Caicos stamp. That way it would look as if there was a whole operation percolating in the Caribbean.

In the 1980s, the Turks and Caicos allowed two types of insurance companies: domestic companies, which it regulated, and "exempt" insurance companies, which it didn't because the companies did their business overseas. Trevitech explained the operation in a 1990 deposition (for a case we'll get to in a bit). He said Colony was "authorized to do business anyplace in the world except the Turks and Caicos Islands." Eugene Palmer, the Austin lawyer asking Trevitech the questions for the deposition,[1] then pressed him: was he allowed to sell insurance in the United States? Well, the Turks charter allowed him to do it, Trevitech explained.

"And this company has never had a certificate of authority to do business in the United States?" Palmer asked.

"That's right, sir," Trevitech answered.

"Do you consider that you personally as a result of this are engaged in the unauthorized business of insurance?" the lawyer asked, incredulous.

"No, sir," Trevitech answered.

"Do you think that you can operate an insurance company without a charter?" Palmer asked.

"The insurance company does have a charter," Trevitech insisted.

"Sir?" asked Palmer.

"I am operating an insurance company under the authority of the country in which the company was incorporated and domiciled," Trevitech said.

"Well, if you issue policies in this country, those policies are subject to the law of the state in which they are issued, are they not?" Palmer asked.

"No, sir," Trevitech boldly responded.

"You can just sell insurance to anybody in the United States without complying with the laws of the state?" Palmer asked. "Yes, sir," Trevitech responded confidently.

"I'm sure the Commissioner in Louisiana will find that to be a novel theory," Palmer concluded.

Eventually Holladay and Trevitech decided they were tired of all the complaints about Colony's exotic locale and decided to shop for an American insurance outfit. Big insurers would have nothing to do with them.

They couldn't set up a real insurance company themselves in the States; that would be too arduous and expensive. Instead they looked for a "front" company, an arrangement that sounds fishy but is legal. A "front" insurance company lends out its name and good standing to a lesser company—for a price.

Trevitech thought himself lucky when he found such a company right across the street from his own Lafayette office.

"I was always on the search for a company that was domiciled someplace in the United States that would be willing to take on the risk of premiums that were offered," Trevitech said in his deposition. "Louisiana Underwriters Insurance Company came to my attention, and so I negotiated a contract with them."

The folks at Louisiana Underwriters even told Trevitech that he was their first client, but that didn't scare him.

The plan was for Louisiana Underwriters to funnel $1.1 million from Colony through its accounts and give $1 million back. Colony would have $1 million left to pay claims and Louisiana Underwriters would keep $100,000 for the use of its insurance license.

What Trevitech and Holladay didn't recognize is that they had just stumbled into a gang of grifters. The people behind Louisiana Underwriters, Ferrell Travis Riley and his wife Cheryll Coon, although acquitted in Louisiana, would eventually be convicted of bribery, racketeering, and fraud. They started up and shut down insurance companies across the country, used the old "I'm not subject to this state's laws because my insurance company is domiciled elsewhere" trick, had registrations in the Turks and Costa Rica and even had a company called Lloyds. They took off with $1.1 million from Colony. According to a 1994 General Accounting Office report,[62] Riley spent $200,000 of Colony's money for a trip to Monte Carlo and $50,000 on "rugs, paintings, vases, scrolls and sculpture for personal use."

Holladay and Trevitech tried to sue them to get the money back—that's the case that Trevitech's deposition was a part of. But Louisiana Underwriters was in bankruptcy, so its case was stayed. Riley didn't give Holladay his money back, but he may have given him some ideas.

With the money gone, Holladay and Trevitech saw in 1989 that they would have nothing to pay off any of Colony's claims.

To put off any potential claims from people injured under Colony's policies, Trevitech got a friend of his, an accountant who just happened to have worked in the state insurance regulator's office, to send out letters saying that Colony had collapsed. Bob Gurnsey of National Survival Games, waterpark operators, and other business owners got the December 12, 1989 letter telling them they no longer had insurance. What had seemed like an outlandish story from Holladay about Louisiana Underwriters turned out to be true.

LEEDS & LONDON (1990–1999)

Holladay and Trevitech could have stopped the operation after Colony's insurance pool was stolen, but instead they thought they could fix the situation by taking in yet more clients and premiums. Looking to drum up business, Holladay went to the gun industry's annual convention, the SHOT Show in Las Vegas. He met Jim Waldorf, who became his first big client in the gun industry.

A month after Howard Holladay collapsed Colony, he took over a new company down in the Turks and Caicos: Leeds & London. Its address was a post office box at a law firm that specializes in setting up offshore companies.

No one is sure exactly how Howard Holladay found Leeds, which had been sitting around waiting for an owner since 1981, but when he animated Leeds in 1990, Holladay found plenty of willing customers for cheap insurance from his new company.

Nine

TIGHTENING THE NOOSE: MORE DOCUMENTS, MORE CASES

If Howard Holladay's insurance empire had been a literal a jigsaw puzzle, Tom McDermott would have formed the corners and edges by 2000. He knew Holladay started Assurance Buyers Co-op to cover restaurants and hotels and had strong backing. But when Holladay let waterparks in on the policy, the big-name companies backed out. He scrambled to find a replacement company and came up with Island Group, run out of the Turks and Caicos. When the owner wanted out, Holladay had Trevitech set up his own company, Colony Insurers. Craving the legitimacy of an onshore company, Holladay turned the money over to Louisiana Underwriters to act as a "front," but that company made off with all the insurance premiums. He and his friend Barry Trevitech collapsed Colony, and Holladay then started Leeds & London.

He felt sure he had enough documents to prove in court that Holladay was really behind all these collapsed insurance entities. Meanwhile, he kept worrying if Holladay was still around. Every once in a while he'd call his Boston townhouse and make a discreet inquiry as to where he was.

But he didn't want to let Holladay blindside him in court, either. So he kept investigating, hoping to find more proof the whole insurance empire had been a farce. He also needed to fill in a few holes in the story. He needed to find out if any state had gone after Holladay's insurance companies. And he needed to know what had happened to Leeds between the time when Holladay took it over in the Turks in 1990 and when it showed up in Costa Rica four years later.

THE STATE CASES: MARYLAND AND TEXAS

McDermott found only two state insurance cases against Holladay. Maryland had discovered Holladay was selling unauthorized insurance to carnival rides, but it didn't punish him. The state just ordered Leeds to knock it off, or, in the words of the consent agreement, "cease and desist . . . until properly registered." Howard Holladay signed the agreement on August 25, 1994.[1]

Compare Holladay to anyone who used the cheap handguns he insured. A robber who got caught holding up a liquor store for $100 would go to jail. Holladay used this insurance to take in millions, but all he had to do was promise not to do it again.

Texas investigated Holladay after Elizabeth Saunders, who ran American Derringer, a small gun company she had inherited from her husband, complained. Here Tom got help from both sides, from the gun company and the shooting victim.

In 2000 Saunders was still, amazingly, writing out monthly checks to Holladay. Once again, it was a surcharge to repay a large claim. A gun fell, went off, and crippled an aspiring actress. Because the surcharge was part of Saunders's plan to get out of bankruptcy, she felt she had to keep paying it.[2] So each month she would send a check to Holladay's company in Boston. Months later the checks would come back, stamped by a bank in the Bahamas.[3]

Saunders was furious at Holladay, frustrated that the Texas insurance department said it didn't think it could find him. Tom was never quite sure if Elizabeth Saunders or her late husband understood what they were (or weren't) getting for the $30,000 a year they were paying.

Meanwhile, Tom had found the injured gun owner, too. Connie Terry had gotten a meager settlement after Holladay threatened her lawyer that if she didn't take this little money, she would get nothing because the insurance company would collapse. Terry's lawyer didn't want Tom to mess with Terry's settlement deal, but Terry helped Tom anyway.

With Saunders and Terry, Tom was able to piece together another part of the puzzle:

American Derringer occupies an old car dealership on a dusty highway not far from the site of the Branch Davidian Compound in Waco, Texas., Elizabeth Saunders, American Derringer's co-owner, has tried to pretty up the grimy office with cheerful floral wallpaper and a battalion of Betty Boop dolls.

Since 1980 American Derringer has made derringers—the kind of tiny, one- or two-shot handguns that killed President Lincoln. Its guns sell for about $400. The company tests each one out back in a shed. When Elizabeth (who has an MBA from nearby Baylor University) introduced the "Lady Derringer" in an effort to sell guns to women, the move was so successful that bigger companies copied it. Soon after Howard Holladay started showing up at the SHOT Shows, her husband met him and signed up for his low-priced insurance.

In 1990, Connie Terry decided to move from her boyfriend's house in Texas to Las Vegas, where she had an acting contract.[4] She'd grown up with guns, felt safer traveling with one, so she packed a recent gift from a family friend, an American Derringer, into her bag. The double safety was on, but when the gun fell out, it shot her in the ankle.

The doctor wanted to amputate her foot immediately, but she insisted on trying to keep it. It would be three years and eighteen surgeries before she could walk again. She had lost three-and-a-half inches off one leg and needed an implanted rod, which was gradually expanded for an excruciating year.

"You have to put a wrench in there and you have to crank it twice a day. Talk about pain," Terry says. "Don't get me wrong: I was thrilled to walk again. But every time I went in, the doctors would say, 'Let's just hope the leg doesn't turn black.'" She blew through an inheritance on the surgeries but a friend put her in touch with a lawyer who researched American Derringer's million-dollar policy with Leeds. "It seemed like it would be okay," Terry says. "It didn't seem like anything would be funny 'til the very end."

In 1993, everyone met in Dallas. By this time, Bob Saunders was dying of cancer. Terry's lawyer went in to the negotiations hoping for $1.8 million. Howard Holladay showed up saying he was there for CSI. He made his first offer: $25,000. Terry sat in a room down the hall and the Saunders family sat in a hotel a few miles away, neither party knowing what was going on in the negotiations between Terry's lawyer and Howard Holladay.

Midway through the negotiations, Connie Terry met Holladay.

"What I remember most of all is I had to go to the restroom," says Terry. "I had these pins on my legs and there was this walker. I had to turn it and kind of jump sideways. If you can imagine trying to hold the walker, jump sideways, turn on the light and hold the door. When I was finished, coming out, there was that man, Mr. Holladay. That S.O.B., I had to hold the door for him. Here I am in a walker and here he is standing with his hands in front of him, folded. It made me feel like he really doesn't give a damn about me as a person, as a human being. I wish I had slammed it on his ass, that S.O.B."

Terry got occasional discouraging updates, then her lawyer came in and told her that $305,000 was the best she could do and advised her to take the offer. The lawyer told her that Holladay had said the company was "a shell upon a shell upon a shell" and if they took it to court, he'd just collapse the company. The lawyer told her, "'This man is a damn crook.' He said I could

look for him and I would waste my time because I could never find him."
"The real kicker" Terry said, was that she had to sign an agreement to keep
her mouth shut. "Here I felt like they made me a victim all over again."

Terry didn't even tell the details to her ex-boyfriend at the time of the accident, who helped her recover, then married her. "My husband said jokingly
to me, 'How can I sue that bastard? He did more for me than anybody.'"

Saunders said she didn't know what was going on in the negotiations—
or that Holladay had just said the insurance was basically worthless.
Months later, after Bob died and Elizabeth took over the business, Holladay would visit Texas and try to woo her to keep the business. He would
take her out to restaurants, buying her $200 bottles of wine and talking
about his yachts.

Meanwhile, Saunders, who looks far younger than her fifty-something
years, had begun to pose on the company website in lingerie to attract business. Plus, she was facing more bills and lawsuits. Holladay told her just to
declare bankruptcy and all the lawsuits would go away. She said she was
skeptical, but he kept nudging her, so finally she put American Derringer
into Chapter 11 bankruptcy protection in 1995.

As soon as she filed for bankruptcy, Saunders said, Holladay's attitude
changed. He said her late husband Bob had agreed to pay a special surcharge to pay him back for the Connie Terry claim. When Saunders filed
for bankruptcy protection, the judge told her to maintain her insurance
coverage—no matter what. So she kept sending the surcharge of $205 a
month to Holladay, even though she was no longer covered by Leeds.

JONES WINS—SORT OF: OCTOBER 15, 2001

The one victory Tom could savor was the Jones case in Kentucky. The Jones
family had effective advocates in Jackie Schroering and Harry Gregory:
they got special permission to litigate their case in Kentucky while the
bankruptcy proceeding was still going on. They added another cause of action: bad faith insurance settlement against Control Systems Inc. and Leeds
& London. Holladay first hired an expensive firm, which moved the case
to federal court, Schroering said, but when the lawyers weren't paid, the
firm withdrew and Jones won by default.

Since the accident, Timmy Jones's parents had been sending what
money they could to Alaska, where Jones's first wife was raising Timmy's
two teenagers, to try to make up for the money Timmy used to send. Myrna
said she still terribly misses Timmy. She describes him as sweetly trusting
and tall and handsome like her husband, with a full head of red-brown
hair: "He used to come by and say, Momma, can you trim my hair? And
we'd laugh and I'd say that his hair is as coarse as horse's hair."

Ownensboro federal Judge Joseph H. McKinley, Jr. ordered Lorcin to pay Jimmy Jones's family $560,000 in the product liability case[5] in March of 2001. Jones was making $20,000 a year as a truck driver, so his lost potential lifetime earnings were modest. The judge ordered $6,500 for medical bills, $3,500 for funeral expenses, and $50,000 for suffering for days before he died.

In his written decision in favor of Jones he found that "the Lorcin pistol was defectively designed and manufactured, and those defects rendered it unreasonably dangerously defective." If the safety hadn't been so lousy, Jones would be alive, he said.

Seven months later, McKinley came back with an even more harsh ruling against Holladay's companies, which he ordered to pay $440,000 in punitive damages, bringing the total to an even million bucks.[5] Because there was no one to pay up, what was more important was his fifteen-page opinion.

McKinley wrote: "It appears fairly obvious to the Court, that neither CSI, nor Leeds, nor its affiliate 'ABC,' never really existed at all, as any kind of bona-fide insurer. . . . Leeds appears to have been a fiction of the imagination of CSI, designed to lend the appearance of credibility and integrity to a financially irresponsible scheme for retention of the unusually onerous risks of product liability claims against Lorcin."

McKinley also wondered in his opinion how many times Holladay's company had wasted some other court's time.

After that victory, Tom thought about a next step: filing a claim on behalf of all the people who had been injured by all of the products that Howard Holladay pretended to insure. He would lure Rusty Brace,[7] an expert in offshore insurance scams, to join his team. Brace, who would often leave his Santa Barbara office when the surf was good, had never intended to handle insurance cases. But he had one elderly client who had been ripped off. No one else had gone after the sprawling international fraud, so Brace decided to do it. He won and even earned a rare letter of praise from a federal judge for his work.

When Brace and McDermott met, they would sheepishly ask each other: "So when are we going to get around to filing that suit?" There was always one more witness to interview, one more document to obtain. But too often, these inquires opened up new avenues of research. They put off filing the case as they looked for more evidence.

DOCUMENTATION FROM TURKS AND COSTA RICA

Tom called down to the Turks registrar's office to find some details on Leeds's formation. He kept getting the same sympathetic clerk who would whisper again and again that it would be a crime to reveal the secret documents. The clerk couldn't divulge who was on the papers—but told Tom something even more interesting: The company had effectively been kicked out of the Turks and Caicos because it could not meet even the islands' rules.

The world was not completely oblivious to the racket these corporate havens had going. Bowing somewhat to international pressure, in 1989, the Turks passed a law that even the "exempt" insurance companies that operated overseas had to start submitting financial applications the next year. In 1990 Leeds met the deadline but not the requirements; the application was rejected in 1991 as incomplete, insufficiently demonstrating its financial stability. Leeds tried again but again failed. In 1992, it was forced to close up shop. Once Tom had all the details, he got a higher official to confirm them for him.[7]

Tom had now nearly pieced together virtually the entire Leeds history and found an incredible gap: For two years—1993 and 1994—Leeds wasn't registered in the Turks or Costa Rica. As far as McDermott knew, it wasn't registered anywhere on earth. And this was while Lorcin was producing 755,846 low-quality handguns, some of which would be blowing up in people's hands, firing when dropped, and otherwise injuring people for decades to come.

Now that Tom had documents showing when Leeds got kicked out of the Turks & Caicos, he had to get the documents showing when it started up again in Costa Rica. Way back on the Hamilton case he had hired the lawyer Rodrigo Soto, who had outlined the basics of the public registration. Holladay's lawyer Raven gave them some additional details and initially said he would cooperate. But like so many people Tom encountered on this investigation, he later seemed to get cold feet. He never sent the documents he promised, he stopped returning calls. Tom had seen this pattern before and he had an answer for it: He showed up in person, unannounced, in March 2001.

Raven's office building, the official address of Leeds & London, was unimpressive even by the low-slung standards of San José. "I'd be hard pressed to realize it was a law office," Tom said. It was a one-story cinderblock house. Inside, however, it was a different story, with plush accommodations and three receptionists. Three businessmen sat in the waiting area.

Tom, wearing a suit and looking official, announced in a loud voice that he was there to see Raven. A receptionist said Raven was in Miami for the rest of the week. Here was the weakness in the dropping-in-unannounced maneuver. "I've come down here from the United States to investigate an insurance fraud that this firm may be involved in," he said. Tom had hired a local former prosecutor to approach the authorities. He noticed the three businessmen stop talking and look over at him. "I have an appointment with the prosecutor's office tomorrow, so by then it may be too late for him." The receptionist in charge ushered him into a conference room and within half an hour, she had Raven on the phone with him. Raven flew back from Miami that night.

The next morning Tom laid out for Raven the documents that showed the story of Holladay's empire. Tom convinced Raven to help, but by now, Raven said, he didn't know where the documents were.

The next morning Raven sent two clerks to a warehouse. At two in the afternoon he called Tom: They had the documents.[9] Raven turned the whole thick file over to Tom. For good measure, Tom also got a proclamation from the Costa Rican government saying Leeds never had permission to run an insurance company there. He got an official translation of the documents from the Ministry of Foreign Affairs and Worship.[10] Tom also got Raven's affidavit telling the whole story.[11] Raven laid out that Holladay had used Raven's law office address, but that there was no real insurance business there and nobody at his firm—not even the clerks whose names were on the Leeds documents—ever worked for or owned any part of the insurance company. The documents were crucial for any court case if Tom ever was able to bring Holladay to court. He was getting closer and closer to catching up to Holladay, but he was perpetually a few steps—or a few Caribbean islands—behind.

Raven's report directly contradicted Holladay, who claimed he didn't have anything to do with Leeds. Holladay used the odd arrangement with the legal assistant proxies to make believe there was some distance between himself and Leeds. When asked what his relationship was to Leeds, Holladay denied there had been anything wrong with his companies or that he controlled Leeds. He called McDermott a "jerk" and his allegations "fabulous" and "ridiculous." He would claim: "Leeds was run by several attorneys and several Costa Rican attorneys' law firm." The documents signing over the company to him? "I lent them my name, yes. But that was at the onset when they were applying for their charter [corporate registration]. You've got to have somebody's name as an officer."[12]

HOW MUCH IS A MANGLED HAND WORTH?
MEDIA, PENNSYLVANIA, APRIL 10, 2002

Tom found the Malcolm and Mary Ann Stritzinger case in the Davis bankruptcy. Malcolm Stritzinger was the part owner of a gun shop. He was a clean dealer; he didn't sell Saturday Night Specials. His motivation wasn't just altruistic: The guns had a low margin and attracted "lowlifes" to his store.[12] But when a woman came in pleading for a cheap gun to protect her from a menacing ex, a clerk took pity on her and ordered her a $50 Davis

.22 from a wholesaler while Stritzinger was out. When she returned days later with a malfunctioning gun, Stritzinger volunteered to fix it himself.

On February 4, 1991, Stritzinger took the gun to the local firing range. On the first shot, the gun exploded. Since then, his right hand has been little more than a fleshy claw.

The Stritzingers' first lawyer gave up on tracking down Holladay. When McDermott revived the case, no one showed up on the defense side. He won, mostly through filing motions.[14] Because Malcolm was a gun professional, no one would have accused him of mishandling the gun or bringing the suit for anti-gun sentiments. Forensics later showed that the firing pin that is supposed to hit the bullet went through the chamber, and the bullet went out the wrong direction. The judge had quickly decided a few months before that Davis Industries, or at least its insurance company, Leeds & London, owed Stritzinger a lot of money. The one thing required was a hearing on April 10, 2002, to determine how much money—illusory or not—the court would award to Malcolm and Mary Ann Stritzinger.

This courtroom, in a posh, Main Line suburb of Philadelphia, wasn't the typical venue for this ethereal, political sort of case. There were no marble pillars or worn hardwood fixtures. This upscale strip mall of a courtroom had fresh, low-pile blue carpeting and practical—not soaring—ceilings. At the metal detector, guards handed out pretend sheriff badges to kids awaiting adoption.

McDermott was now fifty-eight and now looked more like Brian Dennehy; he had a bit less white hair and a few more pounds than when he had faced down Colin Ferguson's Ruger. Tom's enthusiasm and passion were the only things that kept this process going.

The hearing started with McDermott piling document after document on the judge's bench. He realized he had left one in his car trunk. The judge reluctantly agreed to let him fetch it after court "even though it seems like the judgment is probably uncollectible."

Tom had driven down the night before from Long Island so he could be well rested and prepared. Normally a crisp dresser, McDermott was even more fastidious in court. He wore a blue pin-striped suit, yellow tie, and a big smile on his pink face. He wore gold wire-framed glasses, except when he took them off to gesture. In addition to wearing a wedding ring, he wore one of his son Ryan's college lacrosse championship rings. Even his fingernails were polished. No matter the courthouse, McDermott reveled in courtroom manners and procedure. Even in everyday conversation, if he misspoke about anything—driving directions, anything—he would snap, "Strike that," as if interrupting a stenographic record of events.

Malcolm, sixty-one, wore oversized wire-framed glasses and a long-sleeved brown polo shirt over his belly. The couple would later testify these were not fashion choices, but the only options Malcolm could manage because his fingers could no longer manipulate buttons or contact lenses. He was a big man with big, loose movements.

Mary Ann, who now supported the couple with her office job at Sunoco's Philadelphia office, moved in a more nervous and precise way. She wore a beige cashmere twin set and sedate gold jewelry. The Stritzingers had both grown up around Philly and both spoke in its unmistakable accent, pronouncing house "hauwse," very "vurray."

The Stritzingers' first lawyer was an old family friend who hit a dead-end when Davis went out of business. Years later, when McDermott called offering to revive the case, the Stritzingers were uneasy because Tom worked on contingency—meaning he would get paid only if and when he won money. The couple didn't like that McDermott was doing all this work for free. They would have been even more worried if they knew his usual rate was over $300 an hour.

McDermott put Malcolm on the witness stand and asked him to describe getting shot. "It was just like a stick of dynamite going off in my hand. It burned awful," Stritzinger testified. His right index finger was left dangling. His left thumb was broken. Gun pieces had flown in every direction with the force of bullets. Emergency workers would find gun fragments a hundred yards away.

The judge interrupted Stritzinger. "You still seem to have all your fingers," he inquired. For a moment Stritzinger paused in discomfort. He had not expected to become a physical exhibit today, only a witness. He told the judge that the emergency room doctors were just about to cut off his right index finger when the plastic surgeon arrived. The surgeon told Stritzinger that he would never regain use of his finger, "but he could attach it cosmetically." Stritzinger, of course, wanted to keep his finger. "To be honest with you, though, it would've been better if they'd cut it off."

The judge again interrupted. How much could he use his hand? Could he make a fist? Stritzinger obliged once again. He tried to make a fist but showed that the best he could do was cup his hand.

McDermott then went into the damage the gun had done to Stritzinger's life. "With respect to the pain, sir, do you feel pain every day?'

"It's like an explosion," Stritzinger replied. "You see stars."

McDermott asked him to describe his life before the incident. Stritzinger used to hunt, fish and garden in his spare time. Aside from the gun shop, which was more of a hobby than a job, he was a maintenance man for a complex near the Jersey Shore. His whole family, four kids and eight grandchildren, used to spend summers by the beach. He had to quit that job since the accident because he couldn't work the computer.

McDermott asked him to describe his typical day now.

"I get up, drink the coffee my wife has made before she went to work, then maybe eat a Danish. I read a newspaper, then go back to bed. If the pain is too bad, I take Percocet or Oxycontin. It's terrible. I don't like to take either of them. I'll set around for a while. Read another newspaper when I wake up."

McDermott kept an even, upbeat professional tone as he started probing more personal issues. Occasional swearing aside, McDermott has a straight arrow demeanor. No topic would be less likely for him to want to discuss than another middle-aged couple's sex life. But he drilled on, as if the topic were perfectly ordinary. He needed to, because Mary Ann was suing for loss of her husband's "consortium"—that is, sex and companionship.

McDermott asked Stritzinger how the injury had affected his relationship with his wife. Despite McDermott's preparation, Stritzinger was ill at ease.

"I feel sorry for my wife a lot of the time for the way I treat her," Malcolm said. "I'm very short-tempered."

What about their social life, McDermott asked?

"There isn't any, anymore. It's embarrassing. I can't eat. I'm right-handed and you try to eat left-handed and the food falls down."

What about his "marital relations and responsibilities"? Had the injury affected those?

"Yes, it has. She has her own bedroom and I have mine," Stritzinger said. "Yes, we don't have sex no more."

Next Mary Ann took the stand and started talking about their life before the accident. "It was a normal family relationship. It was a good relationship," she said. "We were normal people. We were active. We were able to have a beautiful family."

If she had hoped to fend off more sex questions with that generality, it didn't work. Again, McDermott had to push for a more direct response about their sex life. "Once or twice a week?" McDermott asked.

"Give or take," she responded. "A thought comes to mind what my mother says: every Saturday night whether you need it or not."

At night Malcolm would have nightmares about the gun going off in his hand. He slept restlessly, if at all. He would wake up screaming. If he bumped his hand, he would yowl in pain.

"I think sometimes . . . well, I know," she said, "that the gun goes off over and over again when he sleeps at night."

After she sat down, the judge told McDermott, "I don't think you need to make a closing argument. I think I understand."

"I think you do," McDermott said.

To add to the convivial atmosphere, the judge told McDermott, "Come back to Delaware County any time you need to." McDermott grinned.

After the hearing, the judge called him up to the bench. What was the purpose of all this? He understood the tragedy, but he didn't understand why McDermott was going to all this bother when there was no one to pay at the end.

"Insurance fraud," McDermott was happy to explain. The judge wanted to know how other courts had ruled. McDermott proudly pointed to the recently adjudicated Jones case in Kentucky. Different gun company, same insurer.

Afterwards, McDermott took his clients out for breakfast at a nearby diner. Malcolm showed up for breakfast with his hand bleeding and wrapped up. He'd bumped it on a doorway. Since he had lost most sensation, it often accidentally hit things. Afraid of spilling his food, Malcolm was the only one in the group not to order breakfast.

McDermott assured them once again that he hoped to get them money, not just satisfaction.

"I don't want them to get away with this, I really don't," Stritzinger said. Money, at this point, was not going to solve his problems: He continually tells his wife, "I have no life. They may as well close the box on me now."

McDermott explained again how he was going to find more and more people like the Stritzingers, people who had been injured by products this one insurance company insured. And he would make the man responsible pay.

"This insurance policy is not worth, it's not worth as much . . . as much as . . ." McDermott struggled to find an analogy. "As this menu," he said. He tapped the diner's plastic-coated menu on the table for effect.

"All those people who filed claims got nothing," McDermott says. "What do we do? All those lawyers have disappointed clients. I have proof."

BAHAMAS

There were now only a few pieces missing from the puzzle. Tom wanted a few more documents—even just affidavits—to verify what people had told him.

Tom's last step was Ryan and Co. in the Bahamas, the outfit that had supposedly written to Holladay out of the blue and told him that it was liquidating Leeds during the Davis bankruptcy.

Just after Leeds's collapse, McDermott tracked down Derek Ryan, proprietor of Ryan and Co. Tom found, as he suspected, a young lawyer oblivious to Holladay's larger scheme or his own role in keeping it running. A lawyer at Ryan's previous law firm sent him Holladay's business. When it looked as if Ryan wasn't going to stop working for Holladay, McDermott called the island's insurance commissioner, who told Ryan it was inappropriate for him to liquidate a company that had nothing to do with the Bahamas. Ryan had even told the Davis bankruptcy he was not involved.

Now Tom kept calling Ryan, trying to get documents from him.

"Holy Christ," Tom practically yelled at him. "You are involved in a massive insurance fraud."

Then Tom pulled a McDermott on him.

Tom took Rosemary on a cruise to celebrate their wedding anniversary in 2003. The cruise stopped in the Bahamas. Tom went to Ryan's office at 10:00A.M., telling Rosemary he would take just an hour. Ryan wasn't there. Tom camped out for hours, well into the afternoon, and he had no way to reach Rosemary to tell her what was going on. Ryan finally came in at 4:00P.M. They spent two hours going over Tom's documents. Tom convinced Ryan that Holladay's operation was a fraud, but Ryan worried about attorney-client privilege—and getting sued by Holladay for breaking it. Ryan wanted to get advice from his own lawyer before he committed to anything.

But he did tell Tom something interesting. Holladay had set up two other Bahamian companies in the 1990s: Universal Management and Apex Risk Management. And any funds that came in for Leeds—like Elizabeth Saunders's checks—went into Universal's bank account.

Tom went back to the boat and found Rosemary understandably furious. It was a three-day cruise and Tom had spent an entire day of it with Derek Ryan instead of Rosemary.

He apologized but reminded her of something she herself had once said: that it was annoying for him to spend all this time on his quest, that it was a hassle to have vacations diverted for research and to waste hours waiting for him to interview yet another witness. But it was a lot better than if Tom had succumbed to some inane midlife crisis hobby like racecars or boats.

And it sure beat his being dead. Or needing to be pushed around in a wheelchair.

And those options were the fate they had so narrowly avoided on the 5:33.

For all of his trouble, though, when Tom got back to New York, Ryan changed his mind about cooperating and swearing out an affidavit. Months later he told Tom to stop calling.

Tom was in Florida on business in 2003 and arranged to take a quick flight down to the Bahamas to stop in on Ryan again.

"When he came out of his office, he recognized me, he told me to leave, that I was not welcome," Tom said. "He had no time for me, he didn't care what I did, but I couldn't do it there."

They got into an argument over Ryan's broken promises. Tom had been playing the affable prosecutor long enough. Now he switched gears and blustered a threat to name Ryan as a co-conspirator in a RICO suit. After all, why was Ryan protecting Holladay instead of his own reputation?

On the same visit Tom stopped by the bank that held the account for Universal Management. Tom wrote a $25 check to the account and deposited it. The next day he went back, to the same clerk and asked to check the balance. It was $25.

So Holladay wasn't hiding millions in that account. Perhaps Tom's own persistence had finally put an end to the shell game. But it was a disappointment. If there had been millions in the account, he could have gone after the money for one of his clients.

Meanwhile Tom ran into a former FBI agent he knew, Bob Flaherty. They had worked on a case together once. Flaherty mentioned he was going to the Bahamas for Christmas, and Tom told him about his problems getting the documents from Ryan.

"If you want, I'll check it out," Flaherty said.

"Absolutely," Tom said, excited.

Flaherty didn't get anywhere with Ryan, but he did have some of his law enforcement colleagues check him out. Weeks later an attorney from Miami called Tom, asking if he was investigating Ryan. The probe made Ryan nervous, the lawyer said, and Ryan and his attorney thought they could reach an agreement and send the documents.

Then, unbelievably, after all of that, Tom still got nothing.

The next time Tom ran into Flaherty, Tom hired him to go down and try Ryan again. It was March 2004, and Ryan was upset. "What does this McDermott want? What insurance company does he work for? What kind of money is he expecting to get?" Ryan demanded to know.

Flaherty looked at him surprised. "Don't you know?"

"Know what?"

"Tom's a shooting victim," Flaherty said. "He was shot on the Long Island Railroad by Colin Ferguson. He's not getting any money from this. He's going after this insurance fraud because it helped a lot of bad gun companies."

In all his enthusiasm to be a prosecutor, Tom had never told Ryan—or many of the people he talked to—about why he was pursuing this case with such fervor. It wasn't something he wanted to pull from his ample bag of tricks. But now it was his status as a shooting victim that allowed him to get the evidence that no one else had been able to retrieve. Three days later, Flaherty came back with the documents and a signed affidavit.

MISSISSIPPI

In researching the American Derringer case, Tom found another peculiar lawsuit. In February 2005, he went to the federal archives in Fort Worth to retrieve the case file of a Mississippi firefighter who was shot by a misfired American Derringer gun.[15]

On September 16, 1994, some firemen went out on Natchez's Lady Luck Casino. What nostalgic Mississippi riverboat gambling experience would be complete without an old-time firearm? One guy took an American Derringer pen gun in his pocket. Unluckily, it fell out of his pocket, dropped two feet, and shot his friend, Donald Gibson.

Gibson required five stomach surgeries, and he sued the guy who carried the gun and American Derringer. The suit said "the 'pen gun' is 'unreasonably dangerous per se' inasmuch as it has no sporting purpose (outside of the bizarre "game" of carrying a concealed, defective, and deadly weapon in a crowded public place out of a warped sense of satisfaction and power) and any other remote utility is far outweighed by the enormous dangers and risks to law abiding citizens such as the Plaintiff. . . ." Gibson also sued American Derringer for shipping the one-shot gun, which was designed to be concealed, without checking whether the buyer had a concealed-carry permit.

American Derringer was in bankruptcy protection, but Gibson's lawyer, James Nobles, asked the bankruptcy judge to let him pursue the case outside the bankruptcy and he'd limit damages to the insurance policy. This was what Barnes had asked for in the Lorcin bankruptcy, to no avail. This Texas bankruptcy judge agreed.

But before Nobles got to court, Control Systems sued American Derringer in Texas federal court to get released from paying for the legal defense. The pen gun was produced by another company, but American Derringer had stamped its name on it—a common practice in the gun industry. Holladay entered into evidence a letter that he said he had sent to American Derringer in 1992 that limited the policy to guns the company made itself. The judge had believed Holladay and let him off.

Tom discovered something odd about the letter, though, something that only someone who knew the whole timeline of Holladay and Leeds as well as Tom did would recognize. The letter was dated January 1993, but it used the name and address that Leeds had taken in 1994.

Leeds had incorporated in Costa Rica only on October 5, 1994 (after first trying in June with a name authorities rejected). Before 1994, there was no evidence Howard Holladay or Leeds had set foot in Costa Rica.

Tom believed the letter would show Holladay had defrauded the court.

Chapter 10

GUNS:
JUST LIKE ANY
OTHER BUSINESS

Send lawyers, guns and money
The shit has hit the fan
—"Lawyers, Guns and Money," Warren Zevon

THE NEARER YOUR DESTINATION

For years Tom and Rusty Brace had talked about filing a class action suit on behalf of all the people hurt by companies Holladay insured. Their talk of going to Kentucky began to sound like Chekhov characters' yearning for Moscow. (To be fair, with as slippery a character as Holladay, the more evidence Tom could accrue before filing suit, the more likely his chances of surviving early motions for dismissal and expediting the discovery process.)

Tom figured he could file a case in Kentucky before the judge who had already ruled that Holladay's insurance empire was a sham. They could ask that Judge McKinley be the federal court judge in charge of all the cases from federal courts around the country. If they got approval for McKinley to run a multi-jurisdictional case, they wouldn't even need to be certified as a class, a time-consuming process whose prospects of success were chancey at best.

Time was undeniably running out. Holladay would turn seventy-seven in 2005. McDermott had been investigating him for six years. A long time, but not too bad considering he was working full-time at another job and sending his children off into the world. During that span, though, Holladay had sold his enormous Boston townhouse, and Tom was afraid he'd lose track of him. According to a website, he still hosted weekly game-watching parties for University of Georgia football fanatics at a Boston bar, and as far as Tom knew, he still spent the winter on his Mexican plantation and still had yachts.

Holladay was ostensibly retired—and Tom's pursuit may have a played a role in keeping him from getting back into the insurance business. When asked what he made of all of Tom's accusations, Holladay countered that Tom and his critics hadn't filed a suit yet. (Of course, when Jackie Schroering did sue his company in Kentucky, the federal judge found fraud and bad faith.) Even if Tom never filed, however, his investigation was not a waste. Tom's call to the Bahamian insurance authorities prevented Derek Ryan from doing more work for Holladay. Otherwise, Holladay may well have just set up another company somewhere else— especially if McDermott, Schroering, Kreger, and Stomel hadn't revealed their suspicions about the company. And Jim Waldorf's new company didn't get off the ground in part because it didn't have a certificate of insurance from Holladay to show to distributors.

But Tom wanted to do more. He had tried to get the FBI involved a couple of times. Boston agents interviewed many of the players, but the terrorist attacks of September 11, necessarily diverted their attention.

At some level, of course, a big payday was beside the point. Tom had already written off the $300,000 in work time and expenses he had spent on the case. The main goal of a monetary reward would be to see families like the Stritzingers, Connie Terry, and the Joneses take back some of the money Holladay and his cronies and clients had made helping flood American streets with cheap guns. But his clients had more or less given up hope on seeing Holladay brought to justice before Tom even entered their lives. They had gone along with Tom and his efforts for the same reason he was still pursing this almost a dozen years after being shot. The mission was to make a dent in the number of people hurt by guns, to derive meaning from their tragedies.

GUNS: JUST LIKE ANY OTHER BUSINESS

Tom's journey of the last dozen years—trying to do something about handguns and chasing down Howard Holladay—had not radically changed him. This isn't a "very special episode" of some TV show in which our protagonist comes through on the other side as a different person. He was a decent, uncomplicated guy when he got shot and he's a decent, uncomplicated guy now. Each December seventh the families hurt in the LIRR shooting meet at the Merillon Avenue station for a memorial. They never see the McDermotts there, but the next day they find a wreath from the McDermotts. Told about Tom's quest, many are surprised he's still involved. He doesn't talk about it much. His family has grown up: Ryan McDermott works on Wall Street and is married. Katie lives in the city. Tom still works in the agency that funded improvements to New York racetracks, although the state is considering doing away with it.

Tom may not have changed, but his experience was part of a changing model for crime victims. He stayed true to his original promise of doing something about handguns. But the way he went about it evolved with time. Most crime victims burn out. And they burn out because they devote all their energies to being a walking victim impact statement. Or they take hope in an unrealistic legal challenge and fizzle out in frustration. Or they go right into the maw of the NRA and try to get gun control legislation passed. Many friends from his early days, which he refers to as "my wandering-in-the-wilderness period," have their personal lives and meager political contributions tracked and posted online by gun supporters.

This story could have ended with Tom helping to get the assault weapons ban passed in 1994.

Instead he created a new model for the victims of gun violence in a few ways. Tom never defined his mission as narrowly as preventing the one thing that had gotten him shot. His focus was concentrated on his own shooting at first, but then spread to a broader and broader category of people hurt by guns. He would work on whatever he thought would do the most good, even though it cost him a fortune, was derided as pointless, and would not have prevented the Colin Ferguson rampage.

He sidestepped the forces that prevent meaningful gun legislation and successful products liability lawsuits, namely the NRA and dozens of legal precedents. After so many frustrating episodes in his first few years, he took what he could from the experience of fighting the NRA—it taught him the context and history of the gun issue and where his efforts would be wasted.

By focusing on flaws in the insurance and product design of Saturday Night Specials, he handled cases of people who were not even crime victims. They were hurt by badly made or poorly designed guns. That made their cases much easier to win, but Tom now represented people who owned guns or gun businesses. It's difficult to imagine most gun control activists finding the common ground that Tom did, especially when these same people might have pooh-poohed gun control activists' antipathy for "junk guns" as mere political posturing years before they'd been hurt themselves. Tom was acting like a prosecutor again: going after cases that had the best practical chance and flipping witnesses to his side.

All of this leads to Tom's major contribution to gun control activism: He treated the gun industry like any other business. He wasn't a cartoon vigilante seeking to make gun companies pay for what they'd done and then some—*and this time it's personal.* He wanted gun companies to be responsible enough to pay for the actual damages their products caused. They could pay their way through a big court verdict. Or, if they were simply treated like any other company, gun owners or gun makers would have to buy insurance. They would be paying their way on the installment plan. Merely requiring reliable product liability insurance of gun manufacturers would pull the price of Saturday Night Specials up out of the deep discount range.

If you strip away the premise of guns as a special class of products, deserving of either extraordinary protections or significant limitations depending on your perspective, then you can proceed without the hysteria and inflamed passions that the gun debate typically causes. Some people Tom worked with on the insurance investigation didn't have anything to do with guns; paintballs or waterslides or some other enterprise Holladay insured had hurt them. Tom progressed, in other words, from putting special restrictions on guns to just trying to treat guns like any other product.

Treating guns like any other product is a radical notion in America. It's an idea that in the gun rights-friendly political climate that's developed during the time Tom has been pursuing his mission seems unlikely to take root immediately. But Tom's efforts to consider guns strictly as a financial enterprise point toward a very different world. And although he's not likely the one to reach the summit, others will build upon his work, the same way Tom built upon the efforts of so many.

If you treat guns like any other business, then you see that they're economically insignificant and unworthy of special legal protections. For decades the NRA has promoted the gun industry as a major force in the American economy. In 1967 the NRA promoted a study by Wharton professor Alan Krug, who calculated that gun and ammo sales of $284 million were just a sliver of the gun industry's economic worth.[1] For example, Krug figured hunters wore out nearly fifty thousand tires a year at a cost of $143 million. They also spent $675 million on food, lodging, hunting clothes and gear. In all, they spent $1.2 billion on their sport. Guns, in other words, were good for the economy.

This kind of funky math is embraced by a wide variety of economically insignificant industries—most notably Broadway—trying to impress the public with their might and unappreciated reach and influence. The National Shooting Sports Foundation "hunting and shooting sports generates over $30 billion annually, supporting over 986,000 jobs. And with the multiplier effect, economic activity jumps to over $75 billion annually." That would mean one out of every 149 Americans can thank guns for his or her job.[2] The Fish and Wildlife Service says wildlife watchers spent 86% more than hunters in 2001. So, that would mean industrious backyard squirrels are what's secretly powering the American economy.

In reality, the gun industry in aggregate generates about $3 billion in annual revenues. The United States GDP is $11.7 trillion. If you rolled up the whole industry into one company, it would land in the low end of the Fortune 500. It would be difficult to imagine the federal government exerting so much energy to keep, say, Brunswick (which sells $4 billion of pool tables, bowling supplies, and watercraft) afloat. Even if you accept that the gun industry is essential to our national defense, then America's airline industry is a better analogy. Although often poorly run and the frequent recipient of government bailouts, it takes responsibility for its safety. And as a backstop to make sure that it's following through on its duties, a number of federal agencies oversee it. The FAA has general oversight. The National Transportation Safety Board investigates any crashes.

The gun industry isn't held to the same level of scrutiny. It's averaged 28,000 deaths a year for the last three decades. In 2002, 30,242 Americans died from gun injuries (57 percent were suicides, 40 percent were homicides, and 2.5 percent, or 762, were unintentional, and the manner of the rest was undetermined) and another 65,834 were injured. If 28,000 people died in any year on airplanes, we'd all be traveling by train. Yet guns aren't even subject to the same consumer testing that every other product receives. The ATF, the industry's government overseer, has minimal authority and funds.

National gun policy is increasingly dictated by the NRA and an increasingly narrow segment of gun owners. From 1991 to 2000, NRA membership grew from about 2.5 million[3] to about 4.3 million. But since then, it's slid back. According to a *New York Times* report in December 2003, membership was off about 20 percent to 3.4 million.[4] The drop is understandable for a conservative cause under a conservative administration: people didn't feel as if they had to fight.

The membership numbers are still high, but a look at the numbers makes it clear that the NRA does not represent the interests of all gun owners. About 42 million to 50 million Americans own guns,[5] so less than 10 percent of gun owners bother to join. Those who bother to vote for the board, which largely determines federal gun policy, are even more rare, as Jack Anderson has pointed out.[6] In the 2003 election, the most popular candidate got 89,000 votes. By contrast, another American pastime, *American Idol* claimed 30 million adherents who, when allowed to vote as often as the like, averaged 16 votes each.

The NRA told the press in spring, 2000 that it would donate an awesome $15 million to George W. Bush's campaign.[7] According to the Center for Responsive Politics' election information website, Opensecrets.org, the entire pro-gun lobby gave only $4 million in the 2000 race and the NRA gave little more than 10 percent of that fearsome $15 million figure. In 2004 the NRA told UPI that they would spend $20 million to show Kerry wasn't pro-gun.[8] According to OpenSecrets.org, the whole gun lobby only gave $1.2 million and the NRA only gave $1.1 million. Election data also showed the gun lobby's muscle has been shrinking in muscle for the last four years. OpenSecrets ranks eighty-some industries and interest groups by their relative generosity. The gun lobby fell from number sixty-two in 1998 to seventy-one for the 2004 elections.[9] And they better watch out, because the funeral industry is at their back.

If you treat guns like any other business, then their success or failure isn't predicated on who the president of the United States is. In the 2000 presidential election, the NRA pushed hard for George W. Bush—even though some gun makers privately griped that he'd be bad for business because nothing sells guns like fear of regulation. In a candid moment captured on video, Kayne Robinson, second vice-president of the NRA, sold Bush to an elite group of riflemen in Los Angeles in February 2000, saying, "If we win, we'll have a Supreme Court that'll back us to the hilt. If we win, we'll have a president where we work out of his office. There are unbelievably friendly relations."[10] The Clinton administration worked with Smith & Wesson to have them take responsibility for how they sell their products. The deal was already shaky by the time Bush took office, and his administration let it die.[11]

If you treat guns like any other business, then mythic history doesn't trump common sense. After the September 11 terrorist attacks, when Americans were subject to increased security in all aspects of their life, Attorney General John Ashcroft made one exception. Although he had rounded up 1,200 suspects on U.S. soil suspected of plotting against the United States, he refused the FBI's request to check whether they had tried to buy guns, essentially saying that his theoretical understanding of the Second Amendment was worth more than actual American lives. Later, a General Accounting Office Report found that 58 suspected terrorists had tried to buy guns at stores and 47 succeeded.[12]

Meanwhile, civil liberties like the right to speak to an attorney, which unlike unfettered individual gun ownership had actually been the law of the land, went asunder. Ashcroft threw another bone to the militia crowd: In footnotes to two Supreme Court filings, the Justice Department he slipped in the view that the Second Amendment guaranteed the individual's right to have a gun.[13] Defense lawyers around the country leapt to overturn dozens of gun convictions, the *New York Times* reported.[14]

If you treat guns like any other business, then they don't need or warrant a legal shield built around them. During George W. Bush's first term, the NRA ardently pursued—and very nearly won—legislation that would prevent anyone from suing the industry for negligent distribution claims. Shielding an entire industry is almost unprecedented. It put the NRA in an interesting position: On one hand it insisted that the suits were laughably worthless and doomed, but on the other it held that the health of the entire gun industry—nay, all American industries—depended on what it called the Protection of Lawful Commerce Act.

The Senate passed the bill in 2005. Plaintiff lawyers held out little hope for a Constitutional challenge. Would an equal protection argument work because guns disproportionately hurt blacks? Long shot. The bill seemed sure to become law and create an obstacle to most distribution suits.

In many ways, the negligent distribution suits had served the gun companies well: The NRA and gun company reps could tell reporters that frivolous, politically motivated lawsuits were forcing companies out of business. The truth was, however, that the negligent distribution suits had gotten past discovery only with Judge Weinstein. The other cases were dismissed, either immediately or through an appeals process. A few companies quietly settled. Either way, it wasn't that expensive for an industry that was pooling its resources.

The negligent distribution cases didn't put gun companies out of business. Ring of Fire companies such as Lorcin, Davis, and Bryco went under because they made defective guns. Lorcin didn't lose a negligent distribution suit. Lorcin didn't even fight the *Hamilton* case, the one negligent distribution suit it faced. It just filed for bankruptcy and got protection from the suit. What put it into bankruptcy were all the garden variety product liability suits from gun owners.

If you treat guns like any other business, gun makers would need real product liability insurance. A real insurance policy, which any responsible manufacturer of any consumer product has, would have simply paid off the claims when products hurt users.

To be sure, getting real insurance would have been hard for these Saturday Night Special gun companies. The problem wouldn't have been onerous premiums. In the late 1980s and early 1990s, when the Ring of Fire was taking off, Bob Chiarello says his base rate was about $20 per $1,000 in sales. So insurance premiums would have added just 2 percent to the guns' price, hardly anything for the $35 to $150 handguns.

The major expense would have been the precondition to getting insurance: making the company, building, and product safe enough. The specific product defects cited in court cases involved safety features that would have cost only a few dollars per gun to fix. But getting the clean safety record that standard insurance companies required may well have been priceless.

In the insurance business, the saying is that any risk is insurable—at the right price. So to get real insurance, the low-end gun company's choice would have been either to bring the business up to industry standards in order to get a normal industry rate or to leave the guns unimproved and pay an exorbitant rate.

Insurance is what legal scholars were talking about when they considered requiring gun makers to "pay their own way" for their costs to the American public. Insurance is like paying for a big judgment on the installment plan. Mandatory insurance would incentivize safe behavior and take some of the enormous burden of treating gunshot wounds off taxpayers. It would change the dynamics of the low end of the business. Car owners in forty-three states have to buy insurance so that they can't just run someone over and walk away without paying for it.[15] Even those states that don't require insurance make drivers in an accident to prove they can pay damages or lose their license. Those laws recognize that cars are an exceptionally dangerous consumer product: Someone can buy a $1,000 beater car and do $1,000,000 worth of damage—or worse—to another human being with it. Lawmakers in the early 2000s lack the political courage even to consider such a measure for guns.

But despite all the resistance, many gun manufacturers have been required to have insurance. Not by any law, but by other gun businesses, namely, the distributors. This is the kind of self-regulation that people who share the political views of the NRA regularly embrace. It's the distributors who require manufacturers to have insurance as a precondition of carrying their product, in guns and every other industry. Plenty of handgun makers can and do exist without a major distributor, but without one they can never become a major force on the handgun market as Lorcin did in the early 1990s. In the mess that Tom McDermott uncovered, distributors were either not savvy or not diligent when they evaluated Lorcin's policies from Colony or Leeds. But to go one step further and make insurance mandatory for those that make, sell, distribute, and own guns, would be anathema to the NRA.

The NRA knows the value of liability insurance for guns. It woos potential members with offers of an accidental death and dismemberment policies in case they're injured while hunting. And the NRA helps sell liability insurance to gun businesses and gun professionals such as instructors or collectors through the Lockton Agency (the agency that once sold Holladay's insurance).

Whether you like the tort system or think it's gone too far, it does give Americans the assurance that products are safe. When you go into a store and buy a chair, a teddy bear or paper towel holder, you know not only that the product met the standards of the Consumer Product Safety Division but you know that the company hasn't been sued out of business by an injured customer.

Obviously, just having the product on the shelf doesn't give consumers the right to act stupid and then expect someone else to pay the price, either.

But it does give them the confidence that the product maker has been able to withstand legal challenges. If not, the owner would go out of business. Or at least have to pay exorbitant insurance costs, right? And gun companies don't just go out of business, right?

If you treat guns like any other business, no low-end gun company would have to file for bankruptcy protection when faced with litigation. The highest profile gun company lawsuit in recent years shut down Bryco, the second to last Ring of Fire company. Bryco declared bankruptcy on May 14, 2003, one day after a jury awarded $51 million to Brandon Maxfield, who was seven years old when a Bryco gun paralyzed him.[16] The jury found that the gun had been defectively designed: Users had to take off the safety to unload it. The jury split the blame among the cousin who accidentally shot Brandon; Brandon's parents for lack of supervision; and Bryco, its distributors, and pawnshop retailer. Because Bruce Jennings owned one of Bryco's distributors as well as Bryco, he was on the hook for $24 million.

Bryco was not insured by Holladay. According to Richard Ruggieri,[17] Maxfield's attorney, Jennings had attempted to set up his own offshore insurance company that never got off the ground. Jennings lawyer says that's not true,[18] but, at any rate, when Maxfield was hurt, Bryco was, like so many low end gun manufacturers, riding bare, uninsured.

This case was different from Lorcin because Ruggieri openly challenged whether the bankruptcy court should let the company continue to churn out defective guns. Jennings wasn't officially operating Bryco, but he wanted to sell it to his plant manager. This was a move he'd used earlier in his career, regaining control after the case went away. The Jennings clan insisted they didn't have anything to do with the new company. Ruggieri asked the judge to stop the equipment sale, but when that didn't work, he decided to outbid the manager's original $150,000 offer. The public donated about a half-million dollars to Maxfield's cause, but the manager, Paul Jimenez, ultimately won the bidding. By forcing the manager to raise his bid, however, the move did raise an additional $360,000 for Maxfield and other creditors. Fox Butterfield of the *New York Times* later reported that the winning bid had really come from an entity backed by the Jennings family.

If you treat guns like any other business, they have to contribute to paying the health costs they create. How much do gun injuries cost the American public? In 1992, Dr. Garen Wintemute estimated that taxpayers foot the bill for about $4 billion a year in medical expenses, most of which has been shown to be picked up by taxpayers because shooting victims are disproportionately uninsured.[19] A 2000 book *Gun Violence: The Real Costs,* put the figure at $100 billion a year, including what people do or would spend to avoid getting shot.[20]

As medical advances make it more likely that gunshot victims can be saved, costs rise exponentially. Medieval firearm wounds were treated with potions; guns were thought to work on the devil's power. During the Civil War, those shot in the torso or head were left to die, and those shot in a limb usually did die because of infection.[21] It's only in the post-antibiotic era that there have been many survivors. Still, a 1997 study put the average cost of a firearms injury at $14,482 and a death at $38,000 simply in medical costs.[22]

By those numbers, the medical costs of gunshot wounds alone are approximately $1 billion for injuries and $1.2 billion for deaths in 1997. Medical spending has risen 53 percent since then,[23] so the overall medical cost today is about $3.4 billion, a little more than the gun industry's total sales. If gun makers' portion of the blame is figured in much the way that courts compute it, the total cost might be divided among shooter error, owner negligence, deliberate criminal action, product design, and manufacturing defects. Gun makers would bear all costs for the last two categories, a hefty price.

And if the American public viewed the choice of who should pay simply as a business decision, it would be easy. Gun owners do pay extra taxes, of course. According to the latest figures that the ATF released, in fiscal year 2001 the government collected $298 million in firearms taxes.[24] But much of that is through the Pittman-Robertson Act, the money supports hunters through wildlife restoration and hunter education. The law makes gun owners pay for their extra use of public lands. The payment is imperfect because much of the money is spent on services that go right back to the hunter. It's still better than healthcare, though, where gun owners pay no extra tab for the additional public medical expenses they create.

WHY INSURANCE FRAUD MATTERS TO GUN CRIME

By August 2005, Tom McDermott had still not filed his case against Howard Holladay. He professed that the filing was imminent (as he had for a while). He finally understood not only the chronology of Holladay's operation but the business plan that had evolved over the years.

For the first few years, any liability policy can survive without trouble because it takes that long for a serious claim to get to court. The policy would forestall the big claims but pay out the early little ones, Tom figured, to show it was legitimate.

"You pay the ground balls and the small pop-ups, you don't pay the grand slams because those cost too damn much money," McDermott says. "The cases accumulate and accumulate. The whole mechanism is delay, delay, delay, delay, and then bust out."

Once claims built up, you try to spook the lawyers into taking a lousy settlement by saying the alternative would be to spend the rest of their lives chasing down this "shell upon a shell upon a shell" of a company.

Meanwhile, you advise the owners of the companies you ostensibly insured to file for bankruptcy, which would force all the lawsuits into the madcap world of bankruptcy court, where justice for consumers was a low priority. And then your insurance company would finally collapse and move to another Caribbean haven.

Tom concluded that it was not a coincidence that Holladay insured those companies that were most careless with their sales, most negatively rated by *Gun Tests,* and the frequent target of claims that its guns had drop-fired or exploded in a gun owner's hand. The economic phrase "moral hazard" means it's dangerous to insure people against a risk because if they know they can't be hurt, they'll engage in more risky behavior.

The industry acts as if the efforts of the Tom McDermotts out there put handgun companies out of business. Handgun companies go out of business far more often than people think. Especially the ones Holladay insured. The low-end companies are particularly ephemeral. According to an analysis of ATF production data from 1975 to 2000,[25] the mean survival time is just five years. One hundred thirty-six companies made at least one thousand handguns for one year during that time; thirteen companies survived fifteen years or more. Twenty-four of the companies lasted only a single year. Roughly one-third of the 136 still existed in 2000, the last year the ATF's company data is available. Only twenty of those companies made it to the 2005 SHOT Show held in Las Vegas in February. The other gun entrepreneurs failed on their merits (or lack thereof).

It appears that without Holladay and his insurance, the flood of cheap handguns virtually stopped. The heyday of the Saturday Night Special had seen a near doubling of gun crime rates; their disappearance ushered in a safer era. An analysis of gun price data from 1980 to 2000 shows that when the average price of handguns go down, as when Ring of Fire makers flooded the market, gun sales go up. And when gun sales go up, gun crime goes up. The cheapest guns, the highest sales, and the highest crime rates were in 1992 and 1993, when Lorcin and the Ring of Fire makers were operating at their peak.

In 1987 the average price of a handgun in the United States was $275. Back then, 150 out of every 100,000 Americans would be the victims of gun violence—robbed, attacked, or murdered.

Six years later the Ring of Fire reigned. Although inflation would have made the average handgun price climb to $341, the Ring of Fire's success, fueled by bogus insurance, dropped it to $262. Many guns sold for less than $100. Meanwhile, the average American's odds of staring down the barrel of a criminal's gun went up 50 percent, to 222 in 100,000.

By the year 2000, the Ring of Fire had virtually disappeared. Gun prices were back up to normal levels: The average price was $409. The Cato Institute, a conservative think tank, contends that this price jump is due to gun makers having to pass on the cost of frivolous litigation. But if you analyze the data, the increased cost is in tune with inflation. In fact, it's as if the Ring of Fire never happened. Adjusted for inflation, the $275 handgun from 1987 would have cost $416 in 2000. And the chances of being the victim of gun violence had fallen back, too—by almost half, to 121 in 100,000.

A statistical analysis by Susan Woodward, former S.E.C. chief economist who is now chief economist for Sand Hill Econometrics, showed that between 1980 and 2000 "when the price of handguns *falls* by 10 percent, the gun crime rate *rises* by about 4 percent." If there were no relation between gun prices and gun crime, that result would show up only 7 percent of the time.

Obviously, innumerable factors go into gun violence: everything from drug patterns to pending gun laws to demographic trends. Gun prices, crime rates, and gun sales all influence each other. Consumers' demand for guns rises with the perceived threat from crime. But it's hard to believe—as many gun rights activists claim—that cheap guns don't mean more crime. Cheap guns play a tremendous part.

According to an ATF agent who handled gun traces, cheap guns, priced at less than $150, had an undeniable appeal for gunrunners. Again, consider it as an MBA case study. If a gunrunner had limited capital, say, $3,000, he could buy perhaps thirty Saturday Night Specials and sell each on the street for $300 to $400. Subtract the expenses of traveling the Iron Pipeline, and he'd take home a profit of $9,000 to $12,000. If you purchased higher-end guns that cost $500, the market would only bear a markup of, say, $200. The gunrunner could buy only six high-quality guns and he'd make a $1,200 profit. Simple business math explains why Saturday Night Specials got so popular.

In an age when consumers have been shown to be price sensitive to basic necessities such as prescription drugs and food, it would be extraordinary if consumers were not price sensitive to guns.

And, of course, if gun companies were merely treated like any other consumer manufacturers and required to submit to the standards of the Consumer Product Safety Commission, odds are there would have been no domestic Saturday Night Special industry. When the guns were submitted to California's tests, only one company's passed.

Holladay may have been only an insurance salesman, but he helped the transient companies look real. If they had had real insurance for those rickety guns, the guns would have been far more expensive. His cheap insurance let people sell guns at artificially low prices, which drove up sales—and crime rates—nationwide.

By shining a light on Holladay's activities, Tom played a role in taking those extra (as well as extra cheap and extra lousy) guns off the street. He never expected to get the big courtroom scene and the multimillion-dollar verdict anyway.

The new law shielding gun makers from negligent distribution suits seemingly cut off the end-run around legislation taken by Eliza Barnes and handgun-choked cities. The law, however, created a moral hazard for gun companies, a natural temptation to engage in mre risky and careless sales tactics because they were protected from the consequences. Perhaps that behavior would set the political pendulum swinging in the other direction.

Someday Tom McDermott would pass his research onto someone else, like so many others had given to him. Whether it was through some other lawyer or even this book, someone would make use of his work or his method of treating guns like any other business. Until then, the shooting left Tom not with a disfigurement or disability but a chronic, incurable sense of obligation to prevent more handgun deaths.

He would keep working.

SOURCES

Additional Reading. The endnotes provide specific sources and include websites. The reader should be aware that websites change.

America's Growing Menace: Mass Murder, by James Levin and James Alan Fox, Berkley Books, 1985

American Firearms Makers: When, Where and What They Made From the Colonial Period to the End of the 19th Century, by A. Merwyn Carey, Thomas Y. Crowell Company, 1953

Americans and Their Guns: The National Rifle Association Story, by James Trefethen and James Serven, Stackpole Books, 1967

Bill of Rights, by Akhil Reed Amar, Yale University, 1998,

Citizens in Arms: The Army and Militia in American Society to the War of 1812, Lawrence D. Cress, University of North Carolina Press, 1982

An Equitable Burden: The Decline of the State Militias, 1789–1858, Ph.D. Dissertation, Mark Pitcavage, The Ohio State University, 1995

The Flamboyant Mr. Colt and His Deadly Six-Shooter, By Bern Keating, Doubleday & Co, 1978

Firearms Litigation, Law, Science and Practice, by Windle Turley and James E. Rooks, Jr., McGraw-Hill, 1988

Fired in Anger: The Personal Handguns of American Villains and Heroes, by Robert Elman, Doubleday, 1968

A Good Fight, by Sarah Brady, PublicAffairs, 2002

The Gun and Its Development, 9th Edition, by W.W. Greener, Lyons Press, 2002

Gunshot Wounds, Practical Aspects of Firearms, Ballistics, and Forensic Techniques, by Vincent J. M. Di Maio, M.D., Esevier, 1985

History of Smith & Wesson, by Roy Jinks, Beinfield Publishing, 1977

Landing On Your Feet, Your Guide to Survival in Tough Economic Times, by James Waldorf, 1992

Lawsuit, by Stuart M. Speiser Horizon Press, 1980

Making a Killing; The Business of Guns In America, by Tom Diaz, The New Press, 1999

A Necessary Evil, A History of American Distrust of Government, by Garry Wills, Touchstone, 1999

NRA: An American Legend, by Jeffrey L. Rodengen and Melody Maysonet, Write Stuff Enterprises, 2002

Origins and Development of the Second Amendment, by David T. Hardy, Blacksmith Publishers, 1986

Outgunned: Up Against the NRA, by Peter Harry Brown and Daniel G. Abel, The
   Free Press, 2003
The Party of Fear, From Nativist Movements to the New Right in American History,
   by David H. Bennett, Vintage Books, 1990
The Politics of Gun Control, by Robert J. Spitzer, Chatham House Publishers, 1995
The Saturday Night Special, by Robert Sherrill, Charterhouse, 1973
Shooting Straight: Telling the Truth About Guns in America, by Wayne LaPierre
The Story of the Gun, the History Channel, 1996 A&E Television
Suicide Specials, by Donald B. Webster, Jr., The Telegraph Press, 1958
William Conant Church and the Army and Navy Journal, by Donald Nevius Bigelow,
   AMS Press, 1968

RESEARCH NOTES

Gun production data were supplied by the Bureau of Alcohol Tobacco and Firearms to the Violence Policy Center through a Freedom of Information Act request. The data, which are printed in periodic reports, show manufacturers and the quantities of each gun model produced. The Violence Policy Center uses only companies that have production of at least 1,000 guns.

The price data are from annual *Gun Digest* publications. In cases in which more than one price of a make and model was listed, the mean was used. In cases of unlisted prices, prices were extrapolated from similar models or adjacent years. Prices were then adjusted for inflation.

Statistical analysis by Susan Woodward, chief economist for Sand Hill Econometrics.

Table 1. Cheap Guns, More Crime

Dependent Variable: DLOG(CRIMES)
Method: Least Squares
Date: 02/27/05 Time: 08:47
Sample (adjusted): 1981 2000
Included observations: 20 after adjustments

Variable	Coefficient	Std. Error	t-Statistic	Prob.
C	−0.012104	0.017902	−0.676085	0.5076
DLOG(REALPRICE)	−0.373765	0.194087	−1.925761	0.0701
R-squared	0.170834	Mean dependent var		−0.017957
Adjusted R-squared	0.124769	S.D. dependent var		0.084336
S.E. of regression	0.078900	Akaike info criterion		−2.146633
Sum squared resid	0.112054	Schwarz criterion		−2.047060
Log likelihood	23.46633	F-statistic		3.708554
Durbin-Watson stat	0.932243	Prob (F-statistic)		0.070080

The variables dlog(crimes) and dlog(realprice) are just the percentage changes in each. This estimation says that when the price of guns *falls* by 10 percent, the gun crime rate *rises* by about 4 percent (more precisely, 3.737 percent, read from the "coefficient" column).

The standard error of the estimate (a measure of how much confidence we should have in our estimate) is such that if there were no relation between crime rates and gun prices, we would expect to get an estimate of this value for a sample this size only about 7 percent of the time (read from the probability column). This result convinces me that gun crime rates are related to the price of guns.

Table 2. Gun, Price, Crime Data

Year	Average Handgun Price	Level Price	Real (Inflation- Adjusted) Price	Gun Crime Rate	Handguns Sold in U.S.	Gun Deaths
1980	143.64	82.4	174.32	174	*	33,477
1981	182.59	90.9	200.87	172.9	*	33,778
1982	207.29	96.5	214.81	160.9	*	32,682
1983	246.56	99.6	247.55	141.2	*	30,842
1984	282.65	103.9	272.04	139.4	*	31,078
1985	273.38	107.6	254.07	142.8	*	31,324
1986	248.23	109.6	226.49	156	1,916	33,126
1987	275.68	113.6	242.68	150.3	1,895	32,638
1988	299.43	118.3	253.11	157	1,892	33,757
1989	286.93	124	231.40	165.2	1,923	34,471
1990	300.24	130.7	229.72	198.1	1,958	36,866
1991	288.78	136.2	212.03	217.6	1,997	38,077
1992	262.19	140.3	186.88	221.7	2,027	37,474
1993	284.16	144.5	196.65	225.5	2,022	39,358
1994	361.49	148.2	243.92	208.4	1,958	38,187
1995	378.9	152.4	248.62	192	1,938	35,957
1996	414.95	156.9	264.47	172.8	1,904	33,750
1997	416.68	160.5	259.61	154.9	1,892	32,166
1998	394.1	163	241.78	135	1,891	30,708
1999	412.54	166.6	247.62	124.1	1,875	28,874
2000	409.85	172.2	238.01	121.5	**	26,800*

* ATF says records were not kept

**ATF says 2004 budget forbids release of data

Price Source: Gun Digest, ATF gun make and model multiplied by mean price from Gun Digest

Crime Rate: DOJ

Handguns Produced: ATF, numbers manufactured in U.S., minus exports, plus imports

Gun Deaths: National Vital Statistics Report. The report stopped keeping track of firearms deaths for 2000. Number from news accounts.

Woodward also found that when the real price of handguns rises by $100, the overall industry sales fall by $9,400—not much. She also found that gun sales rise three years after gun crime does.

MAP OF HISTORICAL GUN SITES IN LOWER MANHATTAN

1. First NRA meeting at *Army and Navy Journal* offices, 39 Park Row, on September 4, 1871.

2. NRA regular meetings held at 194 Broadway at John Street, law offices of NRA co-founder George Wingate.

3. *New York Sun* office where NRA co-founder William Conant Church was editor.

4. "Creedmoor, Jr." rifle range in former experimental subway tunnel under Broadway, accessed from 260 Broadway.

5. Bennett Building, only surviving NRA headquarters in New York.

6. The Tombs Prison, where many suspect Samuel Colt blew up the cupola on Nov. 18, 1842 to free his brother, John, who was to hang for murder that day.

7. Samuel Colt's exhibition of a submarine mine at Castle Clinton, July 4, 1842.

8. Site of the murder of a printer on September 17, 1841, near the office of John Colt, who was convicted of the murder.

NOTES

In some references in this book, multiple sources were used and are cited. I used this form of citation for methodological reasons, to illustrate that there were multiple points of conversation in these particular cases.

CHAPTER I

1. Author interviews with Tom McDermott.
2. Barry Meier and Raymond Bonner, "A Deal Done in U.S. Style Dazes an Ex-Soviet State," *New York Times,* Dec. 7, 1993.
3. Francis X. Clines, "Gunman in a Train Aisle Passes Out Death," *New York Times,* Dec. 9, 1993.
4. Rick Hampson, "Shots on the 5:33: 'This is Real Life, Everybody'," The Associated Press, Dec. 8, 1993.
5. Maureen Fan, William B. Falk, Craig Gordon, Michele Salcedo, Kevin McCoy, Rebecca Blumenstein, Susan Forrest, Yolanda Rodriguez, Andrew Smith, Sidney C. Schaer and Beth Whitehouse, "The LIRR Slaughter Nightmare Aboard Car 3," *Newsday,* Dec. 12, 1993.
6. Eric Nagourney and Michael Alexander, "Slaughter Heroes and Victim," *Newsday,* Dec. 9, 1993.
7. Farrell Kramer, "Gunman Kills Four, Wounds 19, in Crowded Commuter Train Terror," Associated Press, Dec. 8, 1993.
8. CityData.com.
9. Shirley E. Perlman, Maureen Fan, Susan Forrest and Phil Mintz, "Slaughter on the 5:33," *Newsday,* Dec. 7, 1993.
10. Carol J. Castaneda, "When Gun Fell Silent, Heroes Took Action," USA Today, Dec 9, 1993.
11. Author interview with Rosemary McDermott.
12. Author interviews with Joel Cohen.
13. Judy Klemesrud, "From Song and Dance to a Tough Cop," *New York Times,* Aug. 28, 1981.
14. *Prince of the City* (1981), Warner Home Video movie, directed by Sidney Lumet, based on the book by Robert Daley.
15. *New York Times,* Feb. 19, 1977, Page 28, Column 4.

CHAPTER 2

1. "Bearing Witness: Headlines Fade and Memories Dim, but the Emotional Scars of Violent Crime Last Forever," *People Weekly,* April 3, 1995.
2. Rebecca Blumenstein, "The LIRR Slaughter: Fighting to Beat the Odds Widow Focuses on Her Injured Son," *Newsday,* Dec 10, 1993.
3. Rebecca Blumenstein, "Kevin's Christmas: A Victim of the LIRR Gunman Gives His Mom a Gift of Pearls—and of Hope," *Newsday,* Dec 26, 1993.
4. Maria Eftimiades, "The Greatest Gift (Long Island Railroad Massacre Victim Amy Federici Was Organ Donor)," *People Weekly,* April 11, 1994.
5. Beth Whitehouse, "LIRR Slaughter: It Was Him Or Me, Says One of the Heroes," *Newsday,* Dec. 9, 1993.
6. Charisse Jones, "In Notes and Past of Accused, Portrait of Boiling Resentment," *New York Times,* Dec. 9, 1993.
7. Jonathan Rabinovitz, "Mass Murder on the 5:33 Police Look for the Spark That Led to the Shootings," *New York Times,* Dec. 10, 1993.
8. Anastasia Toufexis, "Mass Murderer's Journey toward Madness," *Time,* Dec. 20, 1993.
9. Garry Pierre-Pierre, "Suspect's Quiet Roots in Jamaica Suburb," *New York Times,* Dec. 10, 1993.
10. Robert D. McFadden, "A Long Slide From Privilege Ends in Slaughter on a Train," *New York Times,* Dec. 12, 1993.
11. Diana Jean Schemo, "Adelphi Recalls a Student Driven by Rage and Suspended for Making Threats," *New York Times,* Dec. 10, 1993.
12. Robin Topping, "Animal Remark is Defended Anew," *Newsday,* Dec. 21, 1993, and "Ministers Assail Gulotta Remark; Black Clerics Ask Him to Recant 'Affront'," *Newsday,* Dec. 30, 1993.
13. Author interviews with Joyce Goricki.
14. John Marzulli, "NAACP Takes on Gun Industry in New York's Brooklyn Federal Court," *New York Daily News,* April 2, 2003
15. "NRA Leader Wayne LaPierre's 'Homogenization' Quote Most Recent Addition to NRA History of Racist Commentary," Violence Policy Center, May 16, 2000, vpc.org/press/0005nra.htm.

     The other examples included: Paul Blackman, the NRA's head researcher, said "studies of homicide victims—especially the increasing number of younger ones—suggest they are frequently criminals themselves and/or drug addicts or users. It is quite possible that their deaths, in terms of economic consequences to society, are net gains." NRA Board Member Ted Nugent said "apartheid isn't that cut and dry. All men are not created equal."
16. Jack Anderson, *Inside the NRA, Armed and Dangerous: An Expose,* Beverly Hills, CA, Dove Books, 1996, page 40.
17. John R. Lott Jr., *More Guns, Less Crime: Understanding Crime and Gun-Control Laws,* Chicago, University Of Chicago Press, 2000.
18. Timothy Noah, "Finish Rep. Cubin's Thought! A reader contest." *Slate.com,* April 11, 2003. Cubin later said that she was going to say that " . . . sons look

like the Columbine [High School] killers . . . they [should] be prevented from buying guns?" slate.com/id/2081581.

19. Firearms Deaths in 1993: Centers for Disease Control. http://webappa.cdc.gov/sasweb/ncipc/mortrate9.html.

20. International Homicide Comparisons, GunCite.com.

21. Jacob V. Lamar Jr., "'Crazy Pat's' Revenge, A Postman Kills 14 Co-workers in Oklahoma," *Time,* Sept. 1, 1986.

22. "Some Mass Shootings in the United States Since 1980," Associated Press, Dec. 7, 2001.

23. New Rochelle Police Department History, http://www.nrpd.com/history/history.htm

24. "Reinhard," CourtTV's Crime Library, www.crimelibrary.com/notorious_murders/mass/neptune/reinhard_4.html?sect=8.

25. Jim Henderson, "Too Tired to Live: 15th Victim of UT Sniper Chooses to Die after 3 Decades on Dialysis," *Houston Chronicle,* Nov. 15, 2001, page 33. The coroner ruled the death a homicide. "He had a (kidney) transplant, but he rejected it," his mother said. "He like to have died then."

26. "An Arizona Tragedy: Murder and Robbery at a Stage Station, Three Men Killed and a Woman Fatally Wounded," *New York Times,* Jan. 14, 1871.

27. "Two Men Murdered in a Car," *Chicago Daily Tribune,* Dec. 9, 1894.

28. "Took the Lives of Seven People," *New York Times,* Feb. 6, 1896.

29. "Slain by Drunken Fiend; A Tragedy in Minnesota in Which Four Persons Were Slaughtered," The Washington Post, Feb. 17, 1889.

30. CourtTV's Crime Library, *Mass v. Spree,* crimelibrary.com/notorious_murders/mass/howard_unruh/7.html?sect=8.

31. "More Americans Killed by Guns than War in 20th Century," The Brady Campaign, Dec. 20, 1999.

CHAPTER 3

1. *This Week with David Brinkley* (ABC 11:30 A.M. ET), Dec. 12, 1993, Transcript # 633.

2. Author interviews with Michelle Schimel.

3. Katina Johnstone, "The Gun Spoke First," *New York Times,* Dec. 15, 1993.

4. Author Interview with Katina Johnstone.

5. Firearms Deaths 1982–1993: Centers for Disease Control. http://webappa.cdc.gov/sasweb/ncipc/mortrate9.html. Number of deaths: 350,773; Population: 2,466,367,571 (population is multiplied by number of years studied); Crude rate: 14.22; Age-adjusted rate: 13.86.

6. Fox Butterfield, "'Silent March' on Guns Talks Loudly: 40,000 Pairs of Shoes, and All Empty," *New York Times,* Sep. 21, 1994.

7. Thomas F. McDermott, "He Stared Blankly at Me, Then Fired; Of Colin Ferguson and Jim Brady," New York Times, Dec 17, 1993.

8. Julie Salamon, "Crispy Fries and Radical Causes [William Kunstler]," *New York Times,* June 7, 1995.

9. William Kunstler and Ronald Kuby, "Letter to the Editor: An Insanity Defense in LIRR Massacre," *New York Times,* April 28, 1994.
10. "Shooting Suspect Hated Whites, Asians, Certain Blacks, Authorities Said," *New York Daily News,* Dec. 8, 1993.
11. Lucy Friedman, "From Pain to Power: Crime Victims Take Action," The Office for Victims of Crime (OVC), U.S. Department of Justice, Sept. 1998, www. ojp.usdoj.gov/ovc/publications/infores/fptp/welcome.html.
12. Mike Kelly, "Amy's Heart," *Bergen Record,* Dec. 7, 2003.
13. Robin Topping, "'Animal' Remark Is Defended Anew," *Newsday,* Dec. 12, 1993.
14. James Parillo, "Saratoga: The Tide Turns on the Frontier," ParkNet, National Parks Service.
15. "The Story of the Gun," the History Channel, A&E Television, 1996.
16. W.W. Greener, *The Gun and Its Development,* 9th Edition, Lyons Press, 2002.
17. Lawrence D. Cress, *Citizens in Arms: The Army and Militia in American Society to the War of 1812* (Chapel Hill, University of North Carolina Press, 1982).
18. Anonymous, "An Extract From the Prospect Before Us; A New Political Work, Now Ready for the Press, An Answer to the Late Counter Address for the Minority of House Delegates of Virginia," *National Magazine, A Political, Historical, Biographical and Literary Repository,* (1799–1800); 1, 2; APS Online, page 171.
19. David T. Hardy, *Origins and Development of the Second Amendment,* Chino Valley, AZ, Blacksmith Publishers, 1986.
20. Militia Act of 1792, Second Congress, Session I. Chapter XXVIII, Passed May 2, 1792.
21. Mark Pitcavage, "An Equitable Burden: The Decline of the State Militias, 1783–1858" (Ph.D. dissertation, The Ohio State University, 1995).
22. "Fielden Urged Murder: Long Before the Riot He Advocated Using Dynamite," *Washington Post,* July 20, 1886, page 1.
23. "The Lehr Und Wehr Verhein," *New York Times,* July 20, 1886.
24. U.S.S.C., *Presser v. Illinois,* 116 U.S. 252 (1886).
25. *Miller v. Texas,* 153 U.S. 535, 14 S.Ct. 874, 38 L.Ed. 812 (1894).
26. Cynthia Leonardatos, David B. Kopel, Stephen P. Halbrook, "Miller versus Texas: Police Violence, Race Relations, Capital Punishment, and Gun-Toting in Texas in the Nineteenth Century—and Today," *Journal of Law and Policy,* 2001.
27. *U.S. v. Miller,* 307 U.S. 174 (1939).
28. Warren Burger, "The Right To Bear Arms," *Parade Magazine,* Jan. 14, 1990.
29. "The Fight to Bear Arms," *U.S. News and World Report,* May 22, 1995.
30. Wayne LaPierre, *Shooting Straight: Telling the Truth About Guns in America,* Regnery Publishing, Inc., 2002, page 2.

CHAPTER 4

1. Carolyn McCarthy, "Horror on the 5:33," *Ladies Home Journal,* July 1, 1994.

2. Mario Cuomo, "Try Again The Legislature failed to ban assault weapons, but it may yet pass new gun laws," *Newsday,* Jan. 24, 1994.

3. Charles V. Zehren, "LIRR Victim Hails Cuomo Gun Curbs," *Newsday,* Jan 11, 1994.

4. Maureen Fan, "LIRR Victims: Ban Assault Weapons," *Newsday,* March 9, 1994.

5. Author interview with Lucy Friedman.

6. *New York Times,* April 14, 1977, Section 2, page 2, Column 5.

7. "Goetz Gives 'Thanks' To Teens He Shot," Associated Press, April 25, 1988.

8. Transcript, Village of Great Neck Plaza Trustees, March 16, 1994.

9. Transcript, Village of Great Neck Plaza Trustees, April 6, 1994.

10. *Kalodimos v. Village of Morton Grove,* 103 Ill. 2d 483 (1984).
    Quilici v. Village of Morton Grove, 695 F. 2d 261, 270 7th Cir. (1982).

11. Village of Morton Grove Handgun Ordinance, Chronology of Events Surrounding the Ordinance, Morton Grove Public Library, "Webrary" www.webrary.org/Ref/handgun.html, First published on the Web: Jan. 26, 1998, last updated Sept. 16, 2001.

12. Transcript, Village of Great Neck Plaza Trustees, May 18, 1994.

13. Stephen P. Halbrook, "Nazi Repression of Firearms Owners," *The American Rifleman,* Aug. 1999.

14. S. Ollenberg, research and translation. She used the German police site, http://www.polizei-ing.de/content.php/25/0 and the http://www.documentarchiv.de. She found that after two assassinations by gun (Matthias Erzberger, finance minister of the Weimar Republic, was shot down in 1921 and in 1922 Walther Rathenau, foreign minister, was shot to death), the Weimar Republic bans guns. ("Gesetz zum Schutz der Republik" 18. July 1922). On May 12, 1928, Reichsgesetz über Schusswaffen und Munition loosens the law: civilians can own guns, but they must register them. The laws latter enabled Hitler to define who could own guns and on April 12, 1938 Hitler started enforcing these older laws known as law of firearms and munition (Gesetz ucber Schusswaffen und Munition). People who Hitler defined as German citizens got more freedom to own firearms under the Nazi regime. Before Kristallnacht in 1938, the Nazis instructed police to disarm Jews.

15. "Report on the German Volkssturm, a German national militia organized in the last months of WWII," Intelligence Bulletin, February 1945.

16. David K. Yelton, "Ein Volk Steht Auf: The German Volkssturm and Nazi strategy, 1944–45," *The Journal of Military History,* Oct. 2000, Vol. 64, Iss. 4; pg. 1061.

17. "The Story of the Gun," the History Channel, A&E Television, 1996.

18. Author interviews with Whit Collins.

19. Author interview with Ken Stern.

20. Donald Nevius Bigelow, *William Conant Church and the Army and Navy Journal,* edited by the faculty of political science of Columbia University, New York, AMS Press, 1952.

21. Ibid., page 50–51, 60–63.

22. Ibid., page 71, 75, 84.

23. Ibid., page 90.
24. Ibid., page 86, *New York Times,* May 18, 1862.
25. Ibid., page 93–97, 112, 140.
26. Ibid., page 165.
27. Ibid., page 172.
28. Ibid., page 166.
29. James Trefethen and edited by James Serven, *Americans and Their Guns, The National Rifle Association Story Through Nearly a Century of Service to the Nation,* Harrisburg, PA, Stackpole Books, The National Rifle Association of America, 1967, pages 23–26.
30. Ibid., page 184.
31. "Functions of the Militia," *New York Times,* Jan 5, 1898.
32. *Americans and Their Guns,* page 32–33.
33. Author interview with Don Tolzman, director of German-American Studies Program, University of Cincinnati.
34. *Americans and Their Guns,* page 34.
35. Ibid. 38–39.
36. "National Guard Rifle Practice—An Important Movement," *New York Times,* Sept. 5, 1871, page 12.
37. First meeting in 1871: 39 Park Row, Army and Navy Journal offices; First official office, Wingate's office, 194 Broadway; Feb. 7, 1882, meeting at 88 Clinton Place; 1883 executive committee meeting Oct. 30, 1883, at 102 William Street; They also met at the Seventh Regiment and 22nd Armory.
38. *Americans and Their Guns,* pages 40–46.
39. Jeffrey Rodengen, *NRA: An American Legend,* Fort Lauderdale, FL, Write Stuff Enterprises, 2002.
40. *Harper's Weekly,* July, 17, 1875.
41. *Americans and Their Guns,* pages 62–66.
42. *Americans and Their Guns,* page 66.
43. "The Creedmoor Rifles," *NRA: An American Legend,* page 25.
44. *Americans and Their Guns,* page 51.
45. *Americans and Their Guns,* page 82.
46. *Americans and Their Guns,* page 79.
47. *Americans and Their Guns,* pages 86–87.
48. *Americans and Their Guns,* page 89, quoting Wingate's 1907, "Recollections of the National Guard." However, in a Sept. 19, 1882 *New York Times* story headlined "Another Lie Nailed," Gen. E. L. Molineux denies that Cornell was hostile to the NRA at all. In what may have been an insult to Wingate, Molineux said: "He impressed me with the idea, so far as National Guard officers were concerned, that military matters only needed to be placed before him in a business-like way to receive satisfactory consideration."
49. "Searching for a New Range," *New York Times,* Oct. 6, 1886.
50. "The Creedmoor Managers," *New York Times,* Jan. 13, 1886.
51. "Riflemen at Loggerheads," *New York Times,* Jan. 12, 1881.
52. "National Guard Gossip," *New York Times,* Jan. 19, 1890.
53. "The State Gets Creedmoor," *New York Times,* September 4, 1889.

54. Author interview with Jim Trent, director of Queens County Farm Museum, says volunteers at the farm sometimes come across old lead bullets in their fields even though the current farm is far from where the range was.

55. "Will Sue State for $10,000," *New York Times*, April 25, 1896.

56. "Creedmoor Bullets Imperil Farmers," *New York Times*, June 30, 1907.

57. *Americans and Their Guns*, pages 110–112.

58. *Americans and Their Guns*, pages 102–130.

59. Josh Sugarman, *NRA: Money, Firepower & Fear*, Violence Policy Center, 1992.

60. *Americans and Their Guns*, pages 178–189.

61. *NRA: Money, Firepower & Fear*, cites the April, 1926 *American Rifleman* article, which "veteran New York police instructor" John Dietz says "It's the automobile that's making the going tough for the police—not the one-hand gun. A little job of bank-robbery with maybe a killing or two never bothered a crook. What worried him was the get-away. He couldn't make it in the horse and buggy days. But he can make it now with the fast auto."

62. Robert Sherrill, *The Saturday Night Special*, New York, Charterhouse, 1973.

63. Fred J. Hook, "Drawing a Bead on Gun Control," *New York Times*, July 2, 1972. President Nixon declared: "I have always felt there should be a federal law for the control of handguns. . . . I will sign it."

64. Wayne King, "Efforts to Curb Cheap Pistols Called Failure," *New York Times*, June 20, 1975.

65. "Black Caucus in Congress Deplores Wallace Shooting," The *Washington Post*, May 18, 1972. Daley was a strong supporter of handgun laws, advocating gun companies pay for shooting victims funerals. After the assassination attempt on George Wallace, he made an emotional plea saying there is "no reason for handguns being manufactured . . . or imported. Handguns are used to kill one another. You can't hunt with them. A handgun is an encouragement for you to shoot someone else or for him to shoot you. . . . My God, we've had the killing a President, and his brother, the assassination of an outstanding religious leader, and now we have the shooting of a man who is a presidential candidate. . . . My God, what kind of society have we? . . ."

66. David T. Hardy, *BATF's War on Civil Liberties* (Bellevue, WA, Second Amendment Foundation, 1979).

67. Carol Vinzant, "ATF-Troop," *Spy Magazine*, March, 1994.

68. John M. Crewdson, "Hard-Line Opponent of Gun Laws Wins New Term at Helm of Rifle Association," *New York Times*, May 4, 1981.

   Crewdson found that when he was seventeen, Carter shot and killed Ramon Casiano, fifteen. Carter had home to find his mother upset about some Hispanic boys, aged twelve to fifteen, hanging around outside their Laredo, Texas, home. Carter took his shotgun and told the boys to come inside. He and his mom wanted to question them about whether they'd stolen the family car a few weeks earlier. Casiano refused and pulled knife. There was a dispute over how the argument progressed and whether Carter acted is self-defense, as his defense claimed, but not dispute that he shot Casiano. A jury convicted him only a month after the shooting.

Judge J. F. Mullally instructed the jurors: "There is no evidence that defendant had any lawful authority to require deceased to go to his house for questioning, and if defendant was trying to make deceased go there for that purpose at the time of the killing, he was acting without authority of law, and the law of self-defense does not apply."

An appeals court overturned the conviction that Dec., saying the judge should have allowed the jurors to consider the self-defense argument. Prosecutors chose not to retry him because some key witnesses had been convicted of notorious crimes and others could not be found.

The Crewdson report said that Carter "first denied knowledge of the death of Ramon Casiano." His official biography put him at the University of Texas in 1931, when he would have been in jail. Crewdson also found that Carter had changed the spelling of his name, from Harlon to Harlan after his jail stint. He then joined the Border Patrol.

69. *Red Dawn*, 1984, MGM/UA Studios, Directed by John Milius. According to IMDb.com (Internet Movie Database): "The cast underwent a 'realistic,' intensive 8 week military training course before starting work on *Red Dawn*."

70. United States. 37 CONG. Q. ALMANAC 420 (1981); New York Times, Apr. 1, 1981.

71. *Shotgun News,* Copyright © Neal Knox Associates, P.O. Box 3313, Manassas, VA 20108 http://www.nealknox.com All Rights Reserved.

72. Melvin Claxton, "Flawed Guns: Public at Risk, Law Would Shield Gun Makers Against Suits, NRA, Manufacturers Press Congress to Stifle Safety Rules, Despite Evidence of Dangers," *Detroit News,* Dec. 14, 2003.

73. Maureen Fan, "McCarthy Sues Gun, Ammo Firms; Asking for $ 1.5B in LIRR shootings," *Newsday,* May 18, 1995.

74. Lori Montgomery and Tom Infield, "House Votes to Cut Gun Studies, The $2.6 Million for the CDC Was Put to Political Use," *Philadelphia Inquirer,* July 2, 1996.

75. Lauran Neergaard, "Gun Vote by House Gives Victory to NRA, Funds Axed for Disease Center's Research," Associated Press, July 13, 1996.

76. Author interview with Richard Aborn.

77. William Douglas and Glenn Kessler, "A Gun Ban House 216–214, Votes to Outlaw 19 Assault Weapons," *Newsday,* May 6, 1994.

78. William J. Eaton, "Panel OKs Rapid-fire Gun Ban," *Los Angeles Times,* April 29, 1994.

79. Kevin Sacks, "2 Victims of LIRR Shooting Appear in Commercial for Cuomo," *New York Times,* July 20, 1994.

80. "Special Interests Lure Freshmen, Including Frisa," *Newsday,* Aug. 17, 1995 and "Guns in America: National Survey on Private Ownership and Use of Firearms," NIJ Research in Brief, May, 1997, by Jeremy Travis, director.

81. Marie Cocco, "Gingrich Plays Hardball with New York's Money," *Newsday,* Sep. 28, 1995.

82. "Cryptic Fax Was Sent to Stockman," *The Houston Chronicle,* April 24, 1995.

83. James Dao and Don Van Natta Jr., "N.R.A. Is Using Adversity to Its Advantage," *New York Times,* June 12, 1999.

84. "Dole Tells NRA He'll Try to Repeal Weapons Ban," 1995, Congressional Quarterly, *St. Louis Post-Dispatch,* March 19, 1995, P. 3A.

85. Katharine Q. Seelye, "A Life Saved? A Life Lost: Gun Issue Gets Personal; Two Sides Engage With Dueling Witnesses," Apr 1, 1995.

86. Timothy Noah, "The Bellesiles of the Right? Another firearms scholar whose dog ate his data." *Slate.com,* Feb. 3, 2003, http://slate.msn.com/?id=2078084.

87. U.S. Dept. of Justice, Bureau of Justice Statistics, Guns and Crime: Handgun Victimization, Firearm Self-Defense, and Firearm Theft, April 1994, NCJ-147003, http://www.ojp.usdoj.gov/bjs/pub/ascii/hvfsdat.txt.

88. Robert Stacy McCain, "Critics Target Data in 'More Guns, Less Crime'," *The Washington Times,* Jan. 23, 2003.

89. "Report of the Investigative Committee in the Matter of Professor Michael Bellesiles," Emory University, July 10, 2002, http://www.news.emory.edu/Releases/Final_Report.pdf.

90. Randolf Rolf, "Counting Guns: What Social Science Historians Know and Could Learn about Gun Ownership, Gun Culture, and Gun Violence in the United States," Report on Social Science History Association Annual Meeting, Fall, 2001.

91. Author interview with John Donahue.

92. Ian Ayers and John J. Donahue III, "Shooting Down the More Guns, Less Crime Hypothesis," Stanford Law & Econ: Working Paper 247; Stanford Public Law Research Paper 44; Yale Public Law Research Paper 28; Yale Law & Econ. Research Paper 272, National Bureau of Economic Research (NBER), Oct. 2002.

93. Tom W. Smith, "2001 National Gun Policy Survey of the National Opinion Research Center," University of Chicago, www.norc.uchicago.edu/online/guns01.pdf.

94. Erin Stout, "Olin Foundation Gives Away Its Last Cent and Shuts Down," *Chronicle of Higher Education,* Feb, 25, 2005.

95. "Funder of the Lott CCW Study Has Links to the Gun Industry," Violence Policy Center, 1999.

96. http://www.johnrlott.com/ John Lott chose not to comment for this book.

97. A. L. Kellermann and D. T. Reay, "Protection or peril? An analysis of firearm-related deaths in the home," *New England Journal of Medicine:* June 12, 1986, Volume 314:1557–1560.

98. Mark Dugan, "More Guns, More Crime"; National Bureau of Economic Research (NBER) Working Paper No. W7967, Oct. 2000.

99. Daniel Webster and Jens Ludwig, "Myths about Defensive Gun Use and Permissive Gun Carry Laws," Berkeley Media Studies Group, prepared for the "Strengthening the Public Health Debate on Handguns, Crime, and Safety" meeting, Oct. 1999.

100. Ron French, "McVeigh's Bomb Shattered Militia Movement, Too Passionate Patriots Fell Victim to Fear, Boredom," *The Detroit News,* May 6, 2001.

101. Bennett Roth, "Appeal of Arms Ban May be Postponed," *Houston Chronicle,* May 1, 1995.

102. *Stripes,* 1981, Columbia/Tristar Studios, Directed by Ivan Reitman Even this fun, silly movie hints at the widespread belief that any American can learn what the Army teaches in a few hours.

103. Jason Kaufman, Harvard University, "Americans and Their Guns: Civilian Military Organizations and the Destabilization of American National Security," *Studies in American Political Development,* 15 (Spring 2001), 88–102.

104. *Enquirer,* Dec. 1, 1812.

105. *Columbian Centinel,* February 5, 1820.

106. *William Conant Church and the Army and Navy Journal,* page 181, citing the *Journal* February 23, 1867; Nov. 2 and 30, 1867.

107. *The Saturday Night Special,* page 221.

108. Melvin Claxton and William Gaines, "Fire Sale: American Gun Market Unchecked. Part 2: Civilian Marksmanship Program. Through the 94-year-old Civilian Marksmanship Program, thousands of obsolete military firearms are sold to private owners. Trouble is, there are no safeguards on the weapons' resale," *Chicago Tribune,* Dec. 29, 1997.

109. GAO Report: "Military Preparedness: Army's Civilian Marksmanship Program Is of Limited Value," (GAO/NSIAD–90–171) http://archive.gao.gov/d24t8/141431.pdf.

110. GAO Report: "Civilian Marksmanship Program: Corporation Needs to Fully Comply with the Law on Sales of Firearms," GAO/NSIAD–99–41 Jan. 12, 1999, http://www.gao.gov/archive/1999/ns99041.pdf.

111. Carl T. Bogus, "Race, Riots, and Guns," *Southern California Law Review* 66 (1993): 1365.

112. "Extremism in America," Anti-Defamation League Law Enforcement Agency Resource Network Report, article on Lewis Beam.

113. UtterlyBoring.com, blog that originally posted picture, which eventually ran in many media. utterlyboring.com/archives/2003/ 09/30/one_weekend_a_month_my_ass_a_followup.php.

114. Scott Canon, "Fear of Draft's Renewal Exists in Spite of Political, Social Obstacles," *Knight Ridder Newspapers,* May 24, 2004.

115. Roland S. Martin, "Those Refusing to Renew Assault Weapon Ban Stand with Street Terrorists," *Chicago Defender,* Sep.14, 2004.

116. Dun & Bradstreet Report on National Rifle Association Foundation, 2003.

117. National Rifle Association Foundation, IRS Form 990, Part V, Line 75, Compensation Provided by Related Organization. On the bright side, LaPierre only charged the NRA with $1,281 of expenses. http://www.guidestar.org/Documents/2003/521/710/2003–521710886–1–9.pdf.

118. Stephanie Strom, "A Deficit of $100 Million Is Confronting the N.R.A.," *New York Times,* Dec. 21, 2003.

119. "The American Sportsman: Take a Closer Look," Report by the Congressional Sportsmen Foundation, 2001 and U.S. Fish and Wildlife Service 2001 National Survey of Fishing. Hunting and Wildlife–Associated Recreation.

120. Bob Delfay and Doug Painter, "Is the Sky Falling? A Realistic Look at the State of Our Business," *Peterson's Shot Business,* Dec. 1997.

121. New York State Hunter Education Class, 2004.

CHAPTER 5

1. John T. McQuiston, "Suspect in L.I.R.R. Slayings May Dismiss His Lawyer; Colin Ferguson may dismiss William M. Kunstler to avoid an insanity defense," *New York Times,* Oct. 21, 1994.

2. John T. McQuiston, "Ferguson's Insanity Defense Angers Victims and His Lawyers," *New York Times,* Jan. 8, 1995.

3. Maureen Fan, "Ferguson Wants to Face Survivors Will Defend Himself in LIRR Trial," *Newsday,* Dec. 10, 1994.

4. "Defendant in Long Island Train Massacre to Represent Self at Trial," *Los Angeles Times,* Dec. 10, 1994, page 18.

5. "Dubious Counsel (alleged murderer Colin Ferguson)," *People Weekly,* Feb. 13, 1995.

6. David Van Biema, "A Fool for a Client (accused murderer Colin Ferguson)," *Time,* Feb. 6, 1995.

7. Maureen Fan, "Ferguson Opens LIRR Suspect Says He Was Framed; Prosecutor Details Case," *Newsday,* Jan. 27, 1995.

8. "Trial Story; New York v. Ferguson, Murder on the 5:33: The Trial of Colin Ferguson," CourtTV, 1995.

9. Maureen Fan, "'God, Make It Quick' Victim Recounts LIRR Shooting," *Newsday,* Feb. 9, 1995.

10. Sylvia Adcock, "Missing: Mystery Witness," *Newsday,* Feb. 7, 1995.

11. "After Vigil for Verdict, A Plea for Gun Control," *New York Times,* Feb. 18, 1995.

12. John T. McQuiston, "L.I.R.R. Victims Call for Life Sentence; At Court Hearing, Outpouring of Grief by Survivors of Shootings," *New York Times,* Mar. 22, 1995.

13. "Our Broken Hearts: LIRR Victims' Grief and Pain," *Newsday,* Mar. 22, 1995.

14. Author interview with Stephen Glasser.

15. Windle Turley and James E. Rooks, *Firearms Litigation: Law, Science and Practice,* Colorado Springs, CO, Shepard's/McGraw-Hill, Inc., 1988.

16. UMass library in Amherst, Smith and Wesson Archives, show a pre-printed affidavit form the company handed out in the 1920s to address claims from what they called the "Ultimate Consumer."

17. *Henningson v. Bloomfield Motors,* et al., 33 N.J. 358 (1960).

18. Mark Dowie, "Pinto Madness," *Mother Jones,* Sep./Oct. 1977. Mother Jones used company documents to show that Ford Motor Company knew people would burn to death in Pintos. They estimated between 500 and 900 had died.

19. *Rylands v Fletcher* (1868) LR 3 HL 330.

20. Jeffrey O'Connell, "Expanding No-Fault Beyond Auto Insurance: Some Proposals," *Virginia Law Review,* Vol. 59 (1973), page 749.

21. *Ford Motor Co. v. Evancho,* 327 So.2d 201, 204 Fla. (1976).

22. *Moning v Alfano,* 400 Mich 425, 439; 254 NW2d 759 (1977).

23. "Symposium on Firearms Legislation and Litigation," *Hamline Law Review,* Vol. 6, No. 2. (1983): 281.

24. *Richman v. Charter Arms Corp.*, 571 F. Supp. 192 (E.D. La. 1983), revd sub nom *Perkins v. F.I.E. Corp.*, 762 F.2d 1250 (5th Cir. 1985).

25. *Olen J. Kelley et ux. v. R.G. Industries*, INC. et al. (304 Md. 124; 497 A.2d 1143; 1985 Md.).

26. Howard L. Siegel, "Winning Without Precedent: Kelley v. R.G. Industries," *Litigation*, Summer 1988, Vol. 14, No. 4.

27. Webster, D. W., Vernick, J. S., and Hepburn, L. M., "Effects of Maryland's Law Banning 'Saturday Night Special' Handguns on Homicides," American *Journal of Epidemiology* 406, Mar. 2002, 155: 5.

28. Julie Petersen, "This Bullet Kills You Better (Black Talon)," *Mother Jones*, Sep. 1, 1993.

29. Daniel Jeffreys, "Shoot to Kill; The Gun That Killed Amy Federici was a Sturm Ruger. Her Parents Say its Manufacturers are Partly Responsible for her Death. Now They Plan to Sue," *The Independent*, Nov. 21, 1994.

30. Charles Petty, "Black Talon; Design For Defense," *American Rifleman*, Nov. 1992, page 36.

31. Vincent J. M. Di Maio, M.D., *Gunshot Wounds, Practical Aspects of Firearms, Ballistics, and Forensic Techniques*, New York, Esevier, 1985.

32. The bill 1993 S. 179; 103 S. 179 says the tax is 1000 percent (10 x the price) but a *New York Times* by op-ed Moynihan (Guns Don't Kill People. Bullets Do, Dec. 12, 1993) and other news stories say it is 10,000 percent (100 x the price). Moynihan explains his intent is to raise the price of a box of Black Talon bullets from $20 to $2,000.

33. Pierre Thomas, "Winchester to Limit Sales of Controversial Bullet," *Washington Post*, Nov. 23, 1993.

34. Patricia Alex, "Rampage Victims to Sue Arms Makers," *The Bergen Record*, Oct. 26, 1994. John T. McQuiston, "Victims Sue Arms Makers In Shooting On L.I.R.R.," *New York Times*, Oct. 27, 1994; Maureen Fan, "Suit Targets Gun, Ammo Firms," *Newsday*, Oct. 26, 1994; Maureen Fan, "Aiming at Gunmakers," *Newsday*, Oct. 27, 1994; Maureen Fan, "McCarthy Sues Gun, Ammo Firms Asking for $1.5B in LIRR shootings," May 18, 1995.

35. *McCarthy v. Sturm, Ruger and Co., Inc.*, 916 F.Supp. 366 (S.D.N.Y. 1996).

36. Pete Bowles, "LIRR Massacre Suits Meeting Resistance," *Newsday*, March 26, 1996.

37. Ken Moritsugu, "Frisa's Other Opponent: Himself," *Newsday*, Nov. 7, 1996.

CHAPTER 6

1. Author interviews with Elisa Barnes.

2. Crime Gun Trace Reports (2000) National Report, Department of the Treasury Bureau of Alcohol, Tobacco and Firearms, http://www.atf.gov/firearms/ycgii/2000/index.htm.

3. Lynda Richardson, "Challenging Gun Makers to Bear Responsibility," *New York Times*, Oct 22, 2002.

4. Edward J. Schoen, Margaret M. Hogan, Joseph S. Falchek, "An examination of the legal and ethical public policy consideration underlying DES market

share liability," *Journal of Business Ethics*. Dordrecht: March 2000. Vol. 24, Iss. 2, page 141.

5. Paul M. Barrett, "Aiming High: A Lawyer Goes After Gun Manufacturers; Has She Got a Shot?—In a New Approach That Hints At Attacks on Tobacco, Ms. Barnes Goes to Court," *Wall Street Journal,* Sep 17, 1998.

6. Michele Galen, "Legal Affairs The Man Who's Cutting Through the Asbestos Mess—Judge Jack Weinstein Wrote the Book on Settling Injury Megacases," *Business Week,* Jan. 28, 1991.

7. "Vietnam Vets Lose Court Battle Over Agent Orange Exposure," The Associated Press, Feb. 23, 1994.

8. Kathy Sawyer, "Legal Fees Set in Vets' Lawsuit Agent Orange Case Brings $10 Million To 100 Attorneys," *Washington Post,* Jan. 8, 1985.

9. *DeRosa v. Remington Arms Co., Inc.,* 509 F.Supp. 762 (E.D.N.Y. 1981).

10. Jennifer Gonnerman, "Under the Gun," *The Village Voice,* Feb. 2, 1999, Vol. 44, Iss. 4, page 52.

11. *Runaway Jury* (2003), Fox Home Entertainment Studio, directed by Gary Fleder, starring John Cusack, Gene Hackman and Dustin Hoffman, based on best-selling book by John Grisham, *Runaway Jury,* New York, Doubleday, 1996.

12. Author interview with Timothy A. Bumann.

13. Expert Report of Lucy Allen and Jonathan Portes, filed in *Hamilton v. Accutek,* 95-CV-0049 (JBW), U.S. District Court, eastern district of New York.

14. Author interview with Timothy A. Bumann. Bumann says that "across the board, universally, year to year, city to city, 12.5 percent" of guns are traced, but only 10–15 percent of guns traced were actually used in a crime. The rest were traced because when cops pick up on any offense and find a gun, they may trace it.

15. Bureau of Justice Statistics Gun Crime Rate; http://www.ojp.usdoj.gov/bjs/glance/tables/guncrimetab.htm.

16. *Firearms Production in America: A Listing of Firearm Manufacturers in America with Production Histories Broken Out by Firearm Type and Caliber, 2002 Edition,* Violence Policy Center, 2003. The report is based on data obtained from the Bureau of Alcohol, Tobacco and Firearms through Freedom of Information Act requests. http://www.vpc.org/graphics/prod2002.pdf.

17. "Guns Used in Crime," Bureau of Justice Statistics, July, 1995, NCJ–148–201 http://www.ojp.usdoj.gov/bjs/pub/pdf/guic.pdf.

18. ATF Youth Crime Gun Interdiction Initiative (2000), www.atf.gov/firearms/ycgii/2000/index.htm. For 1988 (the year the ATF started doing the studies for the calendar year), the ATF traced 64,637 guns, but there were 364,776 gun crimes reported.

19. "Guns in America: National Survey on Private Ownership and Use of Firearms. National Institute of Justice Research in Brief," May 1997, Jeremy Travis, director, http://www.ncjrs.org/txtfiles/165476.txt.

20. Author interviews with ATF agents at Brooklyn office.

21. *Hamilton v. Accu-tek,* Hass affidavit.

22. Matt Bai, "A Former Insider with a Troubled Conscience Turns on the Increasingly Besieged Firearms Industry," *Newsweek,* Jan. 25, 1999.

23. Violence Policy Center, "Firearms Production in America," Appendix Two, Estimated Wholesale Dollar Value of Firearms Manufactured in the United States. Because handguns are taxed at 10 percent and other firearms are taxed at 11 percent, the figures were extrapolated from the ATF's Firearms Commerce in the United States report, http://www.atf.treas.gov/pub/fire-explo_pub/firearmscommerce/exhibits.pdf, exhibit 6, firearms and ammunition tax collection. After 1996, the ATF stopped providing the public with tax collection figures on firearms categories.

24. Fortune 500 online database. Teleflex had 1994 revenues of $666.8 million. Ventas had 1997 revenues of $2.6 billion.

25. A. Merwyn Carey, *American Firearms Makers: When, Where and What They Made From the Colonial Period to the End of the 19th Century,* New York, Thomas Y. Crowell Company, 1953. The sheer mass of companies covered in this book and *Suicide Specials* suggests American gun companies, particularly the low-end ones, have always been ephemeral.

26. Dave Tinker, "Court Success Doesn't Help Insurance Rates," *Firearms Business,* Vol. 10, No. 3, Feb.15, 2001.

27. "Has Judge Weinstein Flipped-Flopped On What This Case Is About?," National Shooting Sports Foundation News Release, Sept. 26, 2000.

28. *Beretta U.S.A. Corporation v. Federal Ins. Co.,* 2001 WL 1019745.

29. Peter Geier, "No Coverage for Beretta in City Suits," *Bergen Record,* Oct 6, 2000.

30. Roy G. Jinks, *History of Smith & Wesson,* North Hollywood, Beinfield Publishing, 1977. Jinks is the official company historian.

31. Bern Keating, *The Flamboyant Mr. Colt and His Deadly Six-Shooter,* Garden City, NY, Doubleday & Co, 1978.

32. Kathleen J. Hoyt, Colt Historian, quoted in *Tales of the Gun,* "Guns of Colt," History Channel, A&E Home Video, 2000.

33. *Flamboyant Mr. Colt and His Deadly Six-Shooter,* pages 52–55, 62–66.

34. Tales of the Gun, "Guns of Colt," 2000, History Channel, A&E Home Video.

35. *Flamboyant Mr. Colt and His Deadly Six-Shooter,* pages 197–199.

36. Donald B. Webster, Jr., *Suicide Specials,* Harrisburg, PA, The Telegraph Press, 1958, page 1.

37. Duncan McConnell, "Suicide Specials," *American Rifleman,* Feb. 1948, page 36.

38. Robert Elman, *Fired in Anger: The Personal Handguns of American Villains and Heroes,* Doubleday, 1968.

39. Stewart M. Brooks, *Our Assassinated Presidents: True Medical Stories,* Harrisburg, PA, Bell Publishing Co., 1966.

40. *Suicide Specials,* page 16.

41. The low-end companies are particularly ephemeral. According to an analysis of ATF production data from 1975 to 2000, the mean survival time is just five years. The sheer mass of companies covered in A. Merwyn Carey, *American Firearms Makers: When, Where and What They Made From the Colonial Period to the End of the 19th Century,* New York, Thomas Y. Crowell Company, 1953, and Donald B. Webster, Jr.'s, *Suicide Specials,* suggests this has always been the case.

42. Iver Johnson Trivia and Notes (Long Articles), Copyright © 1999, 2000 Ben Sansing, http://www2.arkansas.net/~sws1/iver02.htm.

43. *The Saturday Night Special,* pages 52–53.

44. *The History of Smith & Wesson,* pages 213–214.

45. *American Handguns & Their Makers, A Publication of the National Rifle Association,* Washington, D.C., NRA Books, 1981, page 26.

46. Colt History Society, http://huntingsociety.org/HistColt.html; Colt Collectors Association, Colt Facts, http://www.coltcollectorsassoc.com/ccachronology.htm.

47. "Merger for Colt," *Time,* Oct. 3, 1955.

48. *The History of Smith & Wesson,* page 272–273.

49. Taurus International company history, www.taurususa.com/company/history.cfm.

50. "Lear Siegler to Sell Smith & Wesson Unit For $112.5 Million," *Wall Street Journal,* May 26, 1987. Lear Siegler Corp., a military contractor, bought Bangor Punta, and it was later bought out by renowned private equity firm and leveraged buyout specialist Forstmann Little & Co., which then sold the gun company to Tompkins.

51. E.I. du Pont de Nemours & Co. Records, Hagley Museum and Library, http://www.hagley.lib.de.us/lmss5.htm.

52. "DuPont Plans to Sell Most of Remington to Clayton Dubilier," *Wall Street Journal,* Oct. 22, 1993.

53. Britanica Online.

54. Jennifer V. Hughes, "Du Pont Fights Verdict in Pompton Lakes, N.J., Chemical Contamination Case," *Knight Ridder Tribune Business News,* Jun 28, 2002; Jan Barry, "Pompton Lakes, N.J., Considers Former Du Pont Plant Site for Golf Course," *Knight Ridder Tribune Business News,* Feb 11, 2003.

55. Securities and Exchange Commission Filing, Smith & Wesson Holding Corp., Form 10-Q, Dec. 12, 2004.

56. Jennifer V. Hughes, "Army Drops Colt as M16 Rifle Maker," Associated Press, Oct. 3, 1988.

57. Constance Hays, "State's Big Stake in Colt Clouds Debate on Guns," *New York Times,* July 5, 1992.

58. Colt Company History, http://www.colt.com/CMCI/history.asp.

59. Paul M. Barrett, "Big Bang—Evolution of a Cause: Why the Gun Debate has Finally Taken Off," *Wall Street Journal,* Oct. 21, 1999.

60. Matt Bai, "Unmaking a Gunmaker, The Company of Cowboy Legend and Wartime Firepower is Broke and Nearly out of Business," *Newsweek,* April 17, 2000.

61. Smith & Wesson Holding Corp., Form 10-Q, Dec. 12, 2004.

62. Vanessa O'Connell, "How Troubled Past Finally Caught Up With James Minder, Smith & Wesson Chairman Was Armed Robber in His 20s; Then, He Turned Around 'We Didn't Believe It'," *Wall Street Journal,* March 8, 2004.

63. Securities and Exchange Commission Filing, Sturm Ruger & Co. Inc., Form 10-Q, Nov. 5, 2004.

64. Securities and Exchange Commission Filing, Olin Corp., Form 10-K, March 9, 2005.

65. *Troubled Company Reporter,* Monday, March 26, 2001, Vol. 5, No. 59.
66. Melissa Kendall, "RSR's Revenues Shoot Up Because of Crime, Congress," *Orlando Business Journal,* Oct. 14, 1994.
67. Hoover's Inc. report, http://www.hoovers.com/rsr/—ID__58746—/free-co-factsheet.xhtml.
68. George O'Brien, "Under the Gun: Smith & Wesson Looks to Ride Out a Fluc-tuating Gun Market," *BusinessWest,* Chicopee, MA, June, 1998.
69. Neil Sheehan, "Pistol Production in U.S. Risking, Offsetting '68 Importation Ban," *New York Times,* April 30, 1969. A Washington homicide detective in the story estimated that 40 percent of the guns seized in homicides were Roehms. "Any rookie on the street for two weeks learns to recognize a Roehm," another Washington detective said. The story quoted Lieut. Frank Connolly, a supervisor with the NYPD ballistics section, saying 30 percent of guns seized in New York City were German guns, mainly Roehms.
70. *The Saturday Night Special,* page 105.
71. Ibid., pages 132–4, 146–7.
72. Garen Wintemute, M.D., "Ring of Fire: The Handgun Makers of Southern California," Violence Prevention Research Program, University of California, Davis, 1994.
73. Alix M. Freedman, "Firepower: Behind the Cheap Guns Flooding the Cities is a California Family—The Volatile Jennings Clan Makes the Pistols Favored by Criminals and Kids—A Deal Goes Down in Harlem," *Wall Street Journal,* Feb. 28, 1992.
74. In 1992, 2.6 million handguns were made in the United States the Ring of Fire companies produced 682,321 guns. In 1993, 1.97 million handguns were made, of which 899,422 were from Ring of Fire companies.
75. Police report.
76. ATF Crime Gun Trace Reports, (2000), National Report, Table 14, page 36–38, http://www.atf.gov/firearms/ycgii/2000/generalfindings.pdf.

CHAPTER 7

1. Lorcin Engineering Chapter 11 bankruptcy, United States Bankruptcy Court, Central District of California, Case No. SB 96–27640-RA.
2. See research notes on gun prices. Mean Lorcin gun price taken from *Gun Digest,* 1993.
3. Fox Butterfield, "Saturday Night Special Maker Files for Bankruptcy," *New York Times,* June 24, 1999.
4. Larry Armstrong, "No Surrender from Mr. Saturday Nights Special," *BusinessWeek;* Aug. 16, 1999.
5. Lorcin Bankruptcy, Reply to Debtor's Opposition to Motion for Relief from the Automatic Stay, filed Oct. 20, 1997.
6. Author interviews with James Waldorf.
7. James Waldorf, *Landing On Your Feet, Your Guide to Survival in Tough Economic Times,* 1992.

8. Deposition of James Waldorf, February 19, 1997, in Lorcin Bankruptcy, SB 96–27640 RA.
9. Author interviews with Alan Stomel.
10. Michael Utley, "Empty Shells," *The Press-Enterprise,* Nov. 14, 1999.
11. Sharon Walsh, "The Cheapest Handgun Was Loaded With Profit; For Pistol Firm, Heavy Sales, Then Bankruptcy Protection," *Washington Post,* Aug. 26, 1999.
12. "Hot Guns," *Frontline,* June 3, 1997, edited by Michael Chandler, written, produced and directed by Doug Hamilton.
13. Loren Fleckenstein, "On the Firing Line," *The Press-Enterprise,* Oct. 5, 1997.
14. Editor's Note and "Affordable Protection: Single Action 9 mm Pistols," *Gun Tests,* Jan., 1998. The article also said the Lorcin guns failed to feed about half the rounds. One gun broke and gunsmith found it had a casting flaw. "Bottom Line . . . Failures to function are bad enough; broken frames are a new low for this uncommonly poor firearm—worse than useless as a carry arm. A doorstop maybe . . ."
15. http://www.packing.org/news/article.jsp/6178.
16. Lorcin Bankruptcy, Debtor's Redlined Fourth Amended Disclosure Statement, Event Precipitating the Bankruptcy Filing, filed Dec. 19, 1997, page 16.
17. Estate of Alice Mae Johnson, et al. v. Lorcin Engineering, et al.
18. Jason Booth, "Bankruptcy court overwhelmed," *Los Angeles Business Journal,* March 2, 1998.
19. Lorcin Bankruptcy, Declaration of James Waldorf, Jan., 1998.
20. Lorcin Bankruptcy, Unsecured Creditor's Committee Reply to Oppositions of Debtor and control Systems, Inc., to Committee's Motion to Appoint Ch. 11 Trustee, filed by Alan Stomel, February 12, 1998.
21. Resume of Howard Holladay, submitted as an exhibit in Control Systems, Inc. v. American Derringer Corp., W97CA189, U.S. District Court, Western District of Texas.
22. University of Georgia, alumni website.
23. Author interview with Howard Holladay.
24. Author interviews with Alan Stomel.
25. Kevin Leary, "Federal Agent Plays Madam at Nevada Brothel," *San Francisco Chronicle,* Sept. 20, 1990.
26. "The Liability Risk Retention Act of 1986," International Risk Management Institute, 1995.
27. Massachusetts registration of A-Buyers Co-op.
28. *Jimmy D. Jones v. Leeds & London Merchants Insurance, S.A. and Control Systems Inc.,* 97CI 05181, Jefferson County Circuit Court, Kentucky, Complaint.
29. Charles W. Thurston, "Costa Rica Resolves to Put an End to State Monopolies," *Journal of Commerce,* Aug. 9, 1993.
30. Bufete Soto y Asociados, Rodrigo Soto, faxed report to Tom McDermott, Oct. 3, 1997.
31. Author Interview with Myrna Jones.
32. Kurt Gerstner, letter to Harry Gregory, Sep. 4, 1998.

33. Tom Hays, "Gun Industry Accused of Negligence," Associated Press, Jan. 7, 1999.
34. Jennifer Gonnerman, "Under the Gun," *The Village Voice,* Feb. 2, 1999.
35. Tom Hays, "Jury Finds Gun Makers Liable," Associated Press, N.Y. Feb. 11, 1999.
36. *Freddie Hamilton, et al., v. Beretta, Accu-Tek, et al.,* 2001 NY Int. 40, USCOA,2 No. 36, April 26, 2001.
37. *Commerce in Firearms in the United States,* ATF, Feb. 4, 2000.
38. Mike Robinson, "Daley Hits Gun Industry with $433 Million Public Nuisance Lawsuit," Associated Press, Nov. 12, 1998.
39. *City of Chicago, County of Cook v. Beretta U.S.A.,* et al, Illinois Supreme Court Decision, Docket Nos. 95243, 95253, 95256, 95280, Sept. 10, 2003.
40. John O'Connor, "Court Dismisses Suits Against Gunmakers," *St. Louis Post-Dispatch;* The Associated Press, Nov. 19, 2004.
41. *City of Chicago v. U.S. Dept. of Treasury,* 384 F.3d 429 (7th Cir. 2004)
42. *Regulatory Intelligence Data,* March 17, 2000.
43. Author interview with Ed Schulz.

CHAPTER 8

1. Assurance Buyers Co-op Policy, National Small Manufacturers Division, 1990.
2. Lorcin Bankruptcy, Unsecured Creditors Committee's Objection to Debtor's Redlined Third Amended Disclosure Statement, filed Nov. 14, 1997.
3. Lorcin Bankruptcy, Motion of RSR Wholesale guns of Texas, Inc., to vacate order. RSR attempted to withdraw notice.
4. Lorcin Bankruptcy, Debtor's Fourth Amended Disclosure Statement to Accompany Debtor's Chapter 11 Plan of Reorganization and Committee's Chapter 11 Plan of Reorganization.
5. Lorcin Bankruptcy, Declaration of Howard Holladay, Oct. 27, 1998.
6. Author interview with Robert Pitts.
7. Alan Stomel letter to Craig Barbosh, Feb. 27, 1998, Re: In re Lorcin Engineering Co., Inc. Examination of Howard Holladay.
8. Craig Barbosh, May 8, 1997 letter to Daniel Reiss, Angel and Neistat.
9. Transcript of proceedings to confirm Lorcin Engineering Chapter 11 plan, Oct. 30, 1998.
10. "Shoes to Make Gun Death Statistics Less Abstract," *Weekend Edition,* Sept. 17, 1994.
11. Author interview with Katina Johnstone.
12. D. L. Stanley, "Million Moms to March Mother's Day," *Atlanta Inquirer,* Mary 13, 2000
13. Author interviews with Robert Garvey.
14. Margaret Cronin Fisk, "Kmart Held Liable For Selling Rifle," *The National Law Journal,* Oct. 25, 1993.
15. Eliza O'Grady, "Holding Retailer Responsible for Gunshot Victim," *The American Lawyer,* Dec., 1993.

16. *Sandra Russell Eslinger, et al. v. K-Mart Corp.,* 2:97cv981 S, U.S. District Court, Central Utah.
17. Author interview with Karen Cutts.
18. United States Court of Appeals for the eighth circuit June 2, 1997, ruling in United *States of America v. Arthur A. Blumeyer,* III. No. 96–3003.
19. Author interviews with Larry Keane, National Shooting Sports Foundation.
20. Author interviews with Bob Chiarello.
21. SAIL application.
22. Assurance Buyers Co-operative, State of California registration, April 1986, incorporated in Sarento, CA.
23. Alan Stomel fax to Tom McDermott, Oct. 9, 1997.
24. Author interview with Roger Harrington.
25. Dana Hawkins, "Backyard Paintball Play Leads to Serious Eye Injuries," *U.S. News and World Report,* Aug. 14, 2000, page 52.
26. *James Farrell v. Michael Cichon, National Survival Games, et al,* No. 3: CV–93–0005, U.S. District Court, Middle District of Pennsylvania.
27. Allen Lessels, "Paintball Marks 10 Years of Survival Games Sport Born in State has Army of Loyal Fans," *Boston Globe, New Hampshire Weekly,* Oct 13, 1991.
28. Durty Dan, "Origins of Commercial Paintball," Durty Dan's Paintball Information Service. The article cites *Action Pursuit Games Magazine,* Part 1, Sept. 1992, Part II, Oct., 1992, and *The Official Survival Games Manual,* by Lionel Atwill, New York, Pocket Books, June 1983.
29. Notes of Roger Harrington.
30. Ronald E. Lemay letter to Roger Harrington, Aug. 24, 1993.
31. NSG., Inc. 1990 General Liability Policy, LL10155, with Leeds & London.
32. Kurt Gersner letter to Roger Harrington, Nov. 29, 1993.
33. Author interview with Jean Rooney.
34. Memorandum of Understanding from Gerry Jaggard, National Survival Games, to Jeff O'Leary and Howard Holladay at Control Systems, Inc. Jan. 29, 1993.
35. Letter from CPA, July 1, 1992, to Leeds & London Board, including copy of MKI Securities brokerage statement, dated March 22, 1990.
36. *Matthew Schellenberger, et al. v. Wildwood Lake,* Cuyahoga County Common Pleas Court Case, No. 193890, 1990, which cites Cuyahoga County Common Please Court Case No. CV 119226, judgment of $1 million on March 27, 1990.
37. Author interview with Russell Schellenberger.
38. Author interviews with Peter Weinberger.
39. Hall & Evans, Paul R. Franke, III, (representing Colony) letters to Peter Weingberger, Nov. 1, 1989, Nov. 14, 1989, Nov. 29, 1989, Nov. 27, 1989, Nov. 29, 1989, Dec. 5, 1989, Dec. 11, 1989, negotiating Schellenberger claim, describing Colony's weak financial condition and finally a notice of liquidation of Colony.
40. "Deadly Exceptions: Gun Manufacturers That Would be Protected by the 'Small Business' Cap on Punitive Damages," Violence Policy Center Report, 2000.
41. "Gun Crime in the 18–20 Age Group," Report by the Department of Treasury, Department of Justice, June, 1999, Table 6, http://www.treas.gov/press/releases/reports/report.pdf.

42. "Davis Signs Package of Gun Control Legislation," *Los Angeles Times,* Aug. 28, 1999.

43. Ryan H. Sager, "Sued Shut," *Reason Online,* Dec. 1999, http://reason.com/9912/ci.rs.sued.shtml.

44. US Bankruptcy Court, Central District of California, San Bernadino, Davis Industries, Chapter 11 Bankruptcy, Case No. 9919302, Filed May 27, 1999.

45. Davis Bankruptcy, Howard Holladay declaration, Nov. 12, 1999.

46. Michael Utley, "Bankruptcy Court OKs Gun Maker to Buy Insurance," *Press-Enterprise,* Jan. 12, 2000.

47. Control Systems Inc., quote faxed to Davis Industries, Jan. 5, 1999, an exhibit in Davis Bankruptcy.

48. Congressional Record, Feb. 1, 2000, Statement of Senator Carl Levin on Firearm Related Debts.

49. *Daniel I. Simon v. Control Systems, Inc., a corporation, and Howard K. Holladay,* U.S. District Court, Central District of Florida, Case No. 86 5843JGD (JRX), first amended complaint.

50. Declaration of Howard Holladay in *Simon v. CSI,* Holladay, Jan. 12, 1987.

51. Assurance Buyers Cooperative list of Founding Directors, filed as an exhibit in *Schellenberger v. Colony Insurers.*

52. Frank Seiler letter to American-British Insurance, to "memorialize our agreement," on policy, April 29, 1986.

53. Insurance Binder, Assurance Buyers Co-op policy for Wildwood Lake Water Park, with American British Insurance, Signed James Lodes, May 30, 1986.

54. Assurance Buyers Co-op Inc. Membership Representatives Manual, a 32-page booklet.

55. Peter Strong, Independent Management Group, letter to Chris Koenemann, Lockton Insurance Agency, June 7, 1989.

56. Hannover Re letter to Lockton Insurance Agency, Aug. 19, 1986.

57. Frank Seiler letter to Tom McDermott, Feb. 5, 2001.

58. Author interview with Frank Seiler.

59. Frank Seiler letter of resignation to Board of Directors, Assurance, Buyers Co-op, Boston, Mass., July 25, 1986.

60. Island Group letter to Assurance Buyers Co-op confirming conditions of policy, signed Robert Entin, President.

61. Deposition of Barry Trevithick in *Colony Insurers v. Ferrell Travis Riley,* et al, Bexar County, Texas, 89-CI–21558.

62. GAO Report: "Insurance Industry—Chronology of F.T. Riley's activities and related regulatory actions," GAO/OSI–95–5, Oct. 26 1994.

CHAPTER 9

1. Insurance Commissioner for the *State of Maryland v. Assurance Buyers Cooperative and Leeds & London Merchants Insurance,* Case #MIA–27–8/94, Order-Consent Agreement, Received Aug. 29, 1994.

2. Author interviews with Elizabeth Saunders.

3. Copy of cancelled check.
4. Author interviews with Connie Terry.
5. *Jimmy D. Jones v. Lorcin Engineering,* United States District Court, Western District of Kentucky, Civil Action No. 4:99CV–26M, including: Findings of Fact, Conclusions of Law and Judgment on Damages, March 12, 2001.
6. *Jimmy D. Jones v. Leeds & London Merchants Insurance and Control Systems,* United States District Court, Western District of Kentucky, Civil Action No. 4:99CV–26M, including: Findings of Fact, Conclusions of Law and Judgment on Damages, Oct. 15, 2001.
7. Author interviews with Rusty Brace.
8. Letter from Colin Holde, Superintendent of Insurance, Government of the Turks and Caicos to Tom McDermott, Oct. 13, 1998.
9. Leeds & London Costa Rica incorporation file.
10. Stamped translation by Eugenia Maria Cartin, official translator of the Ministry of Foreign Affairs and Worship of the Republic of Costa Rica.
11. Affadavit of Alberto Raven, Aug. 9, 2001.
12. Author interview with Howard Holladay.
13. Author interviews with Malcolm Stritzinger.
14. *Stritzinger v. Davis* proceedings, Apr. 10, 2002.
15. *Control Systems Inc. v. American Derringer,* U.S. District Court, Western Texas Division, Civil Action W97CA189, including: summons, complaint, response by Control Systems Inc., insurance policies and correspondence, 1992–1997.

CHAPTER 10

1. Robert Sherrill, *The Saturday Night Special,* Charterhouse, 1973.
2. "The Profile of the Shooting Sports," National Shooting Sports Foundation, Sep., 1999.
3. Fox Butterfield, "Depletion of assets alarms NRA leaders," The *New York Times,* June 6, 1995.
4. Stephanie Strom, "A Deficit of $100 Million Is Confronting the N.R.A.," *New York Times.* Dec. 21, 2003.
5. "Guns in America: National Survey on Private Ownership and Use of Firearms. National Institute of Justice Research in Brief," May, 1997, Jeremy Travis, Director.
6. Jack Anderson, *Inside the NRA, Armed and Dangerous: An Expose,* Beverly Hills, CA Dove Books, 1996, page 26.
7. "Gun Lobby Targets Gore, Democrats: NRA Prepares to Play Major Role in Election 2000," CNN, May 23, 2000.
8. "Kerry hunts, campaigns in Ohio," United Press International, Oct. 21, 2004.
9. Center for Responsive Politics, Opensecrets.org. Data for gun lobby is as of Jan. 7, 2005, data for NRA is as of Feb. 7, 2005.
10. George McEvoy, "NRA Circles its Wagons, Throws Bush to the Moms," *Palm Beach Post,* Sep. 16, 2000.

11. Matt Bai, "A Gun Deal's Fatal Wound: As a Landmark Pact to Control Gun Sales Falls Apart, Smith & Wesson Takes the Hit," *Newsweek;* Feb. 5, 2001.

12. Eric Lichtblau, "Terror Suspects Buying Firearms, U.S. Report Finds," *New York Times.* March 8, 2005.

13. Linda Greenhouse, "U.S., in a Shift, Tells Justices Citizens Have a Right to Guns," *New York Times,* May 8, 2002.

14. Adam Liptak, "Defendants Fighting Gun Charles Cie New View of Second Amendment," *New York Times,* July 23, 2002.

15. "The Uninsured Motorist Puzzle," Stephen D. Sugarman, University of California, Berkeley Crossroads 1998, Stephen D. Sugarman, Agnes Roddy Robb Professor of Law, http://www.law.berkeley.edu/faculty/sugarmans/UIWISC. htm.

16. Sherri Cruz., "Costa Mesa Gunmaker Hit with Big Verdict, Declares Bankruptcy," *Orange County Business,* Jun 29, 2003.

17. Author interview with Richard Ruggieri.

18. Author interview with Ned Nashbam.

19. Wintemute, G. J., Wright, M. A., "Initial and Subsequent Hospital Costs of Firearm Injuries," *The Journal of Trauma,* 1992; 34:556–560.

20. Philip Cook and Jens Ludwig, *Gun Violence, The Real Costs,* New York, Oxford University Press, 2000.

21. "Guns of the Civil War," *Tales Of The Gun,* The History Channel (2000), quoting, Russ Pritchard, Director Emeritus, Civil War Library.

22. Cook, P. J., Lawrence, B. A., Ludwig, J., Miller, T. R., "The Medical Costs of Gun Shot Injuries in the United States," *Journal of the American Medical Association,* 1999; 282:447–454.

23. Kaiser Family Foundation study on health costs http://www.kff.org/insurance/7031/ti2004-1-set.cfm.

24. Firearms Tax Collection, 2001, first through fourth quarter, http://www.atf. gov/firearms/stats/index.htm.

25. See gun price analysis in research notes.

INDEX